WALLEYE

WALLEYE
A BEAUTIFUL FISH OF THE DARK

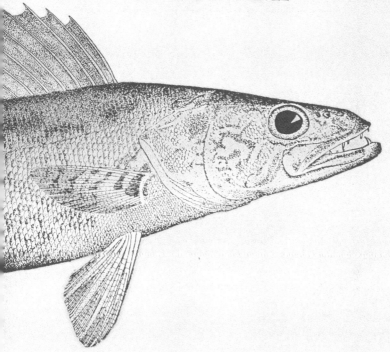

PAUL J. RADOMSKI

University of Minnesota Press
Minneapolis
London

The glossary is reprinted from K. Blackhart, D. G. Stanton, and A. M. Shimada, *NOAA Fisheries Glossary,* U.S. Department of Commerce, NOAA, Technical Memorandum NMFS-F/SPO-69, Washington, D.C., 2006.

Published by the University of Minnesota Press
111 Third Avenue South, Suite 290
Minneapolis, MN 55401-2520
http://www.upress.umn.edu

ISBN 978-1-5179-1363-2 (pb)

A Cataloging-in-Publication record for this book is available from the Library of Congress.

Printed in the United States of America on acid-free paper

The University of Minnesota is an equal-opportunity educator and employer.

30 29 28 27 26 25 24 23 22   10 9 8 7 6 5 4 3 2 1

CONTENTS

PREFACE

There are more than thirty-four thousand species of fish, and we are a better, more intelligent species because of their existence and diversity. Their presence lures us out on the water for sport and sustenance. Freshwater fish are abundant in most ponds, lakes, streams, and rivers. But few fish have as loyal a following as the walleye. The walleye (or, by its scientific name, *Sander vitreus*) is the official state or provincial fish of Manitoba, Minnesota, Saskatchewan, South Dakota, and Vermont. Many towns claim to be the walleye capital of the world, and several walleye statues are scattered across the north to appeal to tourists. Walleye fishing is a challenge. Many anglers spend considerable time honing their walleye fishing skills, and they will travel great distances to fish waters where the bite is good. But perhaps most important, walleye are a delicacy, leading to sustenance harvest for meals with family and friends and commercial harvest for a spot on the menu in restaurants and bars.

Walleye are a fish of large rivers and large northern lakes. As a scientist, I'm amazed by walleye, and I'm a better, more intelligent person because of their existence and abundance. Their nature is fascinating, full of stunning and counterintuitive facts. The name "wall-eye" denotes the uniqueness and importance of this fish's eyes,[1] which evolved to better see in low light conditions and dark water environments. People who view walleye as the "lion of the lakes" are often surprised to learn that rivers are their ancestral habitat; walleye are river fish that adapted to large, cool-water lakes.[2] This book begins with an exploration of the walleye: what they are, where they exist, how they survive, and how people have come to depend on them. I have caught and handled thousands of walleye, and it would be fair to say that I have indisputable walleye fishing skills. I'll describe various ways of catching walleye.

The second part of this book explores the principles (and pitfalls) of managing this dweller of the dark. I start with why walleye are stocked. Since stocking is intoxicating, I'll discuss its history and methods and then deliver perspectives on when and where walleye stocking is prudent. Next, I cover protecting and restoring walleye habitat. Walleye are wild and their habitat is threatened. We live in unprecedented times. Our endless pursuit of the "more is better" axiom discounts future generations, walleye, and the rest of nature. We have polluted our planet at a global scale, fouled its waters with farm and urban runoff, and contaminated them all with chemicals that accumulate faster than nature can bury them or break them down. If walleye can't survive and thrive, maybe we can't either. Our fates are entangled, with more than spooky action at a distance of a rod cast, for the health of us both is dependent on the wellness of our only home. I provide some local habitat protection and restoration solutions and discuss replacing our "more is better" axiom with one that expands our rights to future generations, walleye, and the rest of nature to increase their odds of flourishing. This part then moves to the common ways to manage walleye harvest and, through the use of fisheries dynamics science, how best to manage people to foster sustainable harvests.

There are thousands of waters where walleye exist with associated fisheries. A fishery is made up of fish plus humans; it is a complex, dynamic socioeconomic and biological system.[3] For some fisheries, the facts are clear and the way forward lit. For others, there are mysteries that confront our comprehension and uncertainties that confound our conjecture; that is to say, sometimes we are in the dark. The third part of this book highlights three walleye fisheries, one from Wisconsin (Lake Winnebago) and two from Minnesota (Mille Lacs and Red Lake). I provide a glimpse of their opportunities for fishing and talk with experts who have been involved in their management. Biologists managing these fisheries are working hard to understand their dynamics and to provide great places to fish, but these efforts come with complications.

These fisheries reflect some of the management challenges that many other fisheries, from walleye lakes in the Upper Midwest to Canada, may experience. Plan to visit these lakes and other walleye waters. Explore walleye fisheries close to home and those in distant places. Live according to nature. Our interactions with others and with the rest of nature should be governed by practicing the four cardinal virtues: courage, justice, self-control, and wisdom.

For more than three decades I've worked as a fish biologist and lake ecologist. I have served as Minnesota's lead scientific expert on lake habitat management issues, and I've worked with many lake lovers to protect and restore shorelines, water quality, and walleye populations. My job as a scientist has given me the opportunity to gain a deeper appreciation of walleye and nature. I see great beauty in nature and in the mathematical patterns expressed by plants, animals, and ecosystems. I've always thought of my job as more than a profession; it is a calling, a calling to tend nature. At a young age I wanted to be a state agency biologist, dedicated to restoring and protecting lakes, rivers, and wildlife. Today, I'm an apostle of lake and walleye. This book was conceived as a means to spread the word about walleye fishing, biology, and management.

Are you one who can find beauty in a fish? Maybe you've never thought much about walleye. Or maybe you're the first one out on the lake during the fishing opener, year after year. Whether you're a casual angler or someone who lives for the tug of a walleye on your line, I hope you will find something of interest in these pages. While I understand walleye biology and fisheries management, this book looks beyond the science to real-world opportunities for reducing pollution, protecting fish habitat, and increasing angler involvement in fisheries management decisions. It was written for a broad and diverse audience, but many of its lessons are also applicable to fisheries biologists and managers. This book aims to serve two purposes: first, to beach the knowledge of walleye on a safe shore for nonscientists to examine and appreciate; and second, to row out and then drift offshore to obtain a different perspective of walleye, beyond just a fish to catch at the cabin or resort or a menu item at a restaurant. I believe that this shared journey can lead to a greater appreciation of nature. Walleye are the vessel for this communion, as they are a beautiful fish of the dark.

ACKNOWLEDGMENTS

I thank my wife, Hollie Radomski, for her support and encouragement, and our children, Claire and Wiley, for making life more interesting and fulfilling. Kristin Carlson scrutinized the text, and I owe her an ever-larger debt of gratitude for her help. I thank the many fish biologists and fisheries managers who helped me better understand the Mille Lacs walleye fishery. I appreciate Dr. Andrew J. Carlson, Richard E. Bruesewitz, and Tom Heinrich for sharing their perspectives on fisheries management and for reviewing draft chapters. Kendall Kamke, Adam Nickel, Mike Arrowood, Joe Fellegy, Al Pemberton, Pat Brown, Gary Barnard, Henry Drewes, Thomas Howes, Dana Pitt, and Peter Jacobson generously gave their valuable time to be interviewed, and I am thankful for their patience with my many questions. Brian Borkholder helped in many ways, and I am grateful for his efforts. I thank Dr. Dan Isermann and Dr. Greg Sass for their thoughtful reviews of a draft manuscript. I am grateful to Kristian Tvedten, editor at the University of Minnesota Press, for his encouragement and assistance in polishing a rough collection of walleye facts and stories. I thank those who took me fishing: my parents, Joan and Joseph Radomski; my grandfathers, Harry Grimm and Joseph Radomski; childhood neighbor friends, Dale, Louie, and Carol Gawlik; and work colleagues I fished with for fun and science. Finally, *Dziękuję* (thank you) for reading this book.

PART I

THE FISH OF INTEREST

1
THE WORLD OF WALLEYE
Understanding a Favorite Fish

———◇———

Why a fascination with walleye?[1] This fish has not substantially altered the world, unlike the Atlantic cod, which has influenced world economies and politics for hundreds of years.[2] The freshwater-living walleye could not compete with this prolific ocean fish in captivating industry. Fishing for walleye has not been glamorized in literature and movies, unlike fly fishing for stream trout, as in Norman Maclean's story *A River Runs Through It.* The use of minnow and hook to catch walleye can't compete with the apparent elegance of fishing with lures that mimic drifting or emerging insects. The beauty of walleye has not yet been appreciated by a diversity of artists, unlike the dedication of artists who draw, paint, or carve other animals.[3] Many walleye paintings show this fish grimacing with its tail bent back at ninety degrees, spiny dorsal fin extended, mouth agape, and gills flared; works of art of brook trout often just celebrate the colors of this fish's skin. Despite these facts, walleye have creeled the minds of anglers throughout northern waters. Walleye are fascinating because of their physical beauty, their interesting adaptations, and the fine fillets they produce for our palate. In this chapter, I'll cover each of these topics, and then I'll discuss the importance of walleye in commercial, tribal, and sport fisheries.

In the stark winter whiteness, I pull a fish up through a spiral-scarred ice hole, and a walleye amazes. Their vitality and vividness fresh out of water are powerful, enough to tug one's consciousness to put them back down the long hole into the dark from which they were pulled. They do not belong in the air; they are built to fly in cool waters. Walleye have a fusiform shape, a slender body

MINNESOTA STATE FISH

Popular images of walleye, like this one by artist Roger Preuss, appear frequently on postcards.

with a two-eyed dominant head, two dorsal fins, and a slightly forked tail.[4] They will occasionally grow to a length greater than 2 feet (0.6 m), and only these big fish get chunky. A rare walleye will exceed 15 pounds (6.8 kg). I've caught some monster walleye in my day job of assessing and managing fish populations. With each of these fish there was a sense of urgency to measure and record her attributes, which were written down on wet paper, before she was quickly baptized at the side of the boat and released into the sanctum. Length and weight were recorded, and in some cases a tag number—proof of an earlier encounter with a biologist. Many of these unique fish are likely long dead, but memories of them endure.

Like birds of prey, walleye have evolved over time with a kind of stealth engineering. They are colored to avoid detection. The dorsal is dark and the belly is white or yellowed white. Predators or prey swimming above are less likely to observe a walleye, as the dark dorsal blends in with the dark background, and those below may not see the white underside of the walleye against the diffused lightscape of the top water and pale sky (ichthyologists call this color pattern countershading). The pale underside extends to the lower parts of the pelvic fin, anal fin, and especially the tail, which is brilliantly white tipped. The rest of the tail has alternating spots of yellow and black. Depending on water transparency and inheritance, the sides are colored like a silt-covered beach, gray brown speckled with gold or olive brown and silver. Living in clear water inspires a greater expression of color in walleye. In youth, the sides are sometimes mottled with obvious black or dark saddle-shaped blotches.

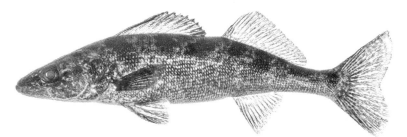

The walleye, or Sander vitreus. *Photograph by Sam Stukel/USFWS.*

Walleye are almost totally covered with scales; only the fins and portions of the gill covers are scaleless. The walleye's scales provide radiance and camouflage. Some fish that walleye prey on, like the various species of minnows, have scales that reflect and distract. Walleye are colored to blend in and evade. They are not showy or fanciful; they express functional beauty. The scales of the walleye expand as the fish grows. Fisheries biologists use this fact to estimate the age of younger walleye.[5] It is often possible to see the distinctive annuli on the scales, formed during the low-growth periods of winter. The annuli are testament of relative time, a record used by biologists working in their laboratories. The scales form an overlapping head-to-tail pattern, providing skin protection and improved hydrodynamics that reduces drag to conserve energy. The anterior edges of the scales are embedded in the skin, and walleye,

like many fish, have an epidermis that covers the scales and ex-
cretes a slimy, slippery mucus. This mucus has many functions,
including protection from pathogens and environmental toxins.[6]
Walleye scales also have small teeth at the posterior edges. For this
reason, walleye have a rough surface to the touch, similar to sand-
paper in texture. The bigger the walleye, the rougher they are.

The fins express a fish's thoughts. When walleye are aggressive,
defensive, or in pursuit of prey, they erect their dorsal fins. These
fins will pop up or lie down as fast as a dragonfly jet. The anterior spiny dorsal fin is composed of a dozen or more sharp spines.
The membranes between the spines are thin and diffusely dark
but blacker at the margin and at the posterior base of the fin. The
second soft dorsal fin begins with one or two spines and continues
with about twenty soft rays that support black-spotted membranes
in rows on a translucent sunset canvas. To keep the fish upright, the
anal fin is usually extended. This light-colored fin has two spines
anterior and about a dozen soft rays. Upfront, the pelvic fins are extended at various degrees depending on the intended flight or kill
path, and any movement of the side-located pectoral fins indicates
subtle changes to direction, including backing up.

The walleye head means business. Wide and stout before taper-
ing to a blunt point, it is a quarter of the walleye's total length. The
head is armed and self-aware. Two bones supporting the gill covers
are weaponized, with the one closest to the mouth serrated on the
posterior edge and other equipped with a short spine located near
the edge of the gill cover opening. The mouth and jaw are large,
like a baseball mitt, designed to improve the odds of a catch with
a desperate grab. Dagger-like teeth are spaced out on the jaw and
the roof of the mouth, with many teeth curved inward to better
hold the surprised and desperate smaller fish caught within. Walleye have color vision and see the longer wavelengths of light (short
to long: blue, green, yellow, orange, red), but not the light in the
ultraviolet range or infrared. A walleye's peak light sensitivity is
for wavelengths in the green portion of the spectrum,[7] which, not

surprisingly, is the same portion of the light spectrum that pene-
trates deepest into lakes.[8] Their large eyes allow more light to enter
and are positioned on the head to look primarily to the sides, limiting binocular vision up close. Walleye eyes can appear glossy or
cloudy depending on your charity. The eye's pupil, the opening of
the iris to the lens, is fixed in size—an unwavering and round dark
aperture into a foreign point of view. The lens is rigid and spheri-
cal, better at focusing on the near than the far. Rimming the pupil,
the iris is a luminescent gold ring. There is no white of the eye to
communicate fear.

A walleye from Upper Red Lake, Minnesota, displays an impressive set of teeth.
Photograph copyright Duluth News Tribune.

Walleye live in a world heavy with twilight and thick with darkness. Water scatters and absorbs radiant energy, so the available
light diminishes with water depth. The wavelengths of the light
that penetrate the depths will shift depending on the quantities of
dissolved organic matter in the water. In clear water, blue light is
more available, and in dark stained waters of the north, yellow and

red light dominates. There are no bright, sunny days in the underworld like those experienced by land animals. Walleye, though, are
adapted to the dark, and they are predators of the waning light.

The walleye retina reflects light.[9] This back-of-the-eye reflector
increases the amount of light hitting the cells of the eye that con-
vert light into electrical signals, as this adaptation gives additional
chances for ricocheting light within the eye to hit a rod or cone
photosensitive cell.[10] Those with this adaptation have better vision
in low light conditions. Humans do not have this adaptation, but
many animals do, including cats, dogs, and horses.[11] Seeing life on
the murky boulder fields and within the dimly lit pondweed forest
canopies is an evolutionary gift, especially when others don't possess the trait. Walleye hunt in very low light conditions, and the
fish they seek lack specialized eyes. Most of their fish-eating competitors also lack this gift. Walleye have the strategic advantage at
night and in low light conditions, allowing them to hunt unseeing
yellow perch and other prey while remaining safe from ambushes
by northern pike and other large predators.

Like light, the transmission and reception of sound are different in water. Fish have adapted to hearing sounds in water, and
humans have adapted to hearing sounds in air. Stop wondering:
there is a difference—fish have ears in their head but not on their
head, whereas people have both, along with ear holes. The speed
of sound is quicker in water (approximately 4.3 times faster than
in air); water also has lower compressibility than air, which allows
the compression wave to gallop in water rather than trot as it does
in the air. A human in the water has a hard time determining the
origin of a sound, because their reliance on small middle ear bones
for hearing prevents them from picking up the difference in sound
arrival time between the left and right ear. Walleye, like many fish,
have a set of three different large otolith inner ear bones on either
side of the skull (these bones are small in humans).[12] These otoliths allow fish to sense low-frequency sound.[13] It is not known
how acute walleye hearing is; however, we do know that they can
hear the breaking of waves, the raindrops strumming the water,

and the racket of anglers in the boat above. Walleye also possess a lateral line—a sensory organ on either side of the body that detects water movement about the body. Compared to other fish species, the walleye version of this organ is simple. Walleye likely use their lateral line to sense and detect movements of nearby prey, like a yellow perch trying to scoot to the side after a strike. Walleye have the sense of the distant touch, analogous to a bobcat's whiskers that feel for the deer mouse underfoot.

Studies on walleye taste and smell are uncommon. Walleye have two nares on their snout, and it is likely they have a good sense of smell that aids in the detection of prey.[14] Do they smell the blooming watermilfoil flowers of summer? Do they smell the gasoline engine exhaust of fishing boats expelled into the surface waters through the hubs of spinning props? I do not know. Walleye have taste buds in their mouth and gills, and this sensory system is likely only used to determine whether what they caught is indeed food.[15] Young hatchery walleye must be conditioned or habituated to eat nonliving food, as the unnatural does not come naturally.[16]

Like many fish species, walleye have a gas bladder that is used to control their buoyancy. This organ consists of two thin-membraned sacs located in the dorsal portion of the body cavity. In walleye the gas bladder uses only their circulatory system. It may be a simple adaptation, but it is effective. The circulatory system, with a connected gas gland adjacent to the bladder, adds oxygen to the sacs to increase buoyancy, and dorsal veins and arteries remove oxygen to decrease buoyancy. A shortcoming of this buoyancy system is that it is slow, which limits walleye from moving up in the water too quickly. If forced to raise too fast, the organ is stressed and could be damaged. Some fish species, like trout, have a gas bladder adapted for quick ascents; a connection between the gas bladder and the gut allows the bladder to be emptied by burping gas (and to be filled by gulping air).[17]

Walleye are sometimes confused with sauger and yellow perch, as all three are in the Perch family (Percidae). Sauger are very similar in size and shape to walleye; however, sauger have definite horizontal rows of black spots on the membranes of the spiny dorsal fin, a black blotch at the base of the pectoral fins, and lack the distinctive white tip of the lower tail fin of a walleye. Sauger have a more reflective eye than walleye, so are better adapted to dim-light conditions or turbid water than walleye.[18] Yellow perch have six to eight wide dark vertical bars on the side of the body and a smaller anal fin than that of walleye. Their body is deeper, and they lack the large canine-like teeth that walleye have. Yellow perch eyes do not reflect and have rod and cone photosensitive cells that have evolved to see in lighted conditions.[19] Yellow perch feed during the day and rest at night; perch and walleye are opposites in this regard. In the shallow shoals at twilight, with perch going out and walleye coming in, the walleye sees the perch and the perch fears what may exist in the shadows. The perch is right to fear, as the walleye diet is often dominated by their kind.

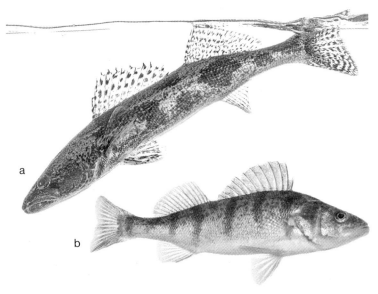

(*a*) *The sauger* (Sander canadensis) *and* (*b*) *yellow perch* (Perca flavescens) *are two freshwater species with a close resemblance to walleye. Photographs by Sam Stukel/USFWS.*

While the description of walleye can be anthropomorphized in a negative or positive light, this fish is a result of millions of years of never-ending simple tests of survival. Walleye have no opinion of humans and demand nothing from them. They live to survive and reproduce, so they consume what they need. Humans, however, have peerless wants that unfortunately result in pollution and global-scale alteration. The further we remove ourselves from other nature, the more stressed we become.[20] In their storms of detachment, the privileged yell their hypocrisy, the majority finds that they are last, and the rest of nature gasps. While this medley occurs, of course, people eat fish. And why not eat the best?

It is not surprising that many walleye fishing stories include a description of how the walleye were prepared for eating or a recipe or two.[21] Walleye have a clean, sweet flavor, and their white finely flaked meat is firm and moist yet delicate, quite distinctive from salmon's rich large-flaked dark fillets and Atlantic cod's dense flaky white meat. Unlike northern pike, walleye fillets have few bones. A modest sized walleye produces a pair of perfect fillets, which can be panfried, baked, broiled, used in a chowder, or, heaven forbid, deep fried.

To follow the tradition of writings on walleye, here is a walleye recipe:

- walleye fillets (sauger or yellow perch may be substituted, but then it is not a walleye recipe)
- butter
- ½ cup of water or milk
- 1 egg
- cracker crumbs or cornmeal (bread crumbs are also suitable)
- seasonings, tartar sauce, or lemon if desired (better not to add salt than to oversalt; actually, I would avoid using seasonings and lemon)

In a container, beat egg with water or milk. Drop fillets into the mixture. Take fillets out and drop them in a container of cracker crumbs or cornmeal until coated evenly. Melt butter in a hot cast-iron skillet. Ease the fillets into the skillet and cook to a light brown on both sides (about 3 to 6 minutes per side). Don't overcook. Remove the fillets from the skillet when the meat is white and tender. Take time to thank the walleye, and then eat.

Besides nourishment, several other reasons explain people's fascination with walleye. Fascination arises from familiarity but limited contact. First, walleye live in the big waters of the eastern United States and much of Canada,[22] so many anglers are aware of their presence. The heart of the walleye mother-water currently consists of the waters of the Laurentian Great Lakes region and the Mississippi River watershed. Their range extends from the Mackenzie River delta of the Northwest Territories in Canada, just before it enters the Arctic Ocean, southeast to the Appalachians of the eastern United States. Walleye can be found in the cool waters from the New River Gorge National Park and Preserve in West Virginia to the Wood Buffalo National Park of Canada and beyond. With stocking, walleye have now populated waters in Montana, Idaho, and the Pacific Northwest. They inhabit the Columbia River. They swim the warmer waters of Lake Meredith of north Texas. They wander the dark and mighty submerged floodplains of the diminished Colorado River in Lake Mead.

Second, since walleye are near the top of the food web pyramid, they are rarely abundant. The hunt for walleye drives passion. When angling is challenging, but wild success possible, many anglers are captivated by the fish that can provide such an experience. Bluegill are often the most sought-after fish where they occur in abundance,[23] yet it is walleye that catch our fascination. It is walleye that we attempt to insert into food webs of bass lakes and faraway waters. Is it human nature to desire the large prize and the inferred majesty of an animal of a high trophic class? For walleye, the hunt just might be for the perfect fillets.

While walleye is not a globally important fish species for human food, they have been and continue to be critical to local communities. Humans have been catching and eating walleye since they arrived at the shorelines of rivers and lakes supporting walleye populations, and it is reasonable to ask if our fishing for them has changed their character.[24] Walleye are vulnerable to capture in the spring when they come into shallow water en masse to reproduce. They spawn on cobble- or rubble-covered shallows, where eggs are protected in cracks and crevices and are not swept downstream or offshore to low oxygen waters. Presumably the first arriving humans focused their harvest on walleye and other large near-shore spawning fish.

TRIBAL HARVEST

More than five thousand years ago, the First Peoples of North America fished with wooden barbed spears, weirs, or funnel traps constructed of rock and wood and with hooks made from bone tied to line made from fibrous plant material.[25] Fishing with nets made from woven grass or other plant material likely quickly followed these earlier capture techniques. In the Great Lakes region, the Anishinaabe people (notably, Odawa, Ojibwe, and Potawatomi) and the Wyandot people relied on fish as a primary food source. On Lake Huron, French immigrants in the late 1600s observed the Odawa people fishing for walleye and other fish using nets. Early European immigrants observed First Peoples using torches composed of pine resin and charcoal to aid in spearing fish; such a technique would be effective for detecting shallow-water-spawning walleye with their reflective eyes. By the early 1800s, Ojibwe people in present-day Ontario were using gill nets along with other fishing techniques to extend the fishing season beyond the spring spawning period.

Tribal members today continue to fish for walleye, and their collaboration in effective fisheries management continues to be key to walleye conservation practices. Over many years, tribal governments in the United States and Canada, through litigation and negotiation, have affirmed or reaffirmed their rights to hunt and fish.[26] One notable litigation example is the Wisconsin Walleye War, which started in 1973 when two tribal members of the Lac Courte Oreilles Band of the Ojibwe speared walleye off their

An Ojibwe couple pulls a net through the ice on Red Lake, circa 1964.
Photograph by Charles Brill. Courtesy of the Minnesota Historical Society.

reservation on a northern Wisconsin lake, which was allowed under the Treaty of St. Peters (1837) and the Treaty of La Pointe (1842) but not allowed under Wisconsin state laws.[27] In 1987, the U.S. District Court ruled that the six Ojibwe tribes had retained their hunting, fishing, and gathering rights in their ceded territory and were not subject to Wisconsin regulation. Today, in Canada, Michigan, Wisconsin, and Minnesota, tribal friends and families gather near the water to create new memories around the harvest of walleye.

Recently, about five hundred tribal members from Wisconsin have spear harvested about thirty-two thousand walleye each spring from about 180 lakes.[28] In Minnesota, similar numbers of walleye have been harvested with gill nets and spears from Mille Lacs.[29] Under commercial fishing quota allocations, Michigan tribal members have harvested a small number of walleye from the Great Lakes. The tribal harvest statistics in Canada are uncertain and less precise than in the States, as most tribal member fishing is family subsistence fishing that generally goes unreported.[30] Tribal member walleye harvest has been substantially less than the recreational sport fishing harvest by the descendants of the non–First Peoples where they co-occur.[31] That does not inhibit members of the latter group from complaining. In many of the Great Lake states, tribal fish harvest and methods remain a contentious issue.[32]

I've spoken with several Ojibwe tribal members on the importance of walleye to their way of life. A conversation with Thomas Howes, a lifelong member of the Fond du Lac Band of Lake Superior Chippewa (Ojibwe), best captured current Ojibwe sentiments on walleye. Thomas was interested in federal Indian law as a young man and received a degree in American Indian studies. More recently he received a master's degree in tribal resource and environmental stewardship from the University of Minnesota–Duluth. He is the natural resources manager for the band, having worked his way up in the agency after conducting a wide range of environmental duties. "I grew up in a time when I was a kid walleye fishing by net and spear, and those things were very outlawed, and treaty rights weren't acknowledged," Thomas said.

I was curious about why walleye were important to him now. Thomas explained, "I've spent a lot of my life as an Ojibwe person trying to maintain culture continuity. I come from an Eagle Clan family, and part of that is being a leader in either maintaining or reclaiming or revitalizing our culture and language—things that have been diminished over time. And so, a lot of that ties to the fishing and hunting and gathering practices that I'm interested in personally. It is a passion, if you will. I have family members who are very involved in arts, language, and education. All that goes into why I am a fisherman. Growing up on the reservation, just up from the St. Louis River, my early adventures as a little kid were going down to the river fishing, not so much targeting walleye initially, but then that evolves over your life. . . . The revitalization of treaty rights to harvest brought me into that realm where now I spear and net each year in the spring for walleye and I do fall netting for tullibee to supplement my family's diet. And when I say 'family' . . . for me,

Fond du Lac tribal members during a night spearfishing event. Photograph by Brian Borkholder.

I'm the fisherman for my broader family, not so much in a nuclear sense. When I fish or hunt it is for family members who can't do certain things physically or for aunties or for people I know who, say, are a single mother or father too busy working or who can't get away, or anyone who needs extra help or just doesn't have those skills. It is a little bit more of a communal way of fishing."

Thomas spoke about the importance of the walleye as a source of food but also about its ceremonial importance to Ojibwe culture. "I live down along the river and there has always been a fishing tradition here for walleye in the spring, and then followed by the sturgeon in the spring, and in the fall, there was a whitefish harvest. Those three fisheries were extremely important in maintaining food, but they were also involved in the ceremonial aspects of Ojibwe life. We always have spring and fall ceremonies that we hold, and these wild foods are a central component of those ceremonies." Thomas and I shared some hunting and fishing stories and discussed the differences between recreational fishing and fishing for subsistence. Thomas explained, "I fish for recreation . . . but gillnetting and spearing of fish is not for recreation; it is for food mostly. . . . Certainly, there are recreational anglers keeping and consuming fish, but mainstream fishing has gone more into catch and release and fishing for entertainment purposes. Ojibwe fishing is definitely a more subsistence-based type of fishing."

Following court decisions in the 1980s and 1990s reaffirming that Ojibwe tribes had retained their hunting, fishing, and gathering rights in their ceded territory, Thomas reclaimed and advanced Ojibwe traditions while he was a young man. "As a Fond du Lac tribal member, we are very fortunate that we litigated and recovered our treaty rights access to a broad area," he explained. "I fish as a provider in the 1837 treaty area, the 1842 treaty area, which is in Wisconsin and the UP of Michigan, and the 1854 treaty area, which is the Arrowhead region of Minnesota. So as a Fond du Lac person, those are the three areas that we have access to under our own regulations, our own licensing process and limitation."

Thomas was quick to note that the Great Lakes Ojibwe have off-reservation treaty rights that have been affirmed but that, besides the Pacific Coast tribes with their tradition of salmon fishing, tribal hunting, fishing, and gathering on ceded lands are quite limited elsewhere in the United States.

Staff of the Fond du Lac Department of Natural Resources take walleye measurements during a lake survey. Photograph by Brian Borkholder.

We discussed the walleye fishery of Mille Lacs, a lake that he fishes each spring. Thomas noted that because of gill net sizes and slot regulations, tribal members harvest mostly male walleye in their spring harvest. The harvest data proves this,[33] and research has found that female walleye are more vulnerable to sport angling than males.[34] Thomas was clear: "We're not out to overexploit the resource. I love those fish. I want my children's children's children to be able to do the same things we're doing. If not, hopefully in a better state. It is not a short-term game for the Ojibwe, and really for anybody it shouldn't be." While Thomas prefers spearfishing, he is a fish provider to a large family. He elaborated, "There is some efficiency in netting. The way I approach it, ideally if conditions are good you do both in a given evening . . . to hedge your bets on catching some fish."

Thomas spoke to why nature was important to him. "Obviously, wild rice and fish are important to us. That is one of the reasons you will see tribal governments and organizations standing up for natural resources. The reasoning for that is philosophical, at least that is how I approach it as an Ojibwe person. All of those resources have been taking care of people for thousands of years. So, when those resources are threatened or are trying to be restored, it's our job to pay that—it is like a life debt or a reciprocal relationship that we have with those resources. They've shared their energy to make our life possible, so we owe them that life debt."

I was curious about his thoughts on the future of walleye fishing and management. "The challenges are our lifestyles as modern-day Americans," he explained. "People are more disconnected and don't spend as much time outdoors. There is a decline in tribal participation, as well as mainstream society, in outdoor activity, whether it is hunting, fishing, or wild rice harvesting." Thomas also noted the challenges with climate change and how it is impacting the walleye range. He ended our conversation on a positive note, as he has been encouraged by the efforts to restore the St. Louis River estuary and the lake sturgeon population, which along with walleye and lake whitefish are critical to the Fond du Lac Ojibwe. He has a strong hope that his grandchildren will have an opportunity to experience the river of his youth, just as his ancestors did.

COMMERCIAL FISHING

Commercial walleye fishing in the Great Lakes commenced in the late 1700s. Each of the lakes had a substantial commercial walleye fishery, caught primarily by gill nets. It was big business. Today only the Canadian waters support a substantial commercial walleye fishery, dominated by the Lake Erie harvest. Records of harvest begin in the late 1800s. In Lake Superior, the walleye harvest generally increased over time, peaking in 1966 at 0.4 million pounds (0.2 million kg); substantially lower harvests soon followed. The commercial walleye fisheries were shut down in Lake Superior's Wisconsin waters in 1956 and in Michigan waters in 1969. Lake Michigan walleye harvest was highest in the 1950s, with a peak in 1950 at 1.1 million pounds (0.5 million kg). Commercial walleye fishing from this lake's Michigan waters ceased in 1969 and from Wisconsin waters ten years later. Lake Huron's commercial walleye harvest was highest in 1899 with an estimated harvest of 3.5 million pounds (1.6 million kg) and declined substantially by the 1950s. Commercial fishing for walleye was prohibited in Lake Huron's U.S. waters in 1970. In the smallest lake of the Great Lakes system, Lake St. Clair, 3.5 million pounds (1.6 million kg) of walleye were harvested in 1891, followed by a sharp decline over the next twenty years. In 1970, high mercury contamination of walleye resulted in the closure of the fishery. The Lake Ontario commercial walleye harvest averaged about 0.2 million pounds (0.09 million kg) through the early 1900s and peaked in 1952. Harvest was broken down by blue-colored walleye and yellow-colored walleye, as prior to the 1960s the blue variety was quite common in this lake as well as in Lake Erie.[35] The commercial walleye fishery closed in the 1970s in the U.S. waters of Lake Ontario.

A commercial vessel from Lake Erie displays a large catch of fish at the dock, 1910. In its heyday the lake supported large populations of walleye, yellow perch, carp, and other species. Photograph by Robert E. Frank. Courtesy of the Sandusky Library.

Lake Erie was and remains the best walleye lake of the Great Lakes from the standpoint of walleye productivity. In 1914, walleye harvest totaled 17.6 million pounds (8 million kg) and expanded to about 29 million pounds (13 million kg) annually through the 1950s (the U.S. commercial walleye fishery closed in the 1970s). In recent years commercial fishers and sport anglers harvested about 6 million walleye annually. The walleye population usually fluctuates between 20 and 80 million for fish two years old and greater.[36]

These dry statistics for wet dead walleye do tell a story—an all-too-common story of commercial fishing. Initially, people think the fishery is bottomless and businesses ramp up. Governments are slow to react or are unwilling to constrain the catch given increased private investment. Then after years of great fishing and large harvests, the fish go missing. Fisheries collapse due to the power of commerce, pervasiveness of greed, and high demand for fish.[37] In addition, technology and knowledge accelerate exploitation. For walleye, the ability to transport fish to markets by new and expanding rail lines, immigrants with fishing backgrounds, steamboats in the 1880s, gas-powered boats in the 1920s, and nylon gill nets in the 1950s all contributed to unsustainable commercial fisheries.

Numerous controls can reduce the likelihood of poor management of commercial harvest. Quota licenses that restrict access to a fish population and annual allowable harvest limits have both proven effective. A fish population could be inexhaustible if harvested carefully. To manage the Great Lakes fisheries, the U.S. and Canadian governments formed the Great Lakes Fishery Commission in 1954. This commission addresses the varied interests of Ontario, the U.S. lake states, and the First Nations through a formalized decision-making process. In addition, this authority implemented an interagency quota management system for walleye and other desirable fish species. An annual allowable catch is determined through analysis of monitoring surveys and past harvests, and then the allowable catch is divided into quotas for each group (state, provincial, and tribal interests). For Canadian waters of Lake Erie, given that Ontario's sport fishing community is small, most of their quota is allocated to commercial fishers.

By the late 1800s commercial walleye fishing had expanded beyond the Great Lakes. Most of this fishing occurred in the large northern lakes and rivers of Canada and a small number of Minnesota lakes. Much of the Canadian commercial walleye harvest from the non–Great Lakes came from Manitoba.[38] Lake Winnipeg, Lake Manitoba, and Lake Winnipegosis were the most important walleye harvest waters, but by the 1980s more than three hundred lakes across the province were being commercially fished for walleye.[39] Early important commercial walleye fisheries in Ontario included Lake of the Woods, Lac Seul, Rainy Lake, and Lake Nipigon. In

Saskatchewan, forty lakes contributed most of the province's commercial walleye harvest, with two hundred or more lakes that added to the total.[40] In Alberta, three lakes supplied most of the commercial walleye harvest for the province: Lake Athabasca, Lesser Slave Lake, and Lake Bistcho. Minnesota's Red Lake, Lake of the Woods, and Rainy Lake had commercial walleye fisheries. Lake of the Woods and Rainy Lake fisheries were closed in the 1980s after considerable walleye population declines and support from sport anglers.

Today, the walleye served in restaurants are primarily wild walleye or wild sauger caught and processed from commercial fisheries in Canada.[41] Commercial fishers in Canada harvest about 17 million pounds (7.5 million kg) of walleye annually, with an estimated value of C$38 million.[42] This is not chicken feed, although to put it into context, Canada produces 2,900 million pounds (1,300 million kg) of chicken annually, with a value of C$2,700 million. To be fair, chicken tastes like chicken and walleye taste better.

SPORT FISHING

People also catch walleye for their own dinner. Most substantial walleye populations support a recreational or sport fishery that is harvest oriented.[43] About 14 percent of the U.S. population fishes.[44] The most sought-after fish in the United States are bass, followed by panfish. About 1 percent of the population fishes specifically for walleye. About 12 percent of U.S. anglers consider walleye one of their target species. States in the heart of the walleye mother-water have higher fishing participation rates (20 to 30 percent), and in these states, like Minnesota, walleye is claimed to be the most sought-after fish species.[45] About 7 percent of Canadians fish, and walleye is the predominant species of fish caught nationally, representing about 26 percent of the total sport catch.[46] For provinces in the walleye mother-water, walleye account for an even greater share of the catch and harvest. The total sport catch of walleye in

Canada in 2015 was estimated to be about 51 million fish, with an estimated sport harvest of about 16 million walleye. Economists have calculated the economic impact of walleye fishing: in both the United States and Canada, it is valued at billions of dollars per year.

It's relatively common for the economist to calculate the economic impact of fishing, but how does the economist place monetary value on the experience of fishing for walleye or the strength of the memories from those experiences? I remember a time out on Mille Lacs when the sun was just rising and slowly lighting up Minnesota. A bank of clouds was tethered to the far eastern shore, ready to capture and reflect the light of dawn. The circle moon was to the west, slightly obscured by the night's remaining haze. I was alone on the big lake. The water was calm and I was at peace. The walleye were stirring. On a human-dominated planet, I was a fugitive, connected to the water and to the moment. The fog was dissipating. With the full emergence of the distant sun, the unfriendly black water of a premature morning slowly transitioned to a gleaming, inviting lake surface. The memory roams the recesses of my mind. It, and many more like it, changed me in unknown and untold ways. The images from those experiences tumble and jumble, and I seek to recreate them by going out into walleye waters again. What value would the economist assign such experiences? The value was more than the sum of my expenditures. Some things are mispriced in this world of economic analysis. Value must mean more than the results of a dubious mathematical exercise. Some things such as fishing for walleye and exploring walleye lakes must be considered priceless. We need to place more value on a future with walleye rather than overvaluing the economic products of today.

Fish and wildlife management agencies are concerned about declining participation rates in traditional outdoor recreational activities like fishing and hunting. Fisheries management is supported in large part by fishing license sales, and any decline in sales affects activities that protect and enhance fish populations

A sport angler casts a line on a northern Minnesota lake. Photograph by Lorie Shaull.

and their habitats.[47] There are many social and physical barriers to fishing. Angling regulations are complicated to those who aren't exposed to the sport at an early age; regulations are often convoluted and contrived rules on the capture or harvest of fish.[48] How will fishing as a sport adapt?

Fishing is an old sport. It is rooted in the need to gather one's own meal. For many in today's world, food is brought to their home—they don't have to go outside, find a plant or animal, and pick them or kill them to survive. These tasks can be delegated, and people can remove themselves from the messy work of being a life extinguisher. A commercial fisher is the delegated; what, then, is the sport angler? The current trend is that sport fishing places a greater emphasis on catching fish than on harvesting fish. Does the angler intend to eat their catch? Is the angler allowed to harvest the fish they caught? If not, then questions arise. Is it reasonable to play with another sentient animal for pleasure? Is it ok to play with someone else's food for some quirky human delight? These are ethical questions, allowed when there is opportunity for free play of the mind.

I ponder these questions often. I have fished all my life, and I still enjoy the thrill of a walleye on the line. I relish being out in the boat on a beautiful day as well as on a rough, wet, and miserable dark night when I'm unsure if there is still a shore to the lake. I find much satisfaction in landing a big walleye. I marvel at its beauty. But what was the purpose, what was my goal? Can I keep it? Shall I eat it? Did I torture this fish for a good reason?

Catch-and-release fishing has merits when used appropriately.[49] This conservation solution started with the dedicated sport anglers of stream trout, largemouth bass, and muskie, who advocated for effective release techniques. Since angler demand for fish always exceeds supply, it is often a pragmatic solution to potentially decrease harvest and increase recreational opportunity. However, for some walleye fisheries, going from a harvest-oriented to a catch-and-release-dominated fishery may not see large benefits in fish growth rates or trophy potential, so the resulting lost harvest opportunities may not be worth the change.[50] The success of catch and release is dependent on fishing methods and time. If the methods and timing are right, catch and release allows the angler to successfully release a fish to be free or caught again. If the methods and timing are not, the angler should not be fishing for walleye when no harvest is allowed.[51] I've concluded that it is ethical to avoid catch-and-release walleye angling when the walleye are deep and the water is warm. In those quiet moments on the water, your conscience is the referee.[52]

2
SURVIVAL SCHOOL
The Life of a Walleye

—◦—

Now that you know what a walleye is, let's look at what their life is like in the water. For a terrestrial being, the life of a walleye is often hard to comprehend. Their watery world confounds. I doubt the fish are as oblivious to the quality of the water as humans are to the polluted air we breathe. For us, a mammal species, the walleye demographic numbers and their long survival odds seem to defy reason. When so many fish die early, the meaning of an individual walleye's life and death is incomprehensible. To understand a walleye's life is to appreciate their purpose. A simple life is better than a complex one.

In the spring, often before lake ice-out, mature male and female walleye congregate in lake shallows, upstream pools, or tributary streams. Some walleye travel great distances to get to these spawning areas. Walleye movements associated with spawning are impressive on large lakes. For example, recently biologists implanted acoustic transmitters into hundreds of Lake Erie walleye and tracked them over several years via an extensive array of acoustic receivers.[1] This telemetry method provides information on individual fish movement, and when aggregated, it allows for the visualization of amazing walleye migrations. After spawning, walleye in the west basin made a spectacular migration east to spread out over the whole lake; then in the winter they would begin to head back west to spawn again in the spring. Often individual fish traveled more than 200 miles (more than 300 km) in just a period of weeks, while others did not stray far from where they spawned (less than 40 miles [64 km]). For east basin spawners, after spawning, some fish also spread out over the whole lake, but migration distances appeared shorter than for west basin spawners. And puzzling to biologists, the Grand River (Ontario) spawners moved little—these walleye generally stayed near the mouth of the river or along the north shore near the river after spawning. The biologists observed high spawning river fidelity; that is, most walleye repeatedly returned to the same river to spawn year after year.[2] In nature, there are usually exceptions.

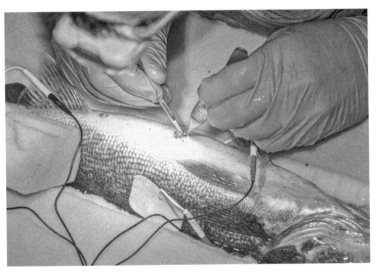

An acoustic transmitter is surgically implanted into an adult walleye. The transmitters help researchers track the fish's migratory movements. Photograph by Joshua Raabe.

At spawning time, the female is full of ripe eggs—tens of thousands or hundreds of thousands of tiny yellow-brown colored eggs.[3] Her fecundity is related to her size; the bigger the female, the more eggs she produces. The environment also plays a role, with walleye from the far north having fewer eggs.[4] For a female walleye, eggs are an energy investment.[5] The probability of egg survival increases with egg fat content and other egg traits.[6] Her eggs were substantially developed by November, and full egg maturation occurred with the increasing water temperatures of early spring.[7] Her ovaries may now constitute 20 percent of her total weight or more. She has sacrificed a large portion of the past year's worth of meals to reproduce this spring. For males the cost of sperm is cheap, but their reproductive investment occurs in the longer time they spend on spawning areas compared to females and competition with other males to spawn with females.[8] Male and female reproductive cycles appear to be group synchronized. Since males and females both experience the same photoperiod and water temperature changes, perhaps nature is synchronizing individual walleye preparedness for sex. If one is making a reproductive investment, then it pays to show up on time.

Spawning occurs in early spring, and it may start under the ice. Water temperature triggers spawning, which begins at about 36°F to 45°F (2°C to 7°C). Peak spawning generally occurs when water temperatures are between 42°F and 50°F (6°C to 10°C).[9] Walleye spawning is a group activity that typically lasts two to three weeks, although the duration can be influenced by periods of cold weather after spawning begins. Males appear at spawning sites first, and they hang around these areas well past when the last female shows up.[10] Females, on the other hand, show up just when they are ready and leave quickly after sex. In a healthy walleye population, this results in a higher percentage of males than females at any one time at a spawning site. The description of walleye sex does not need a warning of graphic content.[11] But be forewarned, walleye are polygamous. They are also nonterritorial during spawning. Spawning generally occurs under the cover of darkness but also during the day, especially at the height of spawning season and when light levels are low. The opposite sexes approach each other at a spawning site and push sideways against each other. As this activity increases, other males and females may join in a group and the pair or group moves forward. At or near the surface the female releases a batch of eggs into the water, and then the male releases his sperm over the eggs, resulting in egg fertilization. The female repeats this act at numerous, nearby spawning sites. The eggs are adhesive for a couple of hours or longer,[12] and this adhesion may allow unfertilized eggs another chance of fertilization by keeping them in an area with male sperm.

EGG

Walleye are broadcast spawners. There is no egg basket, no nest like a male bluegill creates, no redd (spawning bed) like those used by trout. For walleye, a spawning site is simply a place where walleye spawn and deposit eggs. Since walleye eggs can be found in shallow lake environments with muck, silt, sand, and coarse substrates, a reasonable question to ask is, Do walleye select sites that are conducive to egg survival? Based on egg deposition studies, walleye appear to select shallow water with substrates consisting of gravel, cobble, or rubble.[13] In lakes, these areas are often along high-energy shores, on shallow offshore reefs, and around wave-washed points with long fetches. In rivers, these areas are rapids, riffles, and tailwaters below dams. Key to these sites is sufficient oxygen for egg survival. In the Lake Winnebago ecosystem, walleye have unique spawning behavior.[14] Here, most of the walleye migrate up the Upper Fox and Wolf Rivers to deposit their eggs on the flooded marsh vegetation, where the previous years' now-dead plants hold up the now-vulnerable eggs in oxygen-rich flowing water. No matter the spawning site, the eggs are scattered by the female, the sperm is released by the male, and then both the female and the male move on; they do not provide any parental care. The eggs are merely abandoned, as if the walleye fully understand that they have done all they could've done and there is nothing more to do. I have sampled many walleye spawning sites using a fine-screened scap net. Females deposit patches of eggs as they traverse a spawning site, so the embryos tend to be clustered.

A walleye egg's fate is determined in short order.[15] Of course, if the sperm fails to reach the egg, all is lost. Fertilized eggs lose

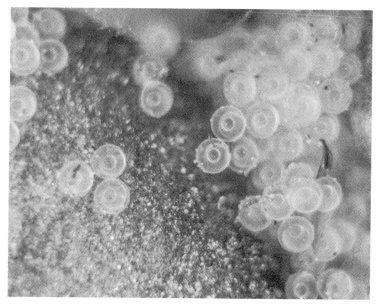

When first deposited, walleye eggs are adhesive and stick together in a cluster.
Photograph by Joshua Raabe.

their adhesiveness and may settle into the rocks or drift with the currents. Embryos will die in low oxygen places, such as in mucky areas. Embryos in shallow water can be buried or damaged by spring storms and wave-shifted sediments.[16] They can also be thrown onshore with those storms, stranded to die on the beach. Persistently cold or declining water temperatures during incubation can decrease the survival of the incubating embryo, exposing them longer to the random forces of mortality. Sometimes the embryo is not viable, and they die quickly after fertilization. When embryos die, they turn cloudy white and a fungus quickly envelops them in a fuzzy mass. It is a rough world for walleye embryos. It is true that each has but one life to live; have compassion for those in the struggle against their end.

The eggs incubate in the shallows while the hermit thrushes move north and the aspen trees start to flower. The chorus frogs comb through their music of love in the wetlands, and sandhill cranes awaken the morning sun, encouraging an output of high noon. The developing walleye are unaware of these terrestrial comings and goings, as they cling to life with unknown force for long moments of indeterministic time. As the embryo develops, it is possible to see the emergence of the walleye's black eyes. In walleye, the eye is the first organ to form.[17] I wonder if the developing walleye observe the spawning of sauger and white sucker or if, at this time, life is a blur. Walleye embryos hatch in about twenty-one days,[18] the same incubation time as a chicken egg. The walleye embryo hatches faster in warmer water, though they can survive low water temperatures; for comparison, a chicken egg needs to be incubated at about 100°F (37.8°C) in the air. Hatching of the walleye embryo is the result of the aggressive movement of the larval fish to escape the bonds of its tiny unshielded space vessel. Once the larval walleye ruptures its weakly protective vessel, they may stay awhile in the rocks or be ejected into the currents.

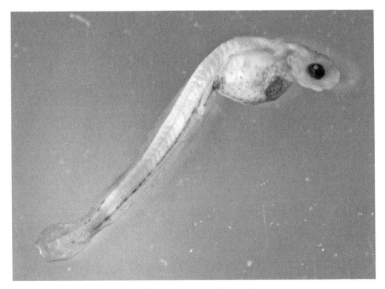

A walleye in the larval stage. Courtesy of the NOAA Great Lakes Environmental Research Laboratory.

Survival rates from fertilization to hatching are low, ranging wildly between 1 and 60 percent.[19] However, the walleye reproductive strategy is clever. Bomb the shore or riffle with millions or billions of eggs, and even at low rates of survival, more than enough will live to replace those that recently died or were killed. Here's a hypothetical example. Assume that the population of mature female walleye in Mille Lacs is four hundred thousand fish and that there is an equal number of mature males. This population of walleye would produce over ten billion eggs in the spring. If all those eggs hatched and grew to maturity there would be no room in the lake for even the water. Walleye egg production almost always exceeds the lake's or river's carrying capacity for walleye.

I'm often confronted about the ethics of harvesting walleye in the spring during spawning. I note that as long as the harvest is sustainable, I see no management or ethical concerns.[20] I tell people to do the math and then tell me why they are really concerned. An argument based on the human or a mammal reproductive strategy is flawed. Thinking about the ethics of spring harvest requires thinking about the walleye's reproductive cycle, which can be vastly different than other fish or wildlife that people fish or hunt. For example, hunting deer is generally restricted to the fall because that year's fawns can survive without the assistance of their mother; killing a doe in the spring often results in the killing of two or more deer—the mother and her likely offspring. For walleye, the new eggs begin developing in a female shortly after spring spawning. Whether she is killed in the summer, fall, winter, or next spring, it is the same—her offspring all die no matter when she is killed. Tell me again why some people are really concerned about harvesting walleye in the spring?

FRY TO FINGERLING

A walleye larva, or fry, just after hatch is a small creature (0.3 inches [9 mm]). They have no functioning gills, so respiration occurs through the skin. They have incomplete fins and are at the mercy of flow, but they are active with jerky upward movements. These awkward movements may propel the fry up into water currents, as they are attracted to the light. A large yolk sac is visible at the belly just posterior to the head, extending about one-third of the larva length. The yolk sac provides the fry with their initial nourishment of protein and fat. This energy drink usually only lasts several days, but in cold water, which reduces metabolism, they may last up to two weeks. In most lakes, the wind-driven currents will distribute fry into open water. In tributary rivers under good conditions the currents will deliver fry to a place with abundant food.[21] About four days after hatch, the little fry begins feeding on tiny zooplankton.[22] With luck, abundant zooplankton is available in the immediate area. If not, because the fry are weak swimmers, they will perish quickly.[23] About ten days after hatch, our diminutive fry is using her newly developed gills to acquire oxygen, and she has inflated her gas bladder. Her life is simple, with the goal of finding and eating zooplankton as efficiently as possible. In about two weeks, walleye fry are also hunting and eating larval yellow perch if available and of the right size.[24] The abundance and the diversity of food are critical for survival. If the timing of spawning and hatch results in the fry living in open water concurrent with a zooplankton bloom and larval perch, then life is good. Yet it is well known but rarely accepted that life is neither fair nor just; unfortunate things happen haphazardly. With luck, our little fry of the northern lake eats well on zooplankton and fish, and she grows quickly.[25]

By early summer our fry is now a fingerling. Her fins are fully developed, and she swims with authority. She has developed scales and shares the wondrous coloration of her parents. Her behavior is also changing. While she was attracted to light as a fry, now she avoids illuminated waters.[26] While she does not sequester to the darkness, she moves in the shadows. Her eyes now begin to reflect.[27] Our young-of-the-year juvenile walleye moves from the open water to nearshore habitats, vegetated littoral areas, and shallow rocky areas. She seeks a piscivorous diet, preferably one

Newly hatched walleye fry at Gavins Point National Fish Hatchery near Yankton, South Dakota. Photograph by Sam Stukel/USFWS.

dominated by devouring in-whole young-of-the-year yellow perch, small darters, confused minnows, and—aghast!—her fellow fingerling walleye. The growth of our fingerling walleye is faster than the growth of young-of-the-year yellow perch, so she will capitalize on her size differential all summer.[28] Our fingerling takes long voyages into mysterious new waters, and as she builds muscle and mass, she spends more time in deeper, darker waters. All the while our fingerling is vigilant, navigating the pondweed forests, desert silt sands, and rocky fjords, seeking meals and evading other fish that are seeking their own lunch. Since our fingerling is small, other fish eaters will hunt her down. A partial list of fish species that would gladly eat her include yellow perch, walleye, northern pike, sauger, smallmouth bass, largemouth bass, and burbot.[29] Our fingerling effectively uses cover and reduces her chances of detection by shifting more of her activity to when the smoldering light on the edges of darkness prevails. By early fall, she is over 5 inches (more than 127 mm) long. For our walleye fingerling, the coming winter is a purgatory. In the fall, she will continue to eat as much as she can.

Young walleye fingerlings at Gavins Point National Fish Hatchery near Yankton, South Dakota. Photograph by Sam Stukel/USFWS.

As our fingerling enters winter, fish biologists make their professional pronouncements about the chance of having good walleye fishing in the future. They speak of year-class strength, or the likelihood of a sizable number of young-of-the-year walleye produced and surviving to a size exploitable by anglers. Their science is good, yet their measures are uncertain.[30] Some variables are known, and many are not. The walleye demographic future is not as well understood as that of the human population. Walleye mortality rates are not easy to predict.[31] Walleye fingerlings have a better chance of surviving winter if they had fast summer growth, if they possessed high energy reserves as they entered winter, and if they had access to plenty of forage fish in the fall and through the winter.[32] Sometimes the fingerling size in the fall can be a good predictor of year-class strength; however, given that adult walleye outcompete and cannibalize young walleye, a high abundance of adults will reduce the number of fingerlings that survive, no matter their size or condition.[33]

YEARLING TO MATURITY

Our fingerling survived her first winter and, as a yearling, is beginning to stretch out. She eats often and grows quickly. She hunts the fish that are most available. If that means bluntnose minnow, Johnny darter, gizzard shad, or yellow perch, then great! But white sucker, rainbow smelt, crappie, carp, and even bullhead will do.[34] While hunting, she moves in on a small fish as fast as the wind, and other times, as if by a miracle, she comes out of nowhere to snatch up an unexamined life. She captures fish from the side with a vicious and sudden grab. She then may manipulate the captive so that its head points towards her gut, which means that when they struggle to free themselves, they only move forward into her tooth-filled mouth and closer to her waiting stomach. This handling also has the benefit of collapsing any spines of spiny-finned fish.

Our yearling also stretches out in her habitat. She now chooses habitat similar to that of adult walleye.[35] She begins to school with her peers, older immature walleye, and adults. In lakes, summer schools of walleye consist of a couple of fish to over a hundred. The larger schools occur in productive areas such as the shallows near the mouths of large tributary rivers. In turbid or dark waters, the walleye's white-tipped tail may provide the visual cue necessary for members of the school to maintain cohesiveness. Our yearling must still be cautious of adults, as a large walleye will occasionally pick off an unwary youngster in the school. During the day, our yearling and other walleye are often resting in contact with the bottom or in the aquatic plant shrubbery. While resting she is often concealed, using the spaces between rocks or under fallen tree trunks. Larger walleye also attempt to hide in the bottom cover; when cover is sparse they might settle to the bottom next to a boulder or sunken log or on top of small rosette plants scattered about on the lake floor. The change in light levels triggers our yearling and other walleye to hunt and feed, whether the changes are from the coming and going of twilight, increased wave action, or "the big, black clouds all heavy with rain"[36] that shadow the lake. As the light wanes, she extends the hunt by moving into shallow shoals or up into the open surface waters for pelagic fish species such as cisco. As the light increases, she extends her feeding time by moving to deeper or more turbid water. By early fall, she is over 9 inches long (more than 229 mm) and is muscular with an attitude.

At the end of another summer, our female walleye's life settles down into a more predictable routine driven by light, water temperature, and dissolved oxygen in the water. She continues to grow at the same rate as her male peers. As a juvenile, her growth is linear and rapid; at the end of her third summer she is 12 inches (305 mm) long, and by the end of her fourth she has reached 15 inches (381 mm). From age 3 to 4 she is of a length most vulnerable to capture by anglers.[37] In a couple more summers, our female walleye will become sexually mature and her growth will slow, although she will grow faster and attain a larger size than the males in her cohort.[38] Walleye, like many fish species, have indeterminate growth; that is, after they mature they can continue to grow in length and weight but at a slower rate. This growth does not continue forever. A walleye may grow to be over 32 inches (813 mm) but may only reach such a large size when abundant large prey fish are present, such as cisco.[39] Fish this size are female, as the biggest male walleye in a population is often about three-fourths the size of the biggest female. Walleye more than 10 pounds (4.5 kg) are impressive but relatively rare. Several 22-pound (10 kg) walleye have been recorded, but most state and provincial angling records are considerably lighter in weight.

WALLEYE ECOLOGY

A walleye's age at maturity and growth rates depend on water temperatures across the seasons.[40] There is some variation in these traits within a population and substantial variation among populations.[41] Walleye growth is generally fastest in summer, except in southern waters where summer water temperatures get too hot for walleye. There, most of the growth occurs in the fall.[42] Walleye mature at a younger age in warmer waters.[43] A walleye may mature by age 2 in the southern United States, and a walleye in northern Quebec may finally reach maturity at age 15.[44] Relatedly, individual walleye growth rates generally decrease from south to north. Females will typically mature one to two years later and at a larger size than males.[45] The average female walleye matures at about 17.7 inches (450 mm) in length and males at about 13.8 inches (350 mm).[46]

Our adult female walleye hunts and eats prey similar to when she was a juvenile. The size of the fish consumed increases as she does. As a juvenile, she wolfed down fish that were half her length.[47] As an adult, she gulps down fish that average a quarter or more of her length,[48] and since she lives in a lake with cisco she will focus her hunting on this energy bar of a fish,[49] especially as she ages and becomes larger. When cisco and walleye share the deep, there are consequences. Walleye often have higher growth efficiencies (weight gained per weight consumed), lower consumption rates (weight ingested per day), and, interestingly, lower activity levels in lakes with cisco.[50]

Cisco strain the filtered essence of blue and yellow light and express it back with unsampled radiance. They are angels of the hellish deep, moving in immense furtive schools and rising to the heavens in the night. Cisco are a slender fish, usually less than 12 inches (305 mm) in length. This species quickly adapts, morphs, and evolves in cold, oxygen-rich lakes, allowing them to diversify in size, shape, and habitat across their range.[51] As a food source, cisco support lake trout, muskie, northern pike, and walleye populations.[52]

How much fish does our walleye eat in a day or in a year? This is a challenging and difficult question to answer with any certainty. I can tell you what I've eaten, and there is guidance on how many food calories I need to survive in the short term (on average, approximately 1,500 calories per day) and how many calories are too many (more than 2,500 calories per day, depending on my activity). Nobody is watching the eating habits of our walleye. She eats what she needs to survive and to reproduce. Consumption studies start with the simple: if you extract walleye stomach contents, what do you find? In Mille Lacs, biologists found that walleye ate primarily yellow perch throughout the year. Larger walleye ate some young walleye, particularly in fall, and cisco were important in the diet when they were available.[53] Add a step. Biologists estimate walleye consumption rates by examining stomachs of juvenile and adult walleye sampled from lakes and then making digestion rate assumptions. In Oneida Lake, New York, biologists estimated that walleye consumption, averaged across weeks, ranged from 0.3 to 6.3 percent of their body weight per day, with consumption rates decreasing with increasing age.[54] Confined walleye tests found that seven-month-old fingerling walleye consumed about 1.5 percent of their body weight per day[55] (to compare, if I recall correctly, my seven-month-old son could consume about 12 percent of his body weight per day). If our 15-inch (381 mm) three-year-old walleye consumes 2.5 percent of her body weight per day, this translates into one yearling yellow perch, about 14 calories, per day. But walleye don't have consistent meals like people, and our walleye might not eat every day or she might eat a lot in a single day. Last, biologists use simple models to estimate walleye consumption indirectly by adding up growth, respiration, egestion, and excretion.[56] There is nothing simple about determining these four variables. This approach was recently used to estimate the consumption of Mille Lacs walleye. Results suggested that adult female walleye ate about 1.5 times more food than males, primarily because they grow larger and use more energy for reproduction (sex matters); adult walleye ate about 5.5 times more food in the summer compared to the winter (water temperatures matter); and adult walleye ate nearly 9 times more food in a year than a yearling walleye (age and size matters).[57]

Our walleye travels a twilight world confined by the edges of the water. That world may be small or large. In small lakes, travel is constrained and the home range will be cramped. In a large, low-productivity lake, our walleye may roam over 100 miles (160 km) a month.[58] She moves alone or in packs of her kind. She cruises at a depth that is comfortable for her, deviating to shallower or deeper contours in her aquatic underworld in response to temperature, light, and oxygen levels. While walleye can achieve bursts of speed, they can't sustain fast cruising speeds. Swimming speed for walleye for a prolonged time ranges from 1 to 2.6 miles per hour (1.5–4.1 km/hour).[59] A human may swim at about this same speed at the water surface.

Everything lives under the laws of nature, including our walleye in her lake up north. These laws were discovered and rediscovered across time and space; they are continually found, tested, challenged, and documented. The law of the conservation of energy and thermodynamic laws determine the fate of energy flows and restrict the shape and number of food web linkages.

For example, about 90 percent of the energy from yellow perch and other walleye prey is lost into the environment as heat that then is not available to walleye. Therefore, there must be substantially fewer walleye than perch and other prey. Walleye use prey energy to survive and reproduce, and they occupy an upper suite in a pyramid-shaped food web. Their growth, reproduction, and mortality rates are dynamic and wobble in time and space due to the changing environment and varying fates of plants and animals on which they ultimately depend.[60] Simple physical laws of this universe constrain the possible but allow the genesis of life to occur where energy is harvestable by metabolic processes. It is not magic that our walleye exists but rather a mix of random luck, natural selection, and the probable.

Our walleye coexists. While she is an effective hunter and, together with her peers, may reduce the abundance of prey, the walleye population also fluctuates with that of their prey. Cause and effect, change and consequence. Large components of the ecosystem show predictable patterns, but fine details such as the status of walleye or yellow perch today and tomorrow are often ambiguous. Young walleye are food for many other fish, including crappie, yellow perch, bass, and other walleye. They are also food for piscivorous waterbirds, such as cormorants.[61] Sometimes these avian predators increase the mortality of young walleye, and other times they have no discernible effect on walleye populations.[62] Walleye compete with other fish predators, and the size of their piece of the pie varies with how well the competition shares their space and time. In waters with abundant northern pike, walleye populations are often lower.[63] When bass are prolific, often walleye populations are less so.[64] Sauger and walleye eat the same fish, and when they share the same habitat they must share the pie.[65]

Walleye face a wide variety of diseases and health challenges. Columnaris is a bacterial disease that afflicts stressed and injured fish, and it can become systemic, resulting in death.[66] Columnaris usually begins as an infection on the body at places of injury or bruising, and then it progresses internally. Symptoms of the disease include bleached-out scales and ulcerations on the skin, but laboratory testing is needed to verify infections. Several viral pathogens affect walleye. One disease that fishers and anglers may notice on fish in the spring is lymphocystis. This viral disease creates white or pinkish growths that erupt from the surface of the skin. These growths often disappear later in the year, and the disease does not appear to cause high mortality.[67] Another viral disease that affects walleye is dermal sarcoma, which looks similar to lymphocystis except the growths are smaller and often patchy on the skin.[68] After initial exposure to the dermal sarcoma virus, walleye appear to develop resistance to reinfection. Walleye also host a large variety of organisms that feed off their blood, tissue, and digestive system[69]—most walleye have a parasite or two,[70] including our female walleye. Leeches, nematodes, trematodes, oh my! Gill lice—parasitic copepod crustaceans[71]—oh wow! Our walleye has also played host to some temporary free riders—several species of mussels. Many mussel species are dependent on fish, although the details of this dependency vary by species. Some mussel species require a particular fish species host, while other mussels are more flexible in their parasitic needs. A female mussel releases her young into the water, and these larvae attach to fish gills or skin to feed on the fish's blood for a short period of time. After the larvae morph into juveniles, they jump ship and fall to the lake or river bottom to live a long action-packed existence of filtering water for food. Our walleye served as both a host and rapid public transport, as her passengers jumped off in a new part of town.

Our walleye has no choice but to adapt to the constraints on her life that are out of her control. Humans can just clear more land for agriculture and pump more pollutants into the ground, water, and air to feed and transport the masses, often creating death so that they may live. Not so for walleye—when their prey is scarce, they suffer. Individual walleye grow slower when their hunting is less productive. Some walleye may die due to food shortages, such as

This walleye, caught in 1949 on Lake Winnebago, shows evidence of lymphocystis, a viral disease. Photograph by Elmer Herman, Wisconsin Department of Natural Resources Collection, University of Wisconsin–Madison Library.

when yellow perch reproduction is poor. When prey numbers are low, our walleye may eat more young walleye or shift to alternative fish often not on her typical menu. The number of walleye in her lake may decline. For a given year, overall walleye reproduction may be reduced due to decreases in growth, increases in mortality, and later sexual maturity. In hard times, each walleye compensates to stay in the game, giving the illusion of a walleye central government. While our walleye does not necessarily starve in these hard times, there are no food shelves or food stamps to help buffer her predicament. It works both ways: the good times are the inverse of the hard times. Ample food leads to higher hunting success, which leads to faster growth, less death, earlier maturation, greater fecundity, and greater reproduction. If this happens, the number of walleye in the population may increase. In addition to prey abundance changing walleye fate, in the same way their own density also influences their destiny.

Fisheries biologists speak of density dependence, which is simply the cumulative fate of individuals rippling across the entire population. For walleye, growth, survival, and reproduction often change due to their population density relative to carrying capacity.[72] At relatively low walleye densities, either the population rebounds from increases in individual growth, survival, and reproduction, termed "compensatory density-dependence effects," or the population continues to decline from decreases in survival, termed "depensatory density-dependence effects."[73] Compensatory effects allow a sustainable harvest,[74] and depensatory effects can result in population collapse.[75] When a walleye population is low due to overharvest, habitat loss, and a changing aquatic community from climate change, walleye recruitment depensation may occur from reduced young walleye survival because of greater predation or competition pressure from traditional or new actors on fewer young walleye in the population.[76]

The number of walleye in a river or lake is dependent on many variables. The quality and fertility of the water, the amount of available walleye thermal-optical habitat, climate, fishing pressure, and the size makeup of the population all influence the density of walleye.[77] In large rivers, walleye can be abundant, and their density may be high, perhaps greater than in some lakes.[78] Across lakes, walleye densities can be highly variable.[79] Most walleye lakes have densities of less than 4 adult walleye per acre of water (10 adult walleye/ha). The median density across a range of walleye lakes was estimated to be about 6 adult walleye per acre (15 adult walleye/ha), although a few lakes had high densities (more than 40 fish/acre [100 fish/ha]).[80] The average walleye density in Lake Erie across many years was about 2 fish per acre (5 fish/ha). To contrast and compare, the human population in Israel currently has a density of 1.7 people per acre of land (4.2 people/ha) and Monaco has 77 people/acre (190 people/ha). The population of gray squirrels in public parks has been estimated to range between 1 and 20 squirrels per acre (2 to 49 squirrels/ha).[81] Simply put, some lakes have few walleye and some have a lot, people are everywhere and they are dense, and some parks have more squirrels than lakes have walleye (just to be clear, I would rather eat walleye than squirrel).

It is important to not confuse abundance or density with productivity. Walleye abundance is the number of walleye present at a specific time. Walleye productivity is a rate. Rates, like fish productivity, are sometimes hard to grasp; take velocity (rate of movement) and acceleration (the rate of change in the rate of movement), each used every day, but each can confuse. Walleye productivity integrates abundance, growth, mortality, and reproduction; it is the total amount of walleye tissue developed in a unit of time. For fish, productivity is measured in the number of pounds per acre per year (kg/ha/year). Walleye productivity, like density, varies over time. Walleye density and production are related;[82] walleye production could be inconsistent with density. For example, walleye productivity could increase because the growth rate of individual fish increased, while walleye density in the lake remained unchanged. Fisheries biologists have detected declines in walleye productivity in northern Wisconsin lakes that are stocked, and they suspect habitat changes along with several other potential factors may account for these productivity declines.[83]

On average about a quarter of the walleye die each year from natural (nonhuman) causes, such as disease, predation, starvation, and old age (termed "natural mortality").[84] Of course, as the walleye population increases, natural mortality may increase with added stress caused by greater competition for prey. Conversely, if a portion of the population is harvested, then the number of walleye that die from natural causes may decrease within the year due to the removal of peer competitors.[85] In addition, the growth and reproduction of walleye may increase in the period after harvest.[86] Thus, walleye population productivity can increase by harvesting the population sustainably. This is one of the foundational theories of fisheries management science. The management challenge is twofold: first, to harvest sufficient walleye to trigger increases in growth and reproduction to gain productivity (compensatory effects); and second, to avoid harvesting too many walleye, which may trigger reductions in reproduction (depensatory effects). Most recognize the latter, but almost all are unaware of the former. Don't save all of today's bounty for a tomorrow that does not come, and don't let yesterday use up too much of today.

It is early spring, and our mature female walleye moves with the other walleye to spawning areas. She has already grafted her lifeline to her gametes, not to extend her life but to extend walleye life itself. While the tree blooms brightest when there may be no tomorrow, her fecundity is related to her fitness. She may follow other walleye to traditional spawning sites or seek the familiar—the sights, sounds, or smells of her youth. Some walleye show high fidelity to a specific spawning area, with some fish swimming to distant waters to reach their preferred spawning site, which suggests a natal homing instinct, a heritable trait, or a learned behavior.[87] And, evidence does indicate that spawning area fidelity, especially for river spawning walleye, might be a common phenomenon.[88]

Our walleye is spawning for the first time; she remains a virgin. She now has a chance to have a daughter or son that can replace her when she dies or is killed. We are not fish, so we can't know if she has emotions and feelings. She may be happy and joyful at this major life event, or she may be emotionless—an avatar in a game of life that is instinctively acting out the script encoded in her DNA. It is easier to believe the former.

Our walleye may have many opportunities to be a mother, perhaps ten or more occasions to rain her eggs on the spawning grounds of her ancestors. Maximum longevity of walleye in a population may be five or thirty years.[89] In the Great Lakes and northern lakes, biologists have observed female walleye older than twenty years old; the oldest males were in their teens.[90] Our walleye will likely outlive most males of her cohort, as in most walleye populations there are more very old females than very old males. The faster they grow the quicker they die of natural causes; thus the warmer their environment the faster the metabolic rate and the faster they expire.[91] Precious is the short life.

Our walleye's life, like our own, has periods of trouble and peace, with freedoms and many dependences. Walleye live in a wild world with no belongings and with cares only of survival. Their eyes see the swift prey in dimly lit waters. They see movement in the shadows, yet are oblivious to their peculiar fate from a so-called superior species. Our walleye is propelled by the forces of nature, yet she is rooted in place, in a dynamic environment and ever-changing web of life. She is unique, yet a commoner in the dark waters of the north.

3
THE THRILL OF THE CHASE
Walleye Fishing

———◦◦◦———

Walleye fishing has many forms and objectives. Besides fishing to acquire tasty walleye fillets, people like getting out into nature, spending time with their kids, socializing, and fishing competitively. Unusual encounters and experiences are part of any fishing adventure. My fellow anglers usually have great expectations and a strong desire to have a good time. A reasonable expectation of catch is the key to a good fishing adventure, so I will give you a little background about fishing. First, not all casts or nets result in fish. I've found that each fishing trip is unique—sights and sounds vary. The sky lightens or threatens; the water is calm or a maelstrom; rain washes away the dust or extinguishes hope of catching walleye. The lessons learned are unpredictable, and no one is too old or too wise to learn. Normally when I'm fishing with friends and family, the conversations we have are about life, mixed with an ample amount of good-natured banter. I find the conversations more important than the catch. Often, the walleye that were to be eaten remain in the lake or river. But if you catch some fish, our distant relatives, it is important to give something important back in return.

Many resources are available to begin or to improve your walleye fishing adventures. If you are like me, perhaps it is best to fish with someone who knows what they are doing. Fish with a family member or a friend or charter a fishing launch or guide. Most large walleye lakes have launch or guide services. Establishments on Lake of the Woods, Leech, Mille Lacs, Winnebago, and Winnibigoshish provide these services, and they are a good way to get exposed to walleye fishing. Be appreciative of those who share their time and fishing expertise, and thank them for their time and help. In addition, watch, learn, and ask a lot of questions. Follow their lead. When among the crows, caw as the crows do. You learn how to fish by fishing. In my trips with the experts, I have learned that there are several important principles for fishing success.

FISH WHERE THE WALLEYE ARE

To fish where the walleye are may seem an indisputable principle, but you'd be surprised how many people fish where there are no walleye or likely to be no walleye. Don't climb a tree to catch a fish. Fishing a new place is fishing the unknown, and the unknown can be exciting and a refuge of hope. Humans have great delusional capacity, and many have faith that they might catch something because they are trying hard. Faith may not determine one's future. Knowing where the walleye are is a huge advantage. If you are fishing just to get out in nature, then by all means fish where it is most beautiful. As you fish, soak up the sweet smell of the exhaling lake or river, absorb the crisp tones of shoreline birds, and reflect on the murmuring complaints of water forced to move.

First-order approximation of good walleye lakes can be assessed quickly by a couple of simple facts. Walleye waters exist between the warm productive bass lakes and the cold, low-productivity lake trout lakes.[1] If you have a lake with northern pike, white sucker, cisco, and yellow perch, then it is possible that it also supports walleye. A lake with abundant leafy aquatic plants is more suited for northern pike, whereas a walleye lake has a greater portion of primary production coming from yellow-brown diatom algae and green algae. Walleye abundance is related to the fertility of the water, with higher density at higher fertility; however, maximal walleye density generally occurs at a medium level of ecosystem productivity.[2] When water fertility is low there are insufficient prey fish to support a large biomass of walleye. Some people tell me that they angle farther north because more walleye are in those lakes. I reply that it is great they are heading north to stay at a resort,

Lac La Croix in the Minnesota Boundary Waters is a good walleye lake and has been luring anglers with its clear, deep water for decades. Photograph by P. Freeman Heim, U.S. Forest Service Records, National Archives.

but the lakes in the southern part of the walleye range have higher walleye densities—they are confusing catchability with abundance. The lakes in the far northern part of the walleye range have lower prey productivity, so those walleye tend to bite at an angler's bait more than the walleye in the more productive lakes to the south. Walleye abundance and productivity are considerably lower in the far north lakes, and because of high catchability, those walleye are also more vulnerable to overfishing.[3]

It is true that self-sustaining walleye lakes are often larger bodies of water, generally those greater than 500 to 1,000 acres (200 to 400 ha) in surface area.[4] Walleye are dependent on ample areas of windswept shore or sufficiently large rivers to provide suitable egg incubating and young fish habitat. Small lakes, even when walleye are dumped into them, usually make poor walleye fisheries.[5] Large lakes allow space for predator fish to spread out and avoid competition with other species.[6] I'm regularly asked by devoted walleye anglers who live on small bass-dominated lakes why the fisheries agencies can't or won't improve their lake's marginal walleye population. My conversation on this topic is often short: I tell them that fisheries managers are constrained by the physical and biological characteristics of the lake and that sometimes it is not possible to impose our will on nature. If they really want to live near the walleye, I suggest that they get a place on a true walleye lake instead.

Good walleye lakes can also be assessed by using knowledge of lake depth. Walleye lakes are often of modest average depth (approximately 20 feet [6 m]) and not extensively shallow.[7] I'm not referring to maximum lake depth, as that lake attribute can mislead the true character of the water. If the average depth is greater than 30 feet (9 m) or most of the lake is very deep and it is way up north, then the lake is likely more suited for lake trout. Average depth of a lake is important because it influences water temperatures and whether a lake will thermally stratify.[8] In deep lakes, the wind may not be able to mix the water sufficiently to create a uniform temperature at all depths. Although the sun warms the surface water, the deep water remains cooler. Thermal stratification often lasts all summer in deep lakes. The lack of water mixing can have consequences on dissolved oxygen concentrations in the water. Algae and aquatic plant photosynthesis produce oxygen. With low nutrient concentrations and organic matter production, the oxygen concentrations are sufficient for fish at all water depths. In more productive lakes, however, bacteria in the bottom sediments consume the oxygen as they eat the accumulated organic matter on the lake bottom, and the oxygen concentration progressively decreases in the deeper water. In such cases, fish will not use these deep parts of the lake. Don't fish the dead water—the fish have left.

Large rivers are also good places for walleye, as walleye are as much a large river species as a northern lake species.[9] Examples include the Mississippi River, Wisconsin River, Rainy River, Detroit River, St. Mary's River, and St. Louis River. Walleye are more accessible from riverbanks than from the lakeshore, and often the walleye population is robust and locally concentrated in rivers. I came to appreciate walleye at a young age while fishing the Wisconsin River close to our home. At the time, my father worked at the nearby paper mill, and he thought it okay if we parked our bikes behind the mill and walked around back to the river. The river flowed through the turbines at the far end of the mill, and beyond the mill the river fell over a low, wide spillway. The eddies of both could be fished for walleye, as could the riffles and pools downstream. The fishing was simple: waders; a basic fishing pole and reel; and a handful of simple jigs, hooks, and sinkers. Cast downstream and jig the lure back, or, while standing on the mill or dam structures, jig the eddies vertically. Occasionally we would use live bait. We did not keep our catch, as my father noted that after dark a foreman would occasionally ask the workers to dump barrels of waste in the tailwaters. The solution to pollution was dilution and collusion. Enlightened hearts and minds, along with the use of water quality standards (e.g., the U.S. Clean Water Act of 1972, the Canada Water Act, and the Ontario Clean Water Act), have returned the Wisconsin River and other rivers to a less polluted state, where walleye and other fish can better survive and flourish. And, often they can be eaten (for details, consult your state, provincial, or tribal fish consumption advisory).

Determining where the walleye are can be quite simple at the waterscape scale. Rather than conducting a systematic, analytical study of agency walleye abundance data by lake and river, talk to those in the know. I encourage sustained periods of fishing for walleye. No good comes from hurrying. Make a vacation out of it. There are hundreds of good family-owned resorts on walleye lakes in the lands up north. These are great places to connect with nature, reaffirm family ties, and explore walleye fishing. Resorts can make fishing for walleye an immersive experience. In the spring and summer, the resort owner can help by providing good fishing advice, a guide, fishing gear, or possibly a tasty meal after a wonderful day on the water. During the winter, many resorts rent ice houses by the day or for the weekend. I've had the good fortune to meet many Minnesota resort owners over decades of working on lake and fisheries issues. I find that they are hardworking menschen. They have chosen a lifestyle that requires multiple talents and considerable patience in serving others, but it is one that allows them to live close to nature while still being social.

I had a conversation about resort vacationing for walleye fishing with Dana Pitt, who with his wife, Cindy, owns and operates Bailey's Resort on Leech Lake. I got to know Dana in 2005, when we served together on a state-organized committee that crafted alternative shoreland development standards for local governments in north central Minnesota. Dana is a thoughtful person with a quiet demeanor. He is active in his community and has served as president of the Community of Minnesota Resorts organization.

A lone ice house sits on Fish Hook Lake, a walleye lake near the resort community of Park Rapids, Minnesota. Photograph by Lorie Shaull.

He is also an avid walleye angler, and with the family resort on Leech Lake, he has many opportunities to help others catch walleye on an outstanding walleye lake. Dana and Cindy bought the resort in 1998. "We had two little kids at the time," he recalled, "and what better place to raise kids than at a resort where you are with them twenty-four hours a day." They eventually raised a family of three children while running the resort business. Dana noted it was perfect for them: "We wanted to be on one of the bigger walleye lakes, more of a destination lake—people knew about it and walleye were the focus, which was kind of what I was interested in, too. So that got us to Leech Lake."

Dana loves living at the lake, working with his family, and running the resort. When I asked him what he liked about the resort, he explained, "Besides the family part of it, you are dealing with people when they are at their best. They are on vacation. They are up here to have fun . . . so you are just promoting that and helping them have that good time. You make a lot of good friends. Being at the resort, you get the repeat customers who come every year and you get to know over the years." On his customers, Dana noted, "During the summer, it's mostly families. It is a lot of the same people coming— the same week every year. They come to the same cabin. They get to know each other. They keep in touch throughout the year too. It is kind of cool to see how other families become friends and get along. I think that is the coolest part of being a resort owner—that and just where we get to live. When I'm having a bad day, I look over the lake and think, 'Wow, it could be a lot worse'!"

I asked Dana how he helps people get closer to walleye. He explained, "There's a couple of dozen or more independent guides on the lake. . . . If a guest wants to take a guide, we line it up and we book the guide. The guide picks them up at our dock and drops them off back here. . . . Even if we are not guiding them or lining up a guide for them, of course we help them any way we can. We bring out the maps . . . and tell them where the bites have been or areas to try. I'll go in their boat with them if they want, look at their tackle and show them what to use and how to rig it. And we sell bait here also. We do what we can. We want them to catch walleye, and if they are catching fish, they are happy. It is a big lake, and you got to point them in a good direction or they could flounder out there for a week if they don't know what they are doing."

Dana noted that their spring and fall guests are mostly dedicated walleye anglers, and while their summer guests do fish, it might be secondary to enjoying the beach and lake. He emphasized the value of resorts: "People will always want to get away and go to the lake. Lakeshore property has gotten so expensive that the average person can't get their own place up here. Resorts are the last place where they can go up and live at the lake. It is different than staying at the local motel and launching your boat at the public access every day. At a resort, you are out on the lake, you come in, you have lunch, you just park your boat at the dock, go up to the cabin, go in and out, you're living at the lake for a week. There is no other way for people to really do that anymore other than at a resort."

Resort owners continue the Minnesota resort tradition of hosting walleye anglers through the years. In this historical photograph, several walleye (and a northern pike) are displayed at Burntside Lodge near Ely, Minnesota, which has been welcoming anglers since 1913. Courtesy of the Ely–Winton Historical Society.

If camping is more your style, find a campground or camping area on a walleye lake or river. Several good locations come to mind, from rugged camping to full-service RV parks. The Boundary Waters Canoe Area Wilderness, administered by the U.S. Forest Service, and Quetico Provincial Park, governed by Ontario Parks, are outstanding wilderness parks for walleye fishing. Voyageurs National Park in Minnesota also has ideal walleye fishing with houseboat camping and rugged campsites among the lakes. Northwest Ontario is home to thousands of walleye lakes and many campgrounds that you could explore for an extended vacation. Many of the U.S. Forest Service campgrounds and several state parks in Michigan, Minnesota, and Wisconsin are on or near walleye waters. If you canoe the waters or walk about the grounds, you can likely start up a conversation about walleye fishing with a fellow vacationer. If you're lucky, someone might give you a tip about where, when, or how they caught some fish recently. If you are fishing near your home and a traditional bait shop still exists there, stop in and ask for gear advice and about where to fish. Most owners are happy to tell you what they've been hearing about the local fishing action, and they will sell you some necessary bait and tackle.

A CREATURE OF HABITS

Once you've identified a lake or a river to fish at, the second principle necessary for the prospect of catching a walleye is to fish when the walleye are most likely to be at a particular place. This is a four-dimensional space and time problem: three dimensions of a lake or river and one dimension of time. Walleye are bottom associates, and the bottom is their sanctuary.[10] However, walleye may move up or suspend in a water column. When walleye are feeding on suspended forage fish, fishing for these midwater walleye by trolling with lures can be highly effective. Therefore, if you know the preferred water depth that walleye are seeking, your space-time problem can reasonably be simplified to a three-dimensional problem: a two-dimensional surface (lake or river bottom plane) and a time dimension. If your time is constrained and adjusting your fishing time is not possible, then your problem may be simplified further to just a two-dimensional surface plane problem. How might you determine the depth that walleye are most likely occupying? If you are fishing in summer on a thermally stratified lake, you can go out to the deepest part of the lake and, with scientific instruments, measure temperature and oxygen systematically from the surface to the lake bottom. If you know walleye preferences for temperature and oxygen, you can then determine what depths you should seek as you begin your fishing expedition. Good luck! Alternatively, you could use sonar equipment (a fish finder) and get a sense of what depths large fish are concentrated in. A fish finder detects air bubbles or air pockets, so the degree of acoustic reflectivity is based on the size of the fish's swim bladder (a fish adaptation that makes them vulnerable to human detection). Or you can do it the old-fashioned way and hunt for walleye at various depths until you are successful (or you see others who are successful) and then continue fishing at those water depths with some variation.

Understanding walleye habits is helpful when fishing for them. There is a seasonal rhythm to walleye haunts. In the spring, walleye move into rivers or along windswept lakeshore to spawn. After spawning they may tarry in rivers and shallow lake waters, and for a week or so after spawning they are less sensitive to light and are vulnerable to daytime angling in shallow water.[11] As summer advances, walleye can also be found more often in shallow waters dawdling and dining. In the summer, in thermally stratified lakes, walleye generally seek out bottom depths where the water temperature is within their preferred range (64–72°F [18–22°C]), light intensity is low (between 8 and 68 lux),[12] and dissolved oxygen levels are sufficient (more than 6 mg/L).[13] This means that walleye are usually dallying at the bottom depth contours of deeper waters, near or at the transition from the warm shallow water to the cool deep water. Sometimes this means that walleye are haltered to a steep slope of a submerged hill, drumlin, or ravine valley. In the fall,

A Wisconsin DNR employee uses an early electronic depth finder during lake survey work in 1957. Photograph by Reese W. Staber, Wisconsin Department of Natural Resources Collection, University of Wisconsin–Madison Library.

walleye are often in the shallow waters, sometimes close to shore, and as water temperature cools they may move to deeper water. As the lake ices up, walleye can be found near shore and often in shallow water. As winter progresses, walleye are more likely to be at deeper depths, where the water is warmest.[14]

In addition to a seasonal walleye rhythm, periodic and daily rhythms occur in walleye movement. Spring and summer storms often stir up lake sediment in the shallow water, creating turbidity and suspending the bottom insects. Minnows and perch feed on the exposed and vulnerable small organisms kicked up by the turbulence, and in turn, walleye feed on those feeding. High river flows of turbid or bog-stained water spilling into lakes can also create conditions favorable for walleye, who find comfort in the turbid water and will feed in and about those murky waters, often in very shallow water. Daily rhythms may be quite distinct on some waters. At dawn, at dusk, and on the dark days of heavy clouds, walleye will move shallow to hunt for yellow perch and other prey. Angler walleye harvest rates are generally higher at dawn and during the evening than at midday.[15] Biologists have accumulated a wealth of data on when and at what temperature (or depth) walleye are inhabiting; acoustic tags provide this information for every minute of the day and night.[16] During high light conditions, walleye are often resting on the bottom, again where the temperature and oxygen are nearest to their preferred range. These locations can be on hard substrate bottoms or even on mud flats like those found in Mille Lacs. Remember, in picking a fishing place, think about the depth contours that walleye are likely to be inhabiting for a given season and time of day. The serious anglers trace these haunts across seasons and by day and night in hopes of becoming professional anglers. Perhaps you just wish to get a bite.

GEAR AND TECHNIQUE

The third principle for catching walleye is to use the right fishing gear. By "right," I mean gear that is likely to be most effective, is allowed by the established rules, and is satisfactory to your conscience. Using a net or fishing pole may be better than praying for fish at the edge of the water. I'll outline the many methods used to fish for walleye. Please check the catch and harvest rules that apply to you and your area. Fishing regulations can be complex, but then again we live in a complex world of variable established rights. First Nation members' regulations vary, but members may have additional rights to walleye using a range of methods.[17] Before heading out to fish, make sure to check your state, provincial, or federal regulations.

Spear and Bow and Arrows

One way to catch a walleye is to take a barbed spear and skewer spawning walleye from the bank of a river or small stream. A spear, a light, and burlap bag to bring the fish home to clean are all you need. As a kid I would spear for white suckers in the rivers close to home. It was mix of elegance and hick, athleticism and awkwardness, normality and lawlessness. Timing was important. Were the fish moving in shallow yet? Was the water too high to get to the best places? Was the water clear? Would school get in the way? It took careful hand-eye coordination to thrust the spear down onto the dark-backed fish as they hesitated in the kill window or moved slowly upstream through it; I tended to ignore the fast-moving ones. If you aim your spear at two fish, both will escape. Bow and arrow use for fishing is also fun and challenging. You can attempt to arrow a fish at a greater distance than with a spear. After several misses, where your arrow whooshes and torpedoes through the water creating a line of air bubbles, you realize that you must adjust your aim lower to account for the light refraction on the surface. The equipment consists of a decent bow, fiberglass barbed arrow, line, and open hand-wrap reel. It is great fun, and while it is rarely allowed for walleye, opportunities to use this gear for suckers and carp may be legal.

Fish Traps

Trap netting for walleye is an efficient yet challenging way to fish, and this gear is routinely used for sampling walleye by fish management agencies. The trap nets I've used consist of a series of steel hoops covered by netting with two internal meshed funnel traps that point inward from the mouth of the trap. The funnels are kept open with lines, and the net ends in a pot that has a line to open and close it. The mouth of the trap is supported by a rectangular steel frame to which a long leader is attached. The trap net is set in shallow water so that the trap is fully submerged. The leader is anchored to shore or at the edge of a littoral break. A slipknot is tied to the pot line, to which an anchor is attached, and a buoy is attached to the anchor. To set the net, the leader anchor is thrown from the bow of the boat, and as the boat backs away, the net is paid out until all slack is gone. The pot anchor is dropped and the buoy thrown free of the boat. There is satisfaction in setting a taut and extended trap net that settles upright on the bottom.

Set depth is critical: the net must be at a depth where it will catch walleye and deep enough that any moving ice will not knock it down. To capture spawning walleye, leave the net to fish overnight and return in the morning. To retrieve the net, grab the buoy line and place the pot anchor in the boat. Being left-handed, when on net duty I tend to work on the port side of the boat. Release the slipknot and remove the thrashing fish by shaking the pot over a large tub. I'm struck that most fish are not spatially aware enough to escape the trap's pot back through the two funnels that they entered. Walleye get in the pot and settle to the bottom, and they see no way out. In years of trap netting, it appeared to me that only bass have some mental capacity and spatial understanding to enter and leave the net with little difficulty. Generally, all fish captured are alive. Release the by-catch (unwanted fish and other animals) back to the water. If you are early in the walleye spawning period, you might also get a few northern pike, as they spawn before walleye and some stragglers may still be close to shore and doing their thing.

My favorite way to catch walleye is trap netting during their spawning season. It is possible to catch dozens of walleye in a single well-placed net provided that your netting effort is well timed. Success depends on getting the nets into the water soon after the ice melts away from shore and as soon as walleye begin to congregate near shore. Sometimes this means breaking up the crystallized and fractured ice with little thought to propeller damage or to the opinions of sequestered humans viewing the action from the comfort of their cabin living rooms. The water on this imagined day might be cold and the weather fickle. But, given that I've adapted to the cold from a lengthy Minnesota winter, the pelting rain and raw wind gusting off the ice sheet do not crush my spirit as they would in November. Howling winds create dangerous conditions as the boat is brought into the shallows. The waves break over the transom. Everything in the boat is wet, I'm wet, and the lunchboxes are

Minnesota DNR employees deploy a trap net into a Minnesota lake, circa 1950s.
Courtesy of the Minnesota Department of Natural Resources.

floating with the remaining buoys at starboard and port. The stern
is heavy. I ignore the sound and fury of the waves and the wind in
my ears while I steer the boat to hold it in place to set or retrieve
a net. A lack of focus and an insufficient throttle in reverse could
throw my teammate and me to shore, to be battered about on the
slippery rocks until engine or human brawn create backward mo-
mentum. The next day might be sunny and warm, with the winds
slight, and the task of setting and retrieving nets of bountiful catch
is a joy. We approach each net slowly and gauge the number of
captures and weight to be emptied. We marvel at the tub full of
beautiful walleye. The fish caught by spring trap netting are heavily
skewed toward males, as they linger longer around the spawning
shoals. On the lake, the speed of time varies not with distance from
mass but from the strength of the wind. On rough water, we eat
lunch quickly while driving between nets, but on calm and sunny
days, we break and eat our shore lunch with deliberate care as we
absorb the sun's power on secluded shores.

Gill Nets

The fishing technique of using gill nets, like trap netting, is a passive approach. This gear is commonly used by tribal and commercial fishers to harvest walleye, as well as by fisheries management agencies to assess walleye populations. The technique is remarkably simple: set a net and hope that fish will encounter it and get caught. How, when, and where the net is set determines the number, sex ratio, and length distribution of walleye captured. A trap net captures fish by entrapment; a gill net captures by entanglement. Setting a trap net to capture walleye on the spawning shoals is sex selective for mature walleye; using a gill net on or near the same shoals is also selective for mature fish, and it is size selective as well. Gill nets are long panels of mesh hung from a float line and connected to a weighted bottom line. The mesh can be constructed of multifilament or monofilament nylon.[18] Multifilament is the conventional material used, and a multifilament net is limp and easy to handle and store. Monofilament nets are stiffer, harder to handle, and more difficult to repair, but they typically capture more fish in clear water than multifilament nets.[19] For the latter reason, monofilament nets are popular. Gill nets are highly size selective, and the mesh size of the net determines the size of walleye captured. Mesh size used for walleye ranges from 1.25 to 2.0 inches (31.75 to 50.8 mm),[20] with the larger mesh capturing a larger average walleye size. In addition, nets with larger mesh sizes fish with greater intensity.[21] A net with large mesh has a higher probability of the walleye hitting or contacting the net because it is less visible to the fish. Selectivity for a gill net is a multiplicative calculation of the probability that a fish encounters the net, the probability that an approaching fish then contacts the mesh rather than detecting and avoiding it, and the probability that a fish contacting the mesh is retained.[22]

Using a gill net to catch walleye is only difficult for the first few net sets, and after those initial experiences you can catch walleye while you sleep. Set up the gill net before you deploy. Remember, well begun is half done, and well done is better than well said.

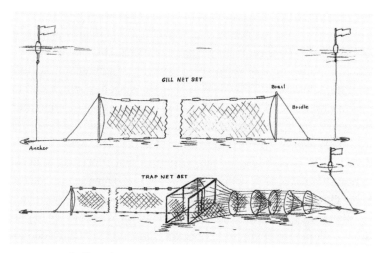

A trap net and gill net in set positions. Courtesy of the Minnesota Department of Natural Resources.

Gill-net deployments for walleye are set on the bottom. Test question: Why the use of bottom sets? Answer: Walleye spend a lot of time near the bottom; so if you wish to catch walleye, fish where they are likely to be. At each end of the gill net attach a wooden brail and the bridle ropes; together these stretch out the end of the net. Attach an anchor line to the end of the bridle, an anchor line to the anchor, and a line from the anchor to the buoy. That is a lot of connections—invest in quality metal trigger snaps or overlay-arm snaps with swivel eyes. Some folks simplify this by eliminating the brail and connecting the anchor to the bridle. Regardless, be sure that the buoy line is longer than the water depths to be fished, or you'll be fishing for your net.

The goal is to set a straight, taut net on the lake bottom. In dark water, you may not be able to see your net, so you'll have to go by feel. If the wind is blowing, it is best to set with the wind, especially in shallow water as the net may roll. To set, throw the buoy and drop brail anchor; then pay out the net over the bow as the boat backs downwind. As the net is spooled out, it will catch on any imperfections or irregularities on the boat or even your clothing, and it is wise to peer out on occasion to see if your buoy still remains at the surface. It is a pisser to not have a buoy at both ends when it comes time to retrieve a gill net, as the wind could shift after deployment and it is nice to have the option of which end to pick up first. I tend to shake out the net as it leaves its container because I don't like tangles in my net sets. Pay out the float and lead lines evenly. As the end of the net is reached, hold the buoy line tight to stretch out the net while the boat continues to back. When the net is taut, drop the brail anchor over the side of the boat. Throw out the buoy and hope you have enough line attached, or otherwise you will see the buoy race forward and under to join the zooplankton. If you're fishing for spawning walleye, you can deploy late in the day and lift the net the next morning when winds are typically light, or if conditions are right, you can deploy in the morning and lift in the evening.

To retrieve the gill net, grab the buoy at the downwind end and pull. If the weather is bad, remove the rigging and feed the net's mesh with the entangled fish into its container. Deal with the ball of fish and mesh back at shore. If the weather is good, you can remove fish as you pull the net in over the side of the boat. Fish are captured by wedging and tangling. Walleye become wedged at several points in their body as they swim through the mesh before they get stuck and are unable to back out; sometimes they get in as far as their dorsal fin. Tangled walleye are captured by their teeth or maxillaries of the jaw. It is quick work to remove tangled walleye as you bring in the net, while wedged fish may take a bit more time, but with practice you will make rapid decisions on whether to pull on the head while dragging the mesh over the dorsal and pelvic fins or to back the fish out by pulling the mesh over the walleye's sharp frontal body protrusions. Using a net pick helps in the fish removal process. Either way your hands will get raw after handling many spiny and rough walleye. Most fish will be either close to death or dead from suffocation caused by constriction of the gills, although

Two fisheries personnel extract a walleye from a gill net, circa 1950s. Courtesy of the Minnesota Department of Natural Resources.

others will still be quite alive. You'll likely get by-catch using this gear. By-catch may be minimized if you are fishing on or near the walleye spawning shoals during spawning season, but even then you might catch and kill a lot of northern pike.

I've fished over one thousand gill-net sets. Fortunately, most of these sets were in the low productivity waters of the north for fall-time walleye population assessments. After months of gillnetting it almost became work, but all nets were retrieved with curiosity. Don't make a toil of pleasure. On pleasant days, anglers would approach our boat as we picked fish out of the nets and ask thoughtful questions. The young and the curious would ask how they could get a job like mine. I would joke that they needed to know someone in government leadership, preferably an elected official—or, alternatively, that they could try bribing the appointing authority.

I always found it interesting that on rough days when we were taking a good beating on the water, no one appeared alongside our boat. On those days, only the cruel cold followed our crashing, careening boat across the unforgiving waters of the north.

Electrofishing

Electrofishing for walleye excites. It is, after all, hunting with electricity.[23] The method is hazardous, so the fishers must be safety conscious. Yet, there is a thrill to performing acrobatic moves to dipnet fish while avoiding contact with the electrified water. Fishing with electricity began in the 1930s, but it was not until the 1950s that fisheries biologists stuck a generator in a johnboat, grounded the generator to the metal hull (cathode), and extended two fiberglass booms off the bow to hold out electrodes (anodes) that were dragged through the water. The usual setup involves one person driving the boat and one or two people (dipnetters) stationed on the bow using fiberglass dip nets to capture the stunned fish and flip them into a live well. Boat electrofishing is effective in shallow water, especially where the bottom consists of hard substrates. Today, several companies manufacture electrofishing boats that are safe and reliable, with waterproof foot switches for the dipnetters, sturdy bow railings adorned with bright lights for night fishing, a control box that allows a range of electric waveforms, and a safety switch on the driver's console. Often a pulsed direct current wave is used, and the boat operator adjusts the control box settings to get an optimal fish response.

Fish response to the electric field depends on the transfer of electric power from water to fish.[24] Water conductivity, which varies from lake to lake, is the major factor in determining power transfer. Fish size also determines power transfer, with small fish, like fingerling walleye, requiring higher electric output. The goal is a fish that is directed by the electric field to move toward the anodes, is stunned, and then recovers quickly within the live well. Too much power and the fish may be injured—too little power and

Students from the University of Wisconsin–Stevens Point conduct an electrofishing survey on a lake in northern Wisconsin. Photograph by Joshua Raabe.

the fish is hard to net. It is most interesting to see fish holding still or moving slowly away from the boat until reached by the electric field. Then they exhibit uncontrolled muscle convulsions that force them to swim to the anode. Once they reach the anode they often are stunned and can be dipnetted. Many biologists will tell stories of horror and fright upon electrofishing the unexpected, such as muskrats and beaver. The trick for those encounters is to switch off the current before they reach the anode; otherwise you may accidentally kill the muskrat or beaver. Let me just say, I prefer the white finely flaked meat of walleye to the dark dense meat of muskrats and beaver.

Electrofishing is illegal for sport fishing in almost all jurisdictions, but it is a common method to assess fish populations. Fisheries biologists use nighttime electrofishing in the fall to evaluate relative abundance of young-of-the-year and yearling walleye, and, in the spring, they conduct night electrofishing to estimate relative abundance of walleye by size and to capture walleye to tag for mark-recapture population estimates.[25] When fish are concen trated, like with spawning walleye, the frenzy of walleye influenced or stunned by the electric field can overwhelm a dipnetter. In those cases, when I was driving the boat, I would, over the noise of the generator, yell encouraging words to the crew on the bow to dipnet faster (e.g., "You're missing them," "Desire all, lose all," and "Keep your stick on the ice").

Angling

This might be your only option to catch walleye, so embrace it. Walleye angling is art. Like life, it requires some patience, practice, and perhaps a predisposition for persistence and failure. Failure is okay; it is not a measure of your worth. Most walleye fishing trips end without catching any walleye.[26] For those angling for walleye in Minnesota and Wisconsin walleye lakes, the mean angler catch rate is about 0.25 walleye per hour,[27] or about one walleye for every four hours of fishing. Angler catch rates do not have a normal, or bell curve, distribution; rather, catch rates are highly skewed, con-sisting of a high proportion of zeros as most walleye fishing trips result in no catch.[28] It is reasonable to say that 10 percent of the anglers catch between 50 and 70 percent of the walleye.[29] These facts may surprise you, but it is why husbands, wives, fathers, and mothers rarely take their wives, husbands, or kids walleye fish-ing. No-walleye-caught days outnumber walleye-caught days, and like gamblers, walleye anglers remember only the good days, lest they become indifferent to the fix of a tugging walleye on the line. It is said that anyone can fish for panfish, bass, or trout, but to be an in-fisherman you need to advance to walleye. And good wall-eye anglers will let you know that this is true (or at least that they firmly believe it).

I've mentioned the whens and wheres of walleye movement that may affect fishing success, but even when those elements are favorable it is another thing for a walleye to check out your bait. A hungry fish may strike when proximate bait is presented and

Anglers prepare for a day of walleye fishing at Mille Lacs, circa 1920. Courtesy of the Minnesota Historical Society.

perceived as prey, but a satiated fish may be disinclined to take the bait. Capeesh? One good tip to follow for walleye fishing is to place your bait close to the bottom, but not on the bottom. You're not fishing for bullheads, and walleye fishing on the bottom only means snags and lost tackle. Develop a keen sense of the water depth you're fishing. Generally, fish are found in shallower water during the spring, in the fall, and in low-light conditions, and they are in deeper water during the summer, in the midwinter, and in the bright of the day. Depending on the lake, the deeper water may be in the range of 12 to 40 feet (4 to 12 m) and associated with slopes or on substrates that rise from the bottom. Fishing the outside edge of an aquatic plant stand may be more productive than fishing in the vegetation. The weather and water conditions may not be important in angling success. One thing is clear to me: when you are angling, you could catch a walleye, and when you are not, then you won't. To state the obvious, the longer you fish, the greater the chance of catching a walleye. If knowing that the lake waves are modest, which some call a walleye chop, helps you decide to head out on a fishing adventure, then great. Low-light conditions may be more conducive to walleye feeding, especially in clear-water lakes; however, good walleye fishing occurs during the day in many waters where walleye feed intermittently.[30] Night fishing in shallow lakes and river waters can be highly effective, but the exact places and timing for productive fishing may be specific to your favorite waters.

Fishing, like life, takes practice. Getting to know your favorite river or lake and fishing with live bait will likely increase your catch rate.[31] You should also fish with someone who knows how to catch walleye; it will help.[32] And, please have some fun while enjoying the great outdoors. Quality of life is measured not by your success but rather by the health of all. Fishing is a good time to reflect on your life. Ponder how to be a better human, how to help your neighbor, your community, and the rest of nature. According to the philosopher Bryan Norton, "The interests of humans and the interest of nature differ only in the short run."[33] He elaborated, "If we look at the broadest human values, the most long-range human values, and compare them with the values of ecological systems, these are really headed in the same direction. If we damage nature, we damage ourselves in the long run."[34]

Jigging

There are several common techniques for walleye fishing. Jigging is the most flexible way to angle for walleye. When jigging, you need a fishing rod, reel, line, and jig. Tie the jig to the end of the line,[35] and you are ready to fish. Good luck. Jigging refers to the up-and-down motion of the jig that you create by moving your fishing rod. One can fish with a jig and not be jigging. The jig is a weighted hook, preferably weighted with a nontoxic metal and not lead.[36] The weight is the head of an imaginary animal and is positioned

Wilbur Isaacson removes a hook from a walleye caught on Lake 13 in Chippewa National Forest, 1958. Photograph by Bluford W. Muir, U.S. Forest Service Records, National Archives.

at the eye of the hook, which is often placed at the top of the head. The rest of the hook comprises the tail of the nonexistent creature, which can be covered in part by a plastic body and tail, feathers, hair, or thread. These jigs are designed to attract the attention of walleye and are produced in various sizes and colors.[37] A bare hook jig is used for live bait. A live minnow is added to a bare hook jig by hooking the minnow through the front of the head (this is not immediately lethal, as the angler wants a lively minnow on the hook). It is vain to fish if the hook is not baited. Jigs are dropped straight down next to the boat, cast out, or trolled with a generous distance behind a drifting or slow-moving boat. You must give the jig motion. Walleye perceive a stationary jig as nonliving, and they seek the living. When vertically jigging, let the jig hit the bottom and then lift the rod, then lower the rod, repeat, repeat, etc. The jigging can be lively or subtle depending on the mood of the angler or the walleye. When casting a jig, cast as far as you can. If fishing a river, cast downstream, across the current, or upstream into eddies. If fishing a lake, cast over the walleye. If you're lucky, your jig will land in water and not on land. For kids, a cast longer than a parent's is grounds for superiority. Let's fish. Be mindful to the task of casting. Cast away. Let the jig settle to the bottom and then lift the rod or sweep it sideways, drop the rod tip down or bring forward, reel in the slack line, and repeat until the jig is upon you. Notice that I assumed you would not catch a walleye on the first cast. Better luck next time.

Trolling

Trolling involves motoring or rowing around the lake while trailing a baited line behind the boat. The advantage of this technique, where allowed, is that you can cover a lot of lake bottom. You can use jigs, Lindy rigs, spinner baits, or lures. The shortcoming is that you must manage the boat and the fishing rod at the same time. In rough conditions, it is best to drift with the wind rather than to troll. You can troll day or night, left or right, right or wrong. I always felt that the motor was doing most of the fishing, but when I caught a fish, I attributed it to my fishing prowess, not random luck delivered by ceaselessly crisscrossing the dark waters by motor. In the spring, as the pastel green leaves of the aspen trees emerge, troll lures in shallow water at dusk and through the darkness. Set the hook as soon as you feel the walleye hit the lure, except when fishing with Lindy rigs, when you should let the fish go by releasing the spool for a count of five to twenty seconds, depending on how hard the bite was, and then set the hook. This latter technique often results in deep hooking, so it is appropriate to restrict its use to those waters where you can harvest fish of all lengths.

Still Fishing

Let's give trolling short shrift and take up a more relaxed approach to walleye angling: still fishing. Fishing rod, reel, line, nontoxic weight, hook, bait, and optional bobber. Simple, effective, and relaxing. The approach allows the opportunity for free play of the mind or quiet time to enjoy nature's bountiful sights and sounds. For the bobberless version, several sinker weight options are available: split shot, egg sinker, or slip sinker. A leader made from a couple feet of monofilament line is terminal from the sinker. The sinker allows a long-distance cast, and when it lands on the bottom the baited hook hangs upward with the buoyancy of the bait. A slip sinker allows the fish to bite without sensing that the food is abnormally leashed to an unknown force of nature. For the bobber option, a small split shot is attached to the line a foot or more from a short-shanked hook. The slip bobber size should match the bait and be no bigger. It needs to float, and using the smallest size minimizes walleye detection of the abnormal. The need for a slip bobber rather than a traditional clip-on bobber is obvious when you are fishing more than a few feet (1 m) deep. To set the fishing depth, a small threaded knot is tied to the line, then a small holed bead is put in place, and, finally, the line is threaded through the bobber. The distance of the threaded knot or bobber stop to the baited hook is the fishing depth. This should be set so that the bait remains close to but not on the bottom. If you cast out and see your bobber lying on its side, your bait is on the bottom, and you need to move your bobber stop down to decrease the amount of line below the bobber. Walleye don't like to grub for a meal. Also make sure that the bobber slips up and down the line; if not, the bait may be near the surface and unavailable to the hungry walleye. Walleye don't like to breach for a meal, either.

Bait your hook and drop your line into the water or cast it out. Let the bobber drift with the wind and current while your bait remains in good walleye water depths. Watch the eagle glide by looking for floaters and land in the nearby white pine. Reel in your slack line as necessary. Observe the loon dive for fish off the break and surface at a distant unpredictable spot. The bobber bounces, announcing that a fish may desire your offering. The bobber vanishes below the surface, so set the hook with a swift rise of your rod. You feel resistance as you reel. It appears that you got something. A large fish is struggling to get away. The fish rips out the drag as they head for the deep. Suddenly, your rod and reel seem inadequate for the task. Keep the rod tip up and reel when possible. Your line moves to the right and then to the left. The fighting creature at the end of the line gets closer, but clearly the fish does not want to come up. They wish to remain in the dark. Keep the tip up! You see a shadow move left and right as you force the fish back to you. And all at once, a golden beauty of head and spine appears at the surface. They are not caught until in the net or hand. Fishing truth: fish get bigger as soon as they get away. Net them and they are yours. Mazel tov! Congratulations—you caught a walleye. Better one today than two tomorrow.

Ice Fishing

Ice fishing is like open-water still fishing. If this becomes your hobby, then you will acquire an array of ice-fishing necessities, including but not limited to augers, chisels, skimmers, dippers, flashers, tip-ups, ice shelters, ice fishing poles, propane heaters, Swedish pimples, insulated and aerated minnow buckets, and the ultimate ice camper. When younger, I regularly walked out on the ice of a Wisconsin or Minnesota lake, careful not to test its strength and the depth of the water with both feet. I carried a minimal amount of gear in a bucket and drilled a hole in the ice by hand. After clearing the hole with the dipper, I baited my Swedish pimple or jig and sat down on the bucket with my short, homemade ice fishing stick. If I hooked a walleye or burbot, I pulled the line in by hand and dropped the fish in the bucket and tried to repeat. The gray clouds touched the ice in the distance. The ice cracked and moaned as the surface shifted with the undetected changing air temperature. On windy days, snow bits bounced about on the ice and followed the wind to my ice hole, where they joined with the freezing water to heal the ice. I had to skim regularly against this force of nature conspiring to protect the fish below. I walked back across the ice when the cold reached my bones and the shakes would not calm, or when I grew weary of the lack of action.

A sport angler uses an auger to drill a hole in the ice of Bass Lake in Superior National Forest. Photograph by Lance Cheung/USDA.

Bait

There are extensive bait options available to walleye anglers. A lure is an artificial bait made of wood, metal, or plastic. It is designed to mimic an animal and to attract a fish to bite. In the store it is often encased in colorful packaging to attract the attention of a passing angler. Fish are nearsighted. The adaptation that allows walleye to see in low light conditions also results in slightly blurred vision. Walleye likely have a much lower visual acuity than humans.[38] A walleye bites at the artificial bait because while they can detect motion in dim-light conditions, they strain to discern the details of the moving object. Live baits used to catch walleye include night crawlers, worms, leeches, and minnows.[39] I have a fondness for leeches and a general preference for minnows.

More than forty species of the minnow family (Cyprinidae), plus many more species from minnow-like fish families (suckers, mudminnows, sticklebacks, etc.), are present in walleye lakes and rivers or connecting waters. All can be used for bait. The minnow nonindustrial complex depends on a few species that they sell to walleye anglers, and, not surprisingly, these species are hardy fish. Probably the most popular species of minnow sold at bait shops is the fathead minnow.[40] This minnow prefers ponds and small lakes, and up north they are found in bog lakes and other dark-stained waters. Fathead minnows can survive in turbid waters with low oxygen concentrations and withstand the rough conditions that come with being trapped, hauled, and held in captivity. These qualities make them desirable for the minnow trade. The creek chub is widely distributed and is one of the most common minnow species in the central and southern portion of the walleye range.[41] Males of this species can reach a length of 10 to 12 inches (254–305 mm). They are readily captured in streams, and as a young boy fishing trout streams in the sand counties of Wisconsin, I delighted in catching this chub that schooled in the larger, deeper pools.

Common shiners are another minnow used extensively in walleye bait fishing.[42] While more common in streams, this minnow can become abundant in lakes. The common shiner is silvery colored with a large diamond-shaped scale pattern. Golden shiners are a popular bait for ice fishing with tip-ups. Golden shiners are a deep-bodied minnow found in lakes and river pools.[43] When possible, I suggest that you capture your own minnows. Seining the shore for minnows gives you another view of the lake. It gives you a greater appreciation for the minnow's life, which may cause you to take more care of these sentient beings before you hook them and cast them into merciless waters. Finally, it gives you the opportunity to

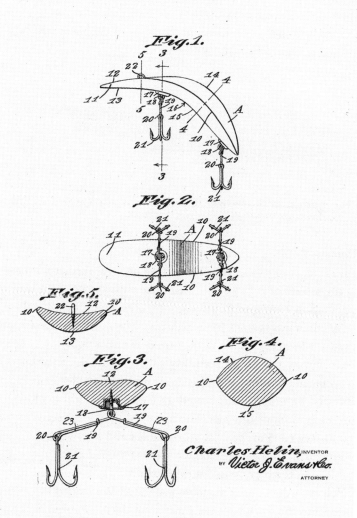

Fig.1.

Fig.2.

Fig.5.

Fig.3.

Fig.4.

Charles Helin, INVENTOR

BY Victor J. Evans & Co.

ATTORNEY

In the 1950s, Charles Helin's patented Flatfish lure became popular in Minnesota and Wisconsin for walleye fishing. Courtesy of the U.S. Patent Office.

better understand the fish community of the water you fish. The diversity of minnows and minnow-like species in a lake is fascinating,[44] and I find it interesting to see which of the many minnow species are the most common across time. Are bluntnose minnows abundant this year in this lake? Can the young-of-the-year mimic shiners be found yet on the sandy nearshore? Where are the emerald and golden shiners today?

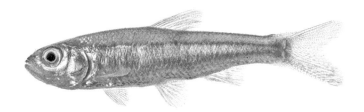

The common shiner (Luxilus cornutus) *is one of several bait fish popular with walleye anglers. Photograph by Sam Stukel/USFWS.*

Camera Traps

On a cold, late October day in 1999, I got out of a warm truck parked in the woods next to a small, clear lake with an abundant walleye population. I stripped down to just my swimsuit. The wet gold and ruby fallen leaves stuck to my pale feet. The north breeze stripped the heat from my hands as they tried to pull a tight, damp scuba wetsuit over my gangly body. My colleague, Dr. Jerry Grant, was working at the shore to get his dual underwater video camera and infrared light apparatus rigged up for an overnight deployment on the bottom of the lake. The apparatus was connected to two 1,000-foot (305 m) coaxial video cables and a power cable, now wrapped around a large wooden spool stationed at the shore. The cable spool, which would stay on shore, was connected to two video recorders and a portable generator. We loaded our equipment into the work boat and pushed off. Jerry motored backward out to the deep part of the lake as I watched to see if the cables were spooling out correctly while holding the apparatus on the bow deck. We anchored and gently finessed the apparatus into the water, slowly lowering it to the lake bottom. I mentally prepared myself for the cold and then flipped back into the water. My first underwater breath through the regulator filled my lungs as the cold water blasted my face and slowly seeped into all corners of the wetsuit. Jerry lowered a large calibration cage into the water, and I guided it to sit just in front of the apparatus without disturbing the silt-covered bottom. Jerry captured some video of the calibration cage and then raised the cage back to the boat as I guided it away from the apparatus. Jerry would now be able to accurately estimate the length of walleye that were recorded.[45] Before going back up to the boat, I spent a bit of time playing hide-and-seek with the fish while marveling at the gleaming crystal-clear pondweed forest beyond the mask. The diffuse light reflecting off the rising air bubbles against a backdrop of a green and blue water world was beautiful. There was no horizon, and I floated carefree. Back at shore, Jerry checked all the equipment, and I stripped out of the wetsuit, doing my best to manage my hypothermia.

At the time of this experiment, camera traps were a novel way to catch walleye. Today, easily deployable, compact underwater video is readily available. Many anglers, especially ice anglers, use underwater video to help them catch fish and to enhance their fishing experience. I wonder if the use of this equipment will ultimately lead a portion of fish enthusiasts to fish for walleye with just underwater video—forgoing the fishing pole. Early wild bird enthusiasts used shotguns to collect birds that they observed, but today they forgo the gun and use binoculars to observe a vast array of birds. Serious birdwatchers keep a life list of birds that they have identified by sight or sound. If birdwatchers could go through an evolution in methods, would it be reasonable to expect that some anglers will move to the capture of live video of fish rather than the need to take possession of the fish with hook and line? Or is the tug of a walleye on the fishing line and the taste of walleye on the plate so stimulating that it would be impossible to give up?

GOOD FISHING
—◆◆◆—

The fourth and final principle for catching walleye is to immerse your mind in the moment. Fishing allows for merging yourself with the artistry of nature. Don't be preoccupied. Focus your attention and awareness, be stimulated by the sounds rippling across the lake, and fixate on the water, the act of fishing, and the caught fish. Observe the waves as they head to shore; they become higher and steeper, until cresting and running ashore. When fishing from shore, I will fixate on a floating object in the waves—maybe a leaf or mayfly exuviae—wondering when it will come ashore as it tumbles and attempts to synchronize with the moving silt and sand. Will it make landfall, or will it be forever trapped in water to be ripped apart and dissolved? Observe the herds of water striders running forth on the water and the stampede of the jet-black whirligig beetles ahead of the boat, as you wonder when they will break formation like pursued bison on the prairie. See the color of the water change with depth and passing cumulus cloud shadows. Smell the decaying pondweed rolled on shore and the fish slime on your hand.

Respect the fish. Before you catch a walleye, it is a good idea to think about what you will do with them. All life is sacred. Harvest only what is needed. If you are releasing the fish back into the wild, then your method of capture should be one that minimizes stress to the fish and you.[46] Angling hooking mortality can be a serious issue, with average walleye hooking mortality rates ranging from 1 to 35 percent. Hooking mortality increases with increasing water temperature and capture depth.[47] Reducing stress to the fish means using hooks and techniques that reduce hooking the fish deep in the mouth or in the gill arch, throat, gullet, or stomach. This might mean that you forgo live bait and angle instead with lures. If you are thinking about eating your catch, then it is important to consult your health agency regarding the likely pollution levels in the fish inhabiting the lakes and rivers you will be fishing. Mercury from coal burning still rains down on our lakes and bioaccumulates in predator fish. Polychlorinated biphenyls (PCBs) from dielectric and coolant fluids still seep into our waters, biomagnifying up the food pyramid and causing cancer in humans. Per- and polyfluoroalkyl substances (PFAS) from a variety of industries whose products were designed without long-term thinking still leach into the water and end up in fish. PFAS is a large class of synthetic chemicals used in many products, including food packaging, water-repellent fabrics, and firefighting foams. Eating fish is good for you, and the benefits outweigh the risks when eating fish low in mercury or other contaminants. Be informed or be polluted.

It is altogether fitting and proper to kill a fish for food, but taking a life is profound, and it is important to respect the fish and ensure the meat will be of high quality. The fish should be killed swiftly to minimize pain and suffering[48] and butchered immediately, or if not possible because of regulations or timing, the dead fish should be placed on ice. I have many fond memories of fishing with my grandfathers. We caught a lot of fish and had great fun and conversation. We would catch fish to eat, and to keep them alive we would put them on a stringer or in a fish basket. When we moved fishing spots, we would pull the stringer or basket out of the water, and the fish would flop on the boat's hull; often the fish died a slow death from stress and suffocation. Water can do without fish; fish cannot do without water.

When people prepare walleye for eating, it is often euphemistically called fish cleaning. The fish were clean before you caught them; nothing is so clean as a fish. A common way to prepare a walleye for eating is to fillet the fish. Butcher the fish on a clean surface, and between fish, clean the surface as necessary. Filleting fish requires a sharp knife with a long, thin blade; a good knife is invaluable. To begin, place newspaper or kraft paper on a flat surface and lay the fish on their side. Make the first cut posterior to the head and pectoral fin, slicing down to the backbone. When the blade touches the backbone, turn the knife and slice along the backbone all the way to the tail fin (you will be cutting through the rib bones). You can cut away this fillet, but I like to stop just short so that the fillet is still attached at the end of the tail. One can elect to remove the rib bones at this time; I tend not to as I'm a minimalist (I remove these few bones when eating, and I tell my guests that there are no boneless fish).

Next, remove the skin (if you'd rather eat the skin, then scale the fish first and skip this next step). Start with a careful slice at the tail end and proceed with a continuous slice along the back side of the skin until the whole fillet is cleared. When done effectively, there should be no meat on the skin. Repeat the process for the other side of the fish. Finally, remove the meat on the head just posterior to the eye. Rinse the fillets with cold water. Roll up the carcass in the paper. If you're in the wilderness, place the carcasses on the rocky shore for the mink; if you are rural, then toss them in the back forty for ravens and crows. In either case, the carcasses will disappear when your back is turned. I encourage you to eat the fish that day or place the covered fillets in the refrigerator for the next day. Use all that was harvested. Give people fish and you feed them for a day; teach them to fish and you set them free for a lifetime. Go, be free.

A fishing party prepares for a meal on the shore near Wisconsin's Turtle River in 1936. Photograph by Eugene Sanborn, Wisconsin Department of Natural Resources Collection, University of Wisconsin–Madison Library.

PART II
WALLEYE MANAGEMENT

4

FISH IN, FISH OUT

Walleye Stocking

——◦◦——

Walleye don't need us. But we would like to eat more of them. To get more walleye, we add walleye to waters where they are not present or are low in number. To protect the walleye populations we have, we need to protect their habitat. When you add people to a walleye population, you get a fishery. To maximize walleye harvest from waters, we manage the harvesters to take the surplus production. This creates complications. Add people to anything and it creates problems. If the problems can be solved, fix them. If they can't be solved, worrying will do no good. Let's cover the important topics on managing fisheries for walleye. A good place to start is stocking, since the politics of stocking is one of the most visible and controversial aspects of a fishery.

Fisheries managers note that their tools are few and weak. Nature sets the constraints of what is possible, and while humans have great capacity to destroy, their powers to improve on nature are often inane and vacuous. The basic activities of a fisheries manager are as follows: put fish in, take fish out, protect habitat, and regulate the harvest. Equally important is the management of people through regulation, education, and other behavioral change. Fisheries managers recognize that they need to measure outcomes instead of activities.[1] When fisheries managers succeed, it is because they have reasonable goals that are measurable and measured. Fish management works best when it takes the path of least ecological resistance. A written plan compels managers to explicitly state their goals and objectives. The plan provides a process for continuity, a means of evaluating the management efforts, a way of documenting issues with the fishery, and a context to listen and include citizen feedback.[2]

When it comes to citizen input, more fish is often the goal, and fish stocking is often the first suggestion or demand.[3] Stocking as the first solution is intoxicating, but it is a sticky and sometimes irritating idea. Walleye are the number one fish species stocked in the United States, and the last available summarized evaluation reported that over a billion walleye are stocked per year.[4] More walleye are stocked in this country today than at any time in history. Walleye stocking, by weight, is more than three times higher today than it was in the 1930s. Most walleye stocking occurs in the Midwest; Minnesota, Wisconsin, and Michigan are at the center of the walleye mother-water. Several states recently doubled down on their walleye stocking, including Wisconsin, with a Walleye Stocking Initiative (2013–present), and Minnesota, with an Accelerated Walleye Program (1999–present).[5] The purpose of walleye stocking is to create fisheries where walleye have failed to immigrate or prosper, to maintain a fishable walleye population in marginal habitat, or to bolster a walleye population to make it easier for anglers to catch them. For some anglers, bigger is better, more is better, and avarice is not a sin. I leave it to you to ask the hard question: what are the direct and indirect consequences of this wealth of walleye stocking besides a warm feeling in a walleye angler's psyche?[6] For Wisconsin's Walleye Stocking Initiative, fisheries biologists recently concluded that walleye stocking is incapable of maintaining or restoring many of their walleye fisheries.[7] For Minnesota's Accelerated Walleye Program, most of the intensively stocked lakes saw no change in their walleye abundance.[8]

In the late 1980s I started my fisheries management life working on the Canada–U.S. border waters for the state of Minnesota. Rainy Lake and boundary waters to the east were the focus of my interest and profession. I worked on two critical issues, which were interwoven. The first issue was the water level management system on Rainy Lake and Namakan Reservoir, which had detrimental effects on fish, wildlife, and navigation. The second was walleye overharvest on Rainy Lake. We advocated for a modification of the international water level management rules that were used by nearby paper mills and for greater restrictions on walleye harvest to restore the Rainy Lake walleye population. For some in the community, these acts were thought to have high economic costs, so they sought to stop their advancement.

Water level changes were expected to increase the operating expenses for the paper mill companies. The water level management system is regulated by rule curves established by the International Joint Commission and implemented by the paper mills at Fort Frances, Ontario, and International Falls, Minnesota. Rule curves are the upper and lower water level elevations within which the dams must be operated to maintain the water levels at any given time. Levels on Rainy Lake are kept higher and more stable than natural conditions to ensure maximal hydropower generation, and water levels on Namakan Reservoir have greater annual fluctuations than natural conditions to provide water storage for Rainy Lake downstream. Dr. Bill Darby of the Ontario Ministry of Natural Resources and I cochaired a group of private citizens and government officials from Canada and United States to study the issue. We compiled the biological and hydrological studies and conducted an extensive public consultation process. After study and public review, we made the case throughout the 1990s for rule curve changes, and in 2000 the International Joint Commission revised the rule curves to address the detrimental effects the past rule curves had on fish, wildlife, and navigation.[9] While the paper mill companies saw increases to their operating expenses due to a reduction in hydropower, the benefits to fish, wildlife, and navigation were realized.[10]

Politicians demanded quick action to solve the consequences of walleye overfishing. The local politicians were savvy, and at least one was a good walleye angler. But, rather than implement greater restrictions on walleye harvest, they proposed a solution of stocking walleye. The action was simple but ill advised, wasting time and resources. The stocking at Rainy Lake failed for several reasons.

A large number of walleye fingerlings died during transport from southern rearing ponds, and there was insufficient fingerling production capacity for the scale of the problem. While we stocked, we also worked with others to move forward on necessary harvest regulations. We collaborated with the Ontario Ministry of Natural Resources on estimating and establishing target-level harvests.[11] With the Rainy Lake Sportfishing Club, whose members were politically connected advocates for the lake, we discussed walleye population projections for a range of creel limit and length-based regulations, including shortcomings and benefits of each regulation option. In the early 1990s, with the support of the public and the club, we proposed and implemented new angling regulations to reduce walleye harvest.[12] The restoration of the Rainy Lake walleye population was successful because people were willing to do the hard, collaborative work rather than just stick to the simple (and incorrect) fix of stocking fingerlings. The collaborative work catapulted the fishery into an outstanding angling destination. Tourism blossomed and all was well.

This experience made a lasting impression on a neophyte biologist. I learned a lesson about the influence that politics can have on fisheries management. I also learned that some anglers have a strong opinion about how to best manage a fishery and that there are unintended consequences to ill-conceived fish stockings. The politics of fish stocking is an example of how government can become ineffective. Abraham Lincoln said, "The best framed and best administered governments are necessarily expensive; while by errors in frame and maladministration most of them are more onerous than they need be, and some of them very oppressive." Lincoln was right: it's not the cost or size of government that is most important; it's the scope that is paramount. A competent and effective government can be more expensive than an inept government, but an inept government has a higher cost as its form endures while its functions are abandoned or corrupted. Government agency leaders need to understand science, whether natural resource management, economic theory, public health, public transportation, or child education. After my work on Rainy Lake, it took years of reflection for me to come to a balanced view of walleye fish stocking as a fisheries management tool. Extensive biological science associated with walleye stocking can help clarify when and where this valuable tool is most effective.

A BRIEF HISTORY OF WALLEYE STOCKING

Walleye propagation has been and continues to be mostly a government-driven enterprise. It is not profitable for capitalists, as the "product" is intended to improve or create walleye fisheries for the recreational angler, not for the restaurant and home food markets. Walleye propagation was first conducted in 1877 at the Sandwich, Ontario, fish hatchery from spawning walleye collected at the mouth of Saginaw Bay and the St. Clair River in Michigan.[13] Soon after, many agencies began walleye fry propagation, and early efforts focused on fry production for direct stocking into lakes and rivers. Five provinces and thirty-six states stock walleye, and currently Minnesota leads them all in both walleye propagation and stocking.[14] While the number of lakes stocked with walleye in Minnesota has changed dramatically over the years, about 1,100 lakes are currently managed with walleye stockings.[15]

Minnesota has a long history of walleye propagation, and its historical arc of methods and management is reflective of other state and provincial programs. Minnesota's walleye propagation program began in 1887.[16] In the early 1900s, walleye spawning take sites were developed on the Rainy River at Birchdale and Pike River, a tributary to Lake Vermilion, at Tower, Minnesota. By 1923, seven seasonal walleye hatcheries had been established across the state, and walleye fry were stocked extensively without regard to lake habitat, fish communities, or effectiveness.[17] Stocking of fingerlings began in the 1940s, and currently hundreds of small lakes and ponds are used to rear walleye through the summer.[18] These shallow waters are fertile and generally have abundant fathead minnow populations for walleye to feed on. With a greater investment of time and resources to raise fingerlings, Minnesota fisheries managers began to steadily apply business management principles to walleye propagation and stocking, first to improve efficiencies in walleye production and increase the number and quality of walleye reared and then later to evaluate, using trial and error, stocking rates and frequencies that best produced walleye of catchable size in stocked lakes and to determine in which lakes stocking was ineffective at creating walleye fisheries. One outcome of these evaluations and reviews was the understanding that walleye stocking is ineffective in lakes with good natural reproduction.[19]

In Minnesota, about 85 percent of the walleye caught and harvested are gifts from nature and not from stocking.[20] Over 3 million all-natural, good old-fashioned, non-human-selected, organic wild walleye are harvested annually from Minnesota's 260 larger lakes

Fisheries personnel at a spawning operation on Red Lake in 1939. Red Lake Agency Photographs, U.S. National Archives.

and rivers. The remaining 15 percent of the walleye harvested (about 0.5 million/year) are the product of a substantial effort. Minnesota annually strips more than 500 million eggs from spawning walleye, which produces over 400 million walleye fry. About two-thirds of the walleye fry are stocked directly into about 600 lakes (the low-cost option), and the remainder are used to produce fingerlings that are stocked into about 550 lakes in the fall (annually more than 2 million fingerlings are stocked in about 300 lakes, the high-cost option). Fisheries managers tend to stock walleye fingerlings where walleye fry stockings have proven unsuccessful. For lakes, stocking every other year is the most common frequency. Walleye stocking has created fishable populations in about 1,300 Minnesota lakes, and fry stocking often results in walleye abundances close to those found in the naturally self-sustaining walleye lakes. Minnesota's walleye stocking program costs about $4 million each year, and the estimated average production cost of a caught stocked walleye is $8.[21]

WALLEYE PROPAGATION

Most agencies obtain eggs from walleye captured in the wild rather than keep brood stock fish in a hatchery.[22] Walleye are usually captured by trap netting or electrofishing during the spawning season. Fish are sorted by sex. Females are checked, and those that are ready to extrude eggs (termed "ripe") are stripped of them. Eggs may be fertilized using either a dry or wet method. In a controlled setting, such as a hatchery, the dry method is used, and elsewhere the wet method is favored. With the dry method, eggs from a couple of females are stripped into a dry pan, semen from males is added, the pan is stirred, and then water is added. For the wet method, about half a quart of water (0.5 L) is added to a stirring pan. The pan is continuously rotated to stir the mixture throughout the process. Semen from one or more males is added to the pan. Then eggs from a couple of females are stripped into the pan while concurrently adding semen from several males. Additional semen is added after the last female is stripped, and the pan is stirred for another minute or two. A bentonite clay slurry (about a half quart [0.5 L]) is added and stirred for several minutes.[23] This clay (or Fuller's earth) is used to prevent clumping of the adhesive eggs. Historically, filtered pond muck was used as a highly effective anti-clumping agent. The mixture, now containing fragile, fertilized eggs, is poured into a filtering cradle that floats next to the working deck, and the eggs are rinsed to remove the anti-clumping agent. After rinsing, the eggs are floated out into tubs to allow them to set and harden for several hours. The water in the tubs is changed periodically during this time. The tubs of eggs are transported to the hatchery, where the eggs will be placed in incubation jars. Females that are not ripe are held in cribs to be checked the next day, and when ripe they are stripped. All fish are released once the walleye egg stripping is complete.

Female walleyes are squeezed to extract eggs. The eggs are then mixed with male walleye milt for fertilization. Photograph by Deborah Rose/Minnesota Department of Natural Resources.

I worked several walleye spawning traps over the years and found the process to be a spectacle of great fun and camaraderie. In International Falls, several of us would go down for a week or so to work either the Pike River[24] or the Cut Foot Sioux walleye trap. When I moved to the Brainerd office of the Minnesota Department of Natural Resources (MDNR), I would occasionally help out at the Pine River walleye trap. Each trap crew had its own unique and time-tested system that covered all parts of the process, including trap setting, placement of holding cribs, morning routines of egg stripping, variations on the wet method of egg fertilization, and afternoon loading of incubation jars. There was an unwritten hierarchy for the trap workers. Often the most experienced one was in charge, regardless of rank. As an out-of-station worker, I often had the pleasure of doing special tasks that helped to reduce the load for the regulars, who had to work the entire duration of the spawn-taking period. Those tasks included sewing chains to the trap's lead in preparation for deployment and quantifying the day's egg collection. Once walleye trapping commenced, the first exercise of the morning was removing the walleye in the trap and sorting fish into the appropriate crib: males, ripe females, and unripe females. Sex was quickly assessed by size and shape (females are larger and rounder), and semen was almost always extruded with quick pressure to a male's abdomen. On cold mornings early in the spawning period, snow often carpeted the work deck and a skim of ice covered the quiet waters. The ice in the shallows and small brooks melted in the afternoon sun, but as the cold air returned those areas froze again with odd fractal patterns. However, spring could not be held back, and there were days of sun and warmth, when the loons flew overhead, hoping to arrive just as the ice opened enough space for landing.

Handling hundreds of beautiful walleye was exciting. There was a frenzy to the sorting, since both walleye and human had a clear purpose and a sense of urgency. For walleye, nature was calling, expressed in elevated serum levels of sex hormones.[25]

For us humans, egg quotas had to be met. The official quota was important, but even more so was the unwritten quota—higher, aspirational, and counted upon. After sorting, eggs were stripped. One person kept a tub loaded with a few females and another tub full of males. One person stirred the pan. One person stripped the females, while one or two people added milt. One person added the anti-clumping agent and worked on rinsing fertilized eggs and loading tubs for egg transport. The flow of teamwork was poetry in motion, like a rugby scrum but with more dexterity. We rotated through the various tasks, signaling that each was equal.

Decades ago, we were fully decked out in our best well-used outerwear. To the outsider, we must have appeared a grungy and grubby fashion show. My black rubber waders were old and hot patched (a technique I had used to patch car tires at a friend's grandfather's corner gas station). My float coat topped my well-layered but raggedy undergarments and shirt, and it still bore the residual fish slime from last fall's gillnetting and every year before that. Over the coat I wore the state-issued yellow rain jacket that had the flexibility of jack pine bark. I suspect the raincoat was yellow to aid in finding my body if I fell in and got sucked into the trap with the fast-flowing water. If it was snowing, I wore insulated rubber gloves that appeared to have been dipped in cat litter to provide magical fish-gripping powers. If it was warm, I used cotton gloves; they provided my hands little protection from the cold water but were a good way to cool down after tossing and sliding walleye into cribs left and right. At lunch the crew would break, often in tight quarters with heaters running or a woodstove burning in the corner to dry clothes, and I recall that the odors were, if sufficiently captured, powerful enough to fertilize several large family gardens. After a week or more of working the walleye trap, I generally felt the need to take some time off to decompress.

Specially designed plastic containers are used to incubate the walleye eggs. Several sizes and configurations are used, but all have concave bottoms that create an upwelling when a water tube is

A net is lifted from the water at the Cut Foot Sioux walleye trap near Grand Rapids, Minnesota. The walleye will then be sorted by sex. Photograph by Deborah Rose/ Minnesota Department of Natural Resources.

inserted within; this upwelling keeps the eggs in suspension. A typical Minnesota seasonal walleye hatchery uses 5-quart (4.7 L) plastic incubation jars. About 2.5 quarts (2.4 L) of eggs, which represents about 300,000 walleye eggs, are placed in each jar. Incubation jars are installed onto the hatch battery, a vertical flow-through system where water enters the top and cascades down through a large array of hatching jars before exiting into holding tanks. These are generally gravity flow systems that are dependable and efficient. Water chillers and water heaters are often added to control the water temperature and subsequent egg hatch timing. Other technology includes water treatment using bubblers or agitators to reduce gas supersaturation, which tends to float eggs out of the hatching jars. The water flow rates are low and vary by the size of the incubation jar. For the typical Minnesota jar, flow rates are generally about one gallon per minute (3.8 L/min) or less. To provide critical dissolved oxygen to the eggs, the flow is continuous, and the low rate ensures gentle movement of all eggs within the jars.

After being extracted and fertilized, walleye eggs are rinsed and then transported to a hatchery for incubation. Photograph by Deborah Rose/Minnesota Department of Natural Resources.

The hatchery layout can also be configured to allow batch marking of recently hatched walleye fry by immersion in an oxytetracycline hydrochloride solution, which produces long-lasting fluorescent marks within the bones of the fish.[26] Obtaining density estimates of natural fry production is a potentially beneficial use of oxytetracycline marking. This technique can be used to differentiate between wild and stocked fish, and using marked fry along with a mark-recapture study allows the evaluation of the contribution of the stocked fish to the walleye population. However, the number of stocked fry should be small, relative to the size of the natural year-class (perhaps less than 10 percent), as only then is it reasonable to assume negligible replacement of natural fry.[27]

Inspecting jars of walleye eggs at the Plum Lake hatchery in Wisconsin, 1957. Photograph by Reese W. Staber, Wisconsin Department of Natural Resources Collection, University of Wisconsin–Madison Library.

Unlike the abandoned walleye eggs on the spawning shoals, the eggs in hatcheries are fretted over, often daily in the larger hatcheries. Dead eggs are removed to reduce fungal growth. Most of these dead eggs were likely not fertilized; however, most fertilization rates for walleye hatcheries are high.[28] Dead eggs float to the top of the egg mass in the incubation jar and are siphoned off. Some hatcheries initially treat eggs with formalin to reduce egg mortality caused by fungi and with iodine to disinfect for viruses.[29]

Over time the eggs in the jars change color, reflecting their development. They start out a golden yellow, appearing, from a distance, like honey from the nectar of delicate fireweed flowers. Slowly, the eggs turn brown and darker, giving a sense of time as they race the nearby leafless trees to leafhood (walleye often win that race; most walleye hatch between the time serviceberry are budding and blooming). The eggs reach the eyed stage in a couple of days.[30] The eyes look back at you. In two to three weeks—faster if the water is warmer—the eggs hatch.[31] After hatching, the walleye fry rise up in the jar and are carried out with the flowing water into the fry holding tanks to await their transport by truck. Most are destined for lakes not suitable for walleye egg life. Others are headed to small, shallow lakes and duck ponds to compete for food and life in a waterscape where, if they live, they will experience another forced transport.

THE ACT OF STOCKING
——•◦•——

From the hatchery holding tanks, fry are seined with a fine-meshed miniature net. Most of these fry are one to three days old. A simple dip into the swarming mass of a black fry cloud captures hundreds of thousands of walleye. Easy walleye fishing! After gently rolling the net to drain some water, the fry are poured into a jug like a maître d' pours wine into a glass. Fry are often transported in 5-gallon (18.9 L) thin plastic jugs. The jug is filled with about 3 gallons (11.4 L) of water and placed on a scale. Then, it is filled with 1 pound (0.45 kg) of fry, which translates to about 100,000 fish.[32] Oxygen is added to the jug through an attached air valve, which along with the oxygen in the hatchery water will provide some additional dissolved oxygen later in the trip as the jugs slosh about in the fish-hauling tanks or the back of the truck.

Walleye fry are stocked into lakes in an attempt to maintain or bolster the walleye population. The stocking rate depends on the condition of the walleye population or the fish community. Under typical conditions, fry stocking rates generally start at 500 fry per littoral acre every year (1,200 fry/littoral ha). Low stocking rates (less than 500 fry/lake littoral acre or less [less than 1,200 fry/littoral ha]) are used when the lake has few or no fish present, such as after a winter kill, or a fish poisoning treatment to the lake, or when the lake is annually stocked. High stocking rates (1,000 fry/lake littoral acre or more every other year [more than 2,500 fry/littoral ha]) are used when past stocking efforts have been ineffective, likely due to high walleye mortality from predation. Stocking frequency is generally every other year, to aid in stocking evaluation. The results of many ad hoc walleye fry stocking evaluations have led to the stocking of 1,000 fry per littoral acre (2,500 fry/littoral ha) in most Minnesota lakes.[33]

Many times walleye fry stocking fails to produce any catchable walleye. Predation of young walleye and competition with other fish limit the number of stocked walleye that survive. Fish assessments rarely determine the reasons for failure. In addition, there is little science on differences in fry stocking success based on how, when, and where the walleye fry are released into lakes. For example, where should the fry be stocked: at single or multiple locations, in deep water or in the shallows? When should they be stocked: day or night? And, does the timing relate to zooplankton abundance? Some fisheries biologists stock walleye fry from a boat in deep water, often on the calm side of the lake. At large lakes, to which a large number of fry have been hauled in fish tanks, biologists often stock directly from the tank to the lake at the public access.[34] When fry are stocked at shore in the daylight it is common to see other fish mob and consume some as they disperse.

The walleye fry that are transported to rearing ponds are often stocked into these small lakes and ponds by boat at high rates (5,000 fry/acre [12,000 fry/ha]).[35] They are left without care, and fisheries biologists return in the fall to harvest the fingerlings for subsequent lake stocking. Cooler water in the fall reduces walleye mortality from trap netting and hauling. Fingerlings are captured with trap nets. By-catch, which includes bullheads, crayfish, salamanders, and muskrats, is common. Boats have holding tanks, to which salt is added to address handling stress. Fingerlings are shuttled to a fish-hauling rig on shore, where biologists estimate the number of harvested walleye. The water in the fish-hauling tanks is also salted (0.5 percent) and oxygenated. Once the fingerlings arrive at their destination, they are typically stocked by pipe from the hauling tanks to the shallow water at a public access. These fingerlings take some time to distribute across the lake.[36]

Walleye fingerling stocking rates are highly variable. In Minnesota, fingerlings are generally stocked at about 1 pound per lake littoral acre every other year (1.1 kg/littoral ha).[37] The size of the fingerling can be an important variable in their survival to a fishable and catchable size; large fingerlings survive better than small fingerlings.[38] Stocking expresses the law of diminishing returns: when walleye are stocked at high rates, survival and growth substantially decline, thus offsetting stocking increases.[39] Fisheries managers adjust their stocking rates based on the average fingerling size; typical walleye fingerling size rates from Minnesota natural ponds range from about 15 to 35 fish per pound (7 to 16 fish/kg) but can be as low as 3 fish per pound (these fish are often yearlings or older due to carryover from previous production years) and as high as 60 fish per pound (1.4 to 27 fish/kg). Walleye fingerling production costs have been estimated to be about $15 per pound ($33/kg).[40] For a given lake, fisheries managers use trial and error in an attempt to find an optimal stocking rate, but the environment is constantly changing, and these efforts are often futile.[41] Often, the management goal is to maximize walleye abundance in the lake.[42] Optimizing to maximize may be a fool's errand, and with a changing environment, fisheries manager intuition is tested and can't be fully trusted.[43] Yet some are lucky. Others have an intuitive sense of what may work, given the constraints imposed by nature, and these managers tend to be successful in working with caring anglers that often demand the impossible.

Distinct genetic strains of walleye are scattered across their native range.[44] Periods of physical isolation, random mutation and genetic recombinations, along with variability in embryonic development, create subtle differences in walleye across North America. Natural selection occurs within a population, and small differences in survival and reproduction of individual walleye over generations and through the expanse of billions of moments result in small but often important distinctive physical characteristics, behaviors, and physiological attributes. Walleye adapt. Fisheries managers have used this recently obtained genetic knowledge to revise agency stocking protocols to provide greater protection of walleye genetic variability. For example, fisheries managers in southern Minnesota protect a small number of genetically distinct and self-sustaining walleye populations that occur in their region, and they conduct modest egg-taking operations of those populations for stocking into nearby waters.

If walleye are to be stocked where they are not currently present, fisheries managers must consider more than whether stocking will result in a walleye fishery. Stocking a fish predator, such as walleye, has substantial ecological consequences. Walleye stocking can diminish forage fish populations, eliminate rare species, and homogenize fish communities, and stocked fish can compete with other fish predators, thereby reducing those populations.[45] Walleye stocking in new waters can produce unexpected and adverse effects on the existing fishery. One approach is to stock walleye within the walleye's historical range but in waters without walleye. This type of introduction is common; agencies have stocked walleye into hundreds of lakes where they could be considered nonindigenous. The other approach is to stock walleye beyond their historical range or their "natural" or "native" spatial distribution—that is, into areas of the continent where walleye did not exist prior to any human intervention. The goal of both efforts is to create fishable populations, preferably ones that are self-sustaining.

Some biologists use the language of war and label a range extension as an "invasion" and the species that is inserted into that place as an "invasive," but strangely these labels are often only applied to species that have been subjectively judged offensive. It should be clearly understood that biologists' value judgments and labels cannot be supported by any science.[46] Given angler desires, walleye have been introduced into many ecosystems to which they did not swim on their own. Some biologists see nature through a binary prism of native or nonnative, and they often fail to see the beauty of the new arrivals. In the age of the Anthropocene, this view is increasingly quixotic. Regardless of your views of new arrivals, anglers will seek out beautiful walleye wherever they are found. It is the responsibility of all people who care about aquatic ecosystems to ensure that fisheries professionals are prudent and wise in their walleye stockings.

THOUGHTS FROM AN UNCOMMON WALLEYE ANGLER

To probe the question of when and where walleye stocking is prudent, I spoke with Peter Jacobson, a passionate walleye angler. Peter, who recently retired, served for thirty-seven years as a fisheries scientist and was instrumental in evaluating walleye stockings and providing guidance to Minnesota fisheries managers. I could ask Peter a hard question and he would walk me through the answer with keen insight and wisdom that had eluded me—and most people. He is the perfect person to articulate walleye stocking prudence.

Our conversation began with the objectives of walleye stocking. I suggested that the purpose might be to create either a walleye harvest–oriented fishery or a catch-and-release fishery. Peter stated, "In Minnesota, walleye have always been traditionally a harvest fish and they remain so. There is a growing interest in catch-and-release, but I think by and large, it is still a harvest-oriented species because it tastes so good and because the populations are usually resilient enough to handle some harvest. In Minnesota, walleye stocking has primarily been targeted at lakes that might not have a very significant walleye fishery to begin with. Many of them are bass-panfish lakes with the goal of trying to create more walleye fishing in the state, and the stocking of naturally reproducing populations is a completely different story."

He then emphasized his point. "The objective of walleye stocking is to create more walleye fishing. I don't know if it always achieves that; in fact, I'm sure in many cases it doesn't. But that's always been the objective, the primary objective. I think the other objective that is related is to *supplant* native reproduction, and that I definitely think does not work; in fact, it may do some damage." I was struck that Peter used the word "supplant" versus the word "supplement," which more often describes fry stocking in walleye lakes with some natural walleye reproduction, but I did not ask why. Later Peter stated that he misspoke; he meant "supplement" but cast a Freudian slip. When I speak, sometimes I wildly grasp for words and end up casting words that confuse more than enlighten. Peter is articulate, and while his word choice was accidental, I believed that it enlightened.

I was curious about the six hundred lakes that the MDNR stocks with fry, and I assumed that many of the southern Minnesota lakes that were fry stocked did not have natural walleye reproduction. Peter told me, "Well, that used to be the thought. In recent years some of the managers down there are finding there's a lot more natural reproduction going on in those lakes than we thought. And that's a pretty fascinating story. A lot of those lakes were places where any strain of walleye was stocked without any regard to hurting any kind of natural endemic strains of walleye. So, they received walleye from all over the state. When they look at the genetics now, they can still detect a native southern Minnesota strain, even on top of all that potpourri of stocking." He continued: "It is remarkable, and I think that story keeps repeating itself over and over. On these lakes that have the ability to naturally reproduce, there simply is nothing better. And the reason is that those fish have evolved to live and reproduce and grow in those bodies of water, and us trying to engineer a better walleye for those lakes just usually fails. Red Lake is a perfect example. You remember that when they first started stocking Red Lake in the recovery phase, they used the Pike River strain of walleyes, and they had very easily detectable ways of measuring those in Red Lake, and for the first few years they made up very high percentages of the walleyes that were in the lake. But over time, the native strain within Red Lake started to dominate once again. There was a discussion on whether to let that lake come back naturally with its own native strain or to supplement it with stocking. I think there were good arguments both ways, but the fry stocking that would kick it in gear as quick as possible won out. But what is fascinating is that those remnant walleyes in that lake still eventually outperformed the stocked walleye. Even in a lake like Red Lake. And that story gets repeated over and over again. And it is so important that we listen to that. Essentially what nature is telling us is that we can't do better than what natural evolution has done. And it is really kind of a concern of mine that we keep trying to do that, especially in lakes that do have significant natural reproduction. We can swamp out a natural year-class with fry stocking . . . and the concern there is we are swamping out the best and optimal genetics for that lake. And where it really becomes concerning is the artificial selection that gets placed on those stocked walleyes."

Peter and I discussed the ways that fisheries biologists are selecting walleye, perhaps maladapted walleye, for the lake that is being stocked. It was an issue that I had not given much thought to, believing that since we were not keeping walleye brood stock fish in a hatchery, any human selection of fish was insignificant.

Peter shattered that belief. "We're selecting artificially the second we take a walleye egg. And we're selecting for eggs that roll around well in that glass jar and we're selecting eggs that hatch in a hatchery setting. And the problem with that is essentially we're losing the pretty big hammer of natural selection. So, in a hatchery setting, we get 60, 70 percent hatch rate or more; in the wild we see far less, considerably less than 5 percent of the eggs, maybe even less, actually hatch and get to the fry stage. In the natural setting, the toughest of the tough are selected. Nature is selecting for those eggs that can handle those wild swings in temperature in the spawning gravels, that can handle some hypoxia and other things that aren't really good for eggs, but they survive, so the lake gets the best of the best. And that's why consistently those native strains outproduce our stocked fish. So, the danger is if you continually swamp those naturally reproduced walleyes with a really inferior fish and an inferior set of genetics at some point, if they hybridize enough with those native strains, you're going to reduce the fitness of those walleye populations. So, to me, not only as a biologist, but an angler, an avid walleye angler in Minnesota, which by the way has some of the absolute best habitat for natural reproduction in the country, you're putting those stocks in jeopardy. And we don't fully understand those risks, and that seriously concerns me."

Peter continued by explaining that we were inserting artificial selection in other ways. "Think about how our walleye runs are managed. Those guys get in there as soon as they can. They're putting the planks and posts in; they're dropping the nets as soon as they can. As soon as they see any inkling of a walleye run, they're fishing. So, every year they take the earliest spawners from that population, and when they get to their goal, they stop. So, there is a real large bias toward early spawners. That's just one example of the shift in selection. What that does, I don't know. I have no idea what that does. But there's a reason that those fish run in a bell-shaped curve. There's an optimal reason why those fish run, and it's in tune to that local lake and we're disrupting that."

In our conversation we both recognized and spoke of the social pressures to stock walleye. Peter explained, "Social pressure has driven our walleye stocking program for over 100 years. It truly has, and it's probably to the point where it is an overused tool. We have a public that has unrealistic expectations of what walleye stocking truly can do. I mean, think about it. Think of all of the school groups that have come and watched walleye eggs roll around in a glass jar with the hatchery tours. Generations of Minnesotans have had that. You wonder why we have a public with unrealistic expectations? We have cultivated those expectations."

I noted that he had estimated that 85 percent of the walleye caught and harvested were from natural reproduction and just 15 percent of the walleye caught and harvested were from MDNR stocking. Peter exclaimed, "Well, that's probably the most important statistic I ever calculated in my career. That's exactly right—85 percent of the walleyes caught in Minnesota are from natural reproduction. So, we're increasing by 15 percent. And for some people, that's fine, that's enough. Again, with the unrealistic expectations, I think people are surprised when they hear it is that low of a bump, but it is something. But as a whole I think it's overused. The expectations are too high. And in the case of natural reproducing populations, it's an actual risk to natural reproducing walleye populations in the state. So, as a whole I think it is an overused tool."

I again pushed Peter on the benefits of walleye fry stocking. Clearly, I thought that it was mostly positive. Peter agreed to a point: "As rule, fry stocking works well, and you tend to have better densities of walleyes in fry stocked lakes [compared to fingerling stocked lakes]. But the problem is a lot of those fry stocked lakes probably have some good natural reproduction. And is it the natural reproduction that's giving you better walleye populations or the fry stocking? There's still a lot of science to decipher what's going on." I pressed Peter: How bad could it be? How many walleye lakes were negatively impacted by this stocking? He said, "It's probably in the realm of 100 lakes by my calculations that have good natural reproduction but are being stocked, and those are the ones that I'm most concerned about." I asked Peter whether, if we created 600 walleye fishery lakes with fry stocking and 100 of those lakes were damaged from inappropriate fry stocking, the benefit of 500 good walleye fishery lakes was worth the cost of 100 damaged lakes. Peter stated forcefully, "If you damaged 100 natural reproducing walleye lakes in this state, that 85 percent, for a lousy 15 percent, I don't think you have to be good at math to know that is not a winning proposition. That's foolishness. That's folly. The treasure in this state are the naturally reproducing walleye lakes—they should be protected at all costs, and anything that threatens them is just wrong." I found his logic interesting and proclaimed that he was making an ethical argument and not a business decision based on a cost-benefit calculation. Peter replied, "Exactly. The first tenet of fisheries management should be 'do no harm.' And we have failed at that as a profession. Think of all the fish we've Johnny Appleseeded around this world and all the damage we've done because of it."

To understand where and how fry stocking harms naturally reproducing walleye populations, I wondered about the use of oxytetracycline (OTC) to mark walleye fry as a method to assess stocking contributions to a fishery. I asked Peter. He roared back, "No, no, that makes it worse. Think of how we can swamp out a year-class with the OTC fry marked fry stocking. We've done it; we've done it on large lakes, we did it on Mille Lacs, Leech Lake, Red Lake. That makes it worse, Paul! Because you're swamping out natural reproduction and you've got an artificially high percent OTC-marked year-class that you've replaced naturally reproduced walleye fry with. It's giving you an extremely biased view of your stocking. The only true way to do it is to figure out the additive component of that stocking and not the replacing. And OTC gives you a replacing component that is incalculable from the way we do it. It's probably one of the most damaging tools that has arisen in recent years because of its ability to swamp out a naturally reproduced year-class. It's a dangerous tool. And people are just enamored with it. . . . People think they're doing something good when they see a big percentage of OTC mark. But think about it. Those inferior hatchery-produced, rolled-around-in-a-jar, scooped-out-of-a-fry-tank fry, and all of a sudden you get a big percentage. No kidding, you get a big percentage. But you've probably damaged that naturally produced year cohort in some fashion. We don't truly understand it all, but we don't have the tools to parse that out. How would you parse that out, Paul? You have to look at an additive model, and that's what we do with that 85 percent–15 percent calculation. We looked at a series of lakes that didn't have any stocking at all for a certain number of years. You look at the signal from that compared to years when you did have stocking and you subtract them out. That's the only way you can do it. You can't look at simply percent OTC mark in one given year because you cannot parse out the additive effect or the replacement effect. You can't do it. And people see those big percentages and they think they're actually doing something. And look at the damage that that's causing."

Peter declared that it is simple to identify the walleye lakes where fry stocking is damaging natural walleye reproducing lakes. Reflecting on some past fisheries management, he said, "You need to stop stocking for a series of years to truly see a population response. You have to stop for three to six years. For example, Dean Ash [MDNR fisheries manager] quit stocking Big Cormorant Lake, a 4,000-acre lake, windswept, gravel shoreline, excellent natural reproduction. Just a tremendous walleye lake, excellent natural reproduction that was stocked for years, because it's such a high visibility lake, the social pressures are so high, they just stocked. Dean Ash had the courage to stop. And when they stopped stocking Big Cormorant Lake, it went from probably on the order of 10 walleye per gill net, maybe 15 on a high year when it was stocked, which is excellent, up to 18, 20, 25 walleye per gill net after they quit stocking. It released that walleye population from that artificial selective pressure of those inferior hatchery fish being put into that system and allowed that natural reproduction to just flourish. It didn't have that burden of those artificial fry stocked, OTC-marked fry, coming out of the hatchery. It's a release phenomenon because those hatchery fish were suppressing the natural year-class of the walleye. . . . I think it was an actual competitive thing at an earlier stage. I really do. You know, fry come out of the hatchery, they're fat and unstressed . . . and they have a competitive advantage over those poor measly but tough [natural] walleye fry that at their egg [stage] were experiencing big shifts in temperature, day and night, big shifts in oxygen. . . . What [naturally] came out were probably a smaller fry with smaller yolk sac, probably a little weaker fry at that point, even though their genetics are superior. . . . This story has been repeated on many good natural reproduction lakes. When you have good natural reproduction, that's been the pattern. That should tell you something."

MDNR stocks about 550 lakes with walleye fingerlings, and I was curious about Peter's thinking about the merits and shortcomings of those stockings. He told me, "There is some benefit to that, no question about it. I will say that when you do look at the creel surveys from those lakes, especially bass-panfish lakes, it's a pretty modest harvest or even catch of walleyes in those lakes. You can get walleyes up to 4 or 5, 6 walleyes per gill net in a bass-panfish lake pretty easily with stocking, but when you look at the actual harvest or even catch—you don't catch very many of them. They are out there, and a handful of people catch a few. But if you add it up, it's not a lot of fish. They're just not good walleye lakes—they're just not. They're trying to make something that just isn't much of a fishery. Now granted, a few cabin owners on the lake catch a few. And, for a few weeks in the spring, some local anglers might catch a few, but it doesn't add up to a lot. . . . At one point I was really concerned about the effects of walleye on the remaining fish community in bass-panfish lakes. But the more I studied it, the more I saw that those walleye populations never really amounted to much; even when we stocked the living snot out of them, they never did. And we have. They just never amount to much. So, I'm not as concerned about those lakes. It seems like they just remain good bass-panfish lakes and the walleye stocking is just secondary. I'm definitely more concerned about the impacts [of fry stocking] on natural reproducing walleye populations."

We got sidetracked with a conversation about the effects of climate change on fish population. Peter has done some important science on the consequences of climate change on cisco and where and how to protect these precious fish. I asked him if walleye stocking would save walleye fisheries in our warming lakes. "Well, the problem is, can you stock your way out of that? So, again, go back to the bass-panfish lake example. You simply can't create much of a walleye fishery with stocking—it doesn't seem to work. It will not be like what it was. So, no, I don't have great hope for walleyes from stocking. Stocking is not the way out of climate change. . . . As a walleye angler I'm concerned about that, and if I liked small-mouth bass I would be happy. And that's the thing with climate change. There will be winners and there will be losers, species of fish. There just will be. There will be some species that benefit from that [climate change] at the detriment of the walleye."

I tried to wrap up our conversation with a summary of what Peter was telling me. First, I noted that fisheries managers needed to have some serious conversations with anglers about some of the lakes that are fry stocked. We need to make the case that if we stop fry stocking in lakes with existing natural reproduction, we might end up with a better fishery. "We owe it to our anglers to do the research to answer those questions," Peter said. Second, we need to express appropriate expectations of fingerling stocking in bass-panfish lakes; anglers should not expect to catch a lot of walleye in those waters. "That's right," Peter agreed. "And there's one more really important point here that I think trumps everything that we've been discussing. So, go back to the 85 percent and 15 percent. Does it make sense to spend a lot of time, effort, funding, money, management, initiatives, on protecting the habitat that's making up that 85 percent? It's always better to protect than restore. . . . Minnesota is blessed with outstanding walleye spawning habitat. Doesn't it make a lot of sense to put as much effort, if not more effort than stocking into habitat protection and restoration in the state? I think it does, and that's how I gravitated my career once I realized that what really is important about Minnesota is the habitat we have. Even with all the impaired lakes and all the issues and land-use change, there still is excellent habitat in this state, and the last half of my career has been spent doing everything I can to protect that. And I think the message to our anglers and our management agency is that they should be spending as much time, and probably a lot more time, and effort on protecting and restoring walleye spawning habitat than they do stocking, and that's critical . . . The [Minnesota] Legacy Amendment, a three-eighths of 1 percent sales tax that is dedicated to clean water and fish and wildlife habitat, is doing more for walleye fishing in this state than the DNR walleye stocking program is doing, by far. And people need to understand that and appreciate that. Protecting that 85 percent of our walleyes and protecting their habitat has to be elevated to the top! . . . And our anglers and our citizens need to realize that we have something special here, and we could easily lose it."

I found Peter's thoughts on walleye stocking wise. The challenge, as Peter noted, is that most anglers, the general public, and elected officials still believe in an all-powerful view of walleye stocking. Walleye stocking is a useful tool in fisheries management when and where it is used appropriately. We will need to accept stocking's limits. And we will need to recognize that to ensure good walleye fisheries we must dedicate most of our resources to walleye habitat protection and restoration.

5

THE LONG EMERGENCY

Protecting Walleye Habitat

———◦◦◦———

At work, I'm apolitical and I can see multiple angles to an environmental problem. Sometimes a solution to a problem is obvious and noncontroversial. Life is not all political. But politics are important for some critical environmental issues.[1] This is especially true today as lakes and rivers are being polluted with new poisons and elevated levels of contaminants. Walleye are threatened with large changes to their habitat. These times require wise and caring leaders. Good leaders appeal to hearts and minds with hope and facts to bring out our best; poor ones appeal to the gut with fear and hate to bring out our worst. The environmental laments that I heard in my youth are again reverberating in my head, with the same rhythm but at a different pitch. Then as now, nature is in serious jeopardy, and when nature stumbles and falls, so will we.

There is little room for error, and scarcities in natural resources appear to be creating higher rates of human conflict.[2] Climate change is altering the environment and forcing people to move to escape flood, inhospitable heat, and drought.[3] Clean freshwater is in high demand around the world, and in many places, the use of water is not sustainable.[4] Humans now use a large share of the Earth's bounty,[5] and human abundance may be near a natural resource limit and carrying capacity.[6] I'm worried for our descendants and for the nature that we and walleye can't live without. It generally comes down to this because people forget about the absurdity of life and community—both can be easily extirpated and razed. While many come north to replenish their spirit, cherished walleye lakes too often become abused, and the beauty of walleye goes unseen. This should not be normal.

While the future is unknown and the public unscientific, there are many among us who are wise. Our knowledge is deep. We appreciate the systematic, iterative, and collective process of science and how it ultimately provides a better understanding of the living and the nonliving than other approaches. An impartial search for facts is best, empirical evidence is gold, and disinterested reporting of the results is the standard. Yet even with science, uncertainties will remain and new and old questions will arise. Since our senses and reason are fallible, our knowledge of nature is probabilistic. As science progresses on a topic, the probability of the result being true approaches, but does not reach, either 0 or 100 percent. Visualize an archeologist at a new dig. She hopes for a whole pot or an entire dinosaur, knowing it is rare. But she assembles the shards found with thoroughness to help understand the past. Can we do the same with nature's shards to understand the future or change our ways? We must use the shards, those pieces of wildness and wildlife, to help human society move to a future better than the recent past. Some say that we don't have the entire skeleton anymore; undomesticated ecosystems and places unchanged by humans no longer exist. But we have wonderful, interesting shards everywhere. People will always need and want to play in, understand, and marvel at nature. We have great walleye lakes and rivers, and we have people like you interested in protecting and restoring these places.

A healthy ecosystem is resilient to outside influences and undiminished in providing critical needs and natural processes for its inhabitants.[7] For walleye, quality habitat can sustain not only the walleye population but also the communities of organisms on which they depend. Walleye habitat includes sufficient physical places to reproduce, grow, and survive. Walleye prey populations must also have healthy habitat, and walleye lakes with cisco require a high level of water quality protection. Many actions can harm water quality and quantity, and many physical alterations of place can jeopardize walleye and their prey populations. These actions and their environmental consequences have been well studied and documented in scientific literature by biologists and scientists as humans have polluted and altered the planet in their quest for food, material, and energy.[8]

Governments don't have policies to ensure that all development and human action will be sufficiently regulated to protect walleye and their habitat. Often, regulations are declared to be socially acceptable at the time they are introduced. While everyone prefers clean water and air, many citizens, developers, business leaders, and local governments prefer a light-handed regulatory approach. Most government environmental regulatory and permitting programs attempt to minimize or mitigate damage to the resource; however, some loss in environmental quality is often expected or granted, and the commodification of the sacred proceeds. The merits of an environmental policy or a project are often assessed by a simple ratio: the monetary benefits of the policy or project divided by the associated costs of the policy or project. The unit of measure is the dollar, an acknowledgment that there is always a fiscal constraint on investing in conservation.

COST-BENEFIT ANALYSIS

Over the years, I've reviewed many cost-benefit analyses for environment projects. Since an analysis includes a measure of the benefits of protecting or restoring nature, provided that benefits don't occur in the distant future, the strength of cost-benefit analysis is that it can be a useful method to rank a suite of potential projects for decision makers.[9] For example, if an agency has $1 million to spend on walleye habitat protection during the next couple of years, cost-benefit analysis can help determine which walleye lakes and their watersheds will provide the best return on investment.[10] However, this analysis has shortcomings.[11] Many benefits may be hard to determine or difficult to monetize; losses of ecosystem services, for example, cannot be easily quantified. Some things get mispriced or artificially priced, and remember, some things, like walleye fishing, are best considered priceless. Most seriously, the cost-benefit method can trivialize future benefits or damage. Cost-benefit analysis discounts the future in two ways. First, it fails to account for the real possibility of low-probability, catastrophic events.[12] It assumes that the economic future will be better than the past, that resources will not be exhausted or can be replaced, and that there will be no disasters in the future. Yet ecosystems are dynamic; they may experience tipping points when thresholds are reached and crossed. The second way cost-benefit analysis trivializes the future is its explicit use of a discount function. Discounting is an economic concept buried within the method, and the reason for using it to assess long-term environmental projects is amoral and illogical. Discounting converts future values (costs, benefits, or damages) into today's dollars, not to adjust for inflation but to determine, much like an investment banker considers future growth, the amount of money needed to invest today to get a specific amount in the future.[13] For example, imagine the pollution of a walleye lake that will result in $1 million in damages in one hundred years. Fixing it today will cost us $200,000. Using a 10 percent discount rate means that we should spend only $73 today; a 5 percent rate means we should spend only about $7,600; a 1 percent rate means spending about $370,000; and a 0 percent rate, or no discounting, means we should spend up to the value of the damage ($1 million).[14] Since most economists use a discount rate in the 5 to 10 percent range, they would recommend against this project because the benefits compute to between $73 and $7,600 (substantially below the $200,000 cost to fix). Thus, an investment banker would do better to invest the project money in the stock market rather than doing a pollution abatement project for the lake. The greater the discount rate the lesser the value of the future environment. If you overvalue money, you undervalue life.

The challenge for people trying to protect walleye habitat is that they need to understand cost-benefit analysis and use it appropriately. Without data and analysis, you are just another person with an unsupported opinion. If you don't like an economist's cost-benefit numbers, just use a zero discount rate, include the unaccounted externalities and ecosystem services, and recompute. Or hire an economist who will use a low discount rate and begin a conversation. How the discounting is done and what discount rate is used are important.[15] A cost-benefit analysis using high discount rates will give low values to future damages, particularly if the benefits or the abated damages accrue much later, and will conclude that policies or projects with high costs today are not justified. This was the case in the example above, and it is also true for analyses of climate change policies.[16] Simplistic cost-benefit analyses fail to recognize that for many environmental issues, including lakes and fish habitat, the damages may be irreversible.[17] So, don't let cost-benefit analysis alone stop the conversation, policy, or project. Speak truth to nonsense.

There are other ways to prioritize walleye habitat protection and restoration besides converting benefits to dollars. Other approaches include "first come, first served," "squeaky wheel," and "those with resources/capacity get more resources." These approaches often appear to be unfair or biased, so many governments and organizations use values-based models in combination with other approaches.[18] Such an approach starts with the creation of a clear objective, for example: "We wish to focus our conservation efforts on lakes with high-quality walleye populations that are at risk." It then proceeds with aggregating criteria that meet the objective with addition or multiplication to calculate a score for each project. Finally, the priority list from the values-based model is ranked using cost-benefit analysis. This combined approach captures the critical need to include what society values and what is also fiscally responsible.

ENVIRONMENTAL ETHICS

In addition to prioritizing the necessary guidance on walleye habitat protection, there is also a human need to assess and aim for the right thing to do. A human is incomplete without the impulses of community, nature, and virtue. Like many people, I've been exposed to several forms of environmental ethics. As a young boy, my parents and grandparents modeled a respect for and love of nature, and through their actions my siblings and I learned that we had responsibilities to care for plants, animals, and the rest of nature. When I was in college, Dr. J. Baird Callicott taught my classmates and me the environmental philosophy of Aldo Leopold's *A Sand County Almanac*.[19] Leopold came to his "land ethic" later in life via the science of ecology. He proclaimed the following principle: *Do not harm the ecological health and beauty of place*.[20] This principle broadens the human obligation to all life, not just human life and community, and it defines the personal responsibilities necessary to foster a greater good, thereby increasing the likelihood for both human and walleye to flourish. Harm to the beauty of place would be any action that decreases the diversity of life and its propensity for future diversity. This principle requires people to have foresight and to speculate about the potential ecological consequences of their actions. Perhaps that is why this moral principle has not been embraced by many people.

Late in life I've learned of another way to think. The culture of the Ojibwe and other First Nations includes a philosophy that asks people to think about how a decision or an action may affect the next seven generations.[21] As I understand it, the Ojibwe ethic is founded on the belief that plants, animals, and the Earth are kin or family relatives.[22] The Ojibwe came to their environmental ethics long ago, practiced by their ancestors and passed on through the generations: a creed advanced by a subsistence way of life. Their familial, reciprocal relationship with the Earth fosters a social stewardship of nature.[23] When you are taught early in life that all living organisms are family members, the right thing to do is to practice restraint and reverence toward nature. These environmental ethics should be of interest to all those who care for walleye and their habitat. We could all have a nonhierarchical view of the importance of life, where humans have the same power and rights

Blue-green algae blooms (like this one on Wall Lake near Fergus Falls, Minnesota) are the result of excess phosphorus, which can impair walleye habitat. Courtesy of the Minnesota Pollution Control Agency.

as the rest of nature with governing principles of reciprocity. We could all recognize that we are part of nature, inseparable from it, united with it. We could all believe that land and nature cannot be owned and that all have obligations in its use.

Some people see no immediate value in the rest of nature, and others simply may not care for any life they deem of no or little value. It is not important that some people believe this. What is important is that most people will endeavor to live with the rest of nature and that they will strive for sustainability and justice in their life and work. It is a journey, with dead-end routes and failed solutions, and we will need to play the long game in negotiating what's possible in the quest for flourishing walleye populations in northern waters. To avoid a dystopian future, although counterin-tuitive, human survival rests on the ability to expand obligations rather than contract them.

In employing the need to do what is right, there are many op-portunities for walleye habitat protection or restoration. While a top-down, regulation-based strategy attempts to change human be-havior by deploying rules, education, and enforcement, a bottom-up, values- and rights-based strategy attempts to change human behavior by moving or changing the social norm, that is, by normalizing the good behavior with effective principles of persuasion.[24] The habitat management toolbox for this strategy includes working with farmers, shoreland owners, and forestland owners using a range of options that include plans for best management land practices, grants, cost-sharing projects, restoration of shoreline function and natural beauty, economic incentive programs to protect land and forest, conservation easements, and land acquisitions.

WATER QUALITY

To protect water quality for walleye, we need to protect the environment from various insults. These insults may originate in the watershed of a lake or river, which could be some distance from the walleye water or near its shore.[25] They may also originate in faraway lands, outside the watershed. For example, air pollution, such as acid rain that originates from coal-fired electric plants without adequate sulfur controls,[26] obeys no boundaries and falls on walleye lakes hundreds of miles away. Industrial and mining wastes contaminated with toxic metals and other persistent chemicals can reduce walleye reproductive success, alter walleye behavior, and affect walleye survival. These pollutants may be discharged directly into the water, they may be dumped in the ground and carried by groundwater to connecting waters, or they may be emitted or leaked into the air, but eventually we find that which has been dumped. Plastic dumped in waters and falling from the sky is polluting lakes and rivers.[27] Road salt pollution increases sodium and chloride concentrations in lakes and rivers, harming or killing plants, frogs, and fish.[28] Chemicals released from household, agriculture, and industrial waste or products can interfere or disrupt hormones in the bodies of fish, wildlife, and humans, resulting in negative health consequences.[29] For fish, the disruption of the endocrine system may impact sexual development, which may degrade reproductive success.[30]

Pollution of America's waterways reached an apex in the 1970s, prompting a new environmental awareness and better regulations. This photograph taken by Ted Rozumakski in 1973 shows a paper mill on a heavily industrialized section of the Fox River in Wisconsin. Environmental Protection Agency Records, National Archives.

The discharge and drainage of excessive amounts of waste and nutrients into lakes and rivers can reduce dissolved oxygen, increase algal production, and alter food webs. Waters that receive large amounts of waste with a high biological oxygen demand often have reduced oxygen concentrations, leading to stressful or lethal conditions for walleye.[31] Excessive nutrient pollution from agriculture and urban runoff can produce noxious algal blooms,[32] accelerating the loss of deepwater oxygen as the algae settle and decompose, reducing walleye summer habitat or increasing summer or winter mortality due to low oxygen (summerkill or winterkill). Failure to manage rainwater from construction, agriculture, or forestry practices results in erosion, and its sediment and accompanying pollutants from that erosion degrade water quality. Runoff from residential areas also increases sedimentation and toxic pollution, leading to reduced fish reproductive success and survival.[33]

Intensive industrial agriculture practices strongly conflict with high water quality walleye lakes. Runoff from these lands is typically very high in phosphorus, an important plant nutrient naturally abundant in many North American soils. This is a serious concern, as it only takes small additions of phosphorus to lead to large reductions in lake water quality.[34] Intensive agriculture also depletes soil and water resources, changes the magnitudes and patterns of surface water hydrology, depletes groundwater, and impoverishes surrounding ecosystems through often excessive use of fertilizers, pesticides, and herbicides.[35] Walleye-friendly farm practices and policies are needed, such as better management of nutrient additions, sustainable use of groundwater, alternative manure management, wetland restoration, and extensive use of riparian buffers to capture a proportion of nutrient-rich runoff.[36]

Agriculture is expanding, and in the walleye motherland, forestlands are being converted. Targeted forests include those with flatlands, sufficient soil, and available shallow groundwater for pivot irrigation. It appears to happen slowly. Scattered woods bulldozed. Thousands of trees here, thousands there. Soon I'm pointing to potato and corn fields and telling the kids or wife that I

Forested rivers and streams filter pollutants from agriculture runoff and reduce pollutants reaching water and fish. This photograph shows the west branch of the Susquehanna River in Pennsylvania. Photograph by Will Parson/Chesapeake Bay Program.

used to hunt deer there. I share memories of walking through thick young white pine forests or red brush and aspen parklands. I suspect they think it odd that I mourn such losses (or they figure that my memory has failed). Large amounts of forestland are converted to agricultural lands within a lifetime, and the speed of change will likely increase.[37] To protect walleye, it is necessary to protect or advance forests and working forest and forestry practices.[38] Filthy water can't be washed.

Wetlands and forests protect water quality and walleye habitat. Wetlands and their associated plant cover provide critical ecosystem services, such as groundwater recharge, to walleye lakes. A forested watershed filters and absorbs water. Plants use and recycle the nutrients within the forest, thereby limiting the excessive movement of nutrient-rich waters to lakes that may lead to lake eutrophication or an accelerated rate of lake aging. Water quality in many forested lakes of the north has changed little, with phosphorus concentrations remaining low. A lake with a forested watershed is not polluted with nutrient-rich runoff like lakes with agricultural or urban-dominated watersheds.[39] However, as land use in these forested watersheds changes from forest to agricultural or urban, nutrient loads to lakes increase. Large protected land areas within a lake's forested watershed provide benefits to freshwater ecosystems and fish communities.[40] With these understandings, fisheries managers are collaborating with various land use organizations to reduce runoff pollutants within lake watersheds.

For example, Minnesota is working with citizens to protect private forestlands in lake watersheds with moderate disturbance (agricultural or urban land use less than 25 percent) but levels of protection (public ownership or conservation easement) less than 75 percent. These efforts use volunteer conservation easements to keep private lands forested, with the goal of having at least 75 percent of the lake's watershed covered in forest.[41] Initial efforts have been successful. Agency biologists and scientists have educated landowners and lake residents on the science of limnology. Advocates who care about fish and lakes have amplified the message about the importance of forests to protect lake water quality. Various agencies and organizations have collaborated with private forest landowners to craft conservation easements that allow working forests.[42] This is slow work, so it takes perseverance and endurance. Those involved recognize the need to play the long game of fish habitat protection.

PHYSICAL CHANGES

Physical changes to rivers and lakes can be damaging to walleye populations.[43] In North America, pervasive damming of rivers and water control structures on lakes have changed the amount and quality of walleye habitat. In the United States, more than three thousand dams exist in the walleye mother-water.[44] Dams reduce water flow variability, and the loss of high or low flows changes the location, character, and quality of shallow water foraging and spawning habitat. Dams reduce connectivity, often fragmenting walleye populations in river segments with reduced amounts and diversity of habitats available. Water level alterations in reservoirs often do not track natural seasonal patterns, and these changes may impact walleye growth and survival. Juvenile walleye survival may be reduced by entrainment and impingement on intake screens to hydropower turbines, or they may drift or swim over dams on a one-way trip downstream.

Fisheries managers use several in-water practices to restore walleye habitat. Removing dams and converting dams to rapids (nature-like fishways) are usually very beneficial walleye habitat restoration projects.[45] Dam removal can result in upstream migration, where those movements were formerly stopped, and often fish migrations return quickly after dam removal and restoration of connectivity.[46] In addition to allowing greater upstream walleye spawning migration, dam removal projects restore river channels, hydrology, floodplain habitat, and water temperature regimes. Bypass fishway projects can also be very beneficial for walleye and other fish species. These projects construct a smaller-sized river channel that connects the reservoir to the tailwater to allow fish migrations in spite of a dam. Restoring river connections can be critical for many walleye populations. For example, in the Winnebago System, organizations have invested in restoring spawning areas by reconnecting the river again to its floodplain. Finally, fisheries managers have attempted to create or improve walleye spawning habitat with the addition of rock to these shallow water areas. These projects often have limited success.[47] On using artificial spawning areas or adding coarse substrates to existing walleye spawning areas, the first question to be asked and assessed is whether there are inadequate existing spawning areas for a walleye fishery in the system.

After decades of use as a shipping corridor and a waste conduit, the waters of the St. Louis River estuary near Duluth, Minnesota, became highly contaminated, spurring a massive environmental restoration effort that involves careful monitoring of mercury and PCB contamination levels in both water and fish. Courtesy of the Minnesota Pollution Control Agency.

The threats to fish habitat are also global in consequence, which exacerbates local environmental losses. We've polluted our air with greenhouse gases, and scientists are beginning to understand the ecological consequences.[48] Our winters and summer nights are warmer, and we are experiencing more extreme weather.[49] Walleye are more exposed and vulnerable than some organisms. Climate change is altering lake and river hydrology and temperature regimes.[50] In lake and river systems this pollution has resulted in warmer waters, a change in the character and strength of temperature and oxygen stratification in lakes, reductions and high variability in lake ice cover duration, longer growing seasons, and wicked winds that alter lake mixing.[51] Rain and snow are delivered in more severe storms, altering river flows and increasing land erosion, pollutant runoff, and algal blooms. This alteration of the water cycle also brings more dissolved organic matter, the leachate of plant matter, to lakes and rivers, resulting in increased browning of waters.[52] Climate change and runoff pollution are now synergized to imperil walleye today and into the distant future.[53] As the future unfolds, there will be large expected and unexpected consequences,[54] and failure to acknowledge and act will only result in more calamity.

Climate change has altered fish growth rates, the timing of maturity, reproduction rates, productivity, and fish distributions.[55] The sensitivity of a walleye's home to our atmospheric insult depends on the size of the waterbody, its location, its depth, its fish community, and the clarity of the water.[56] Water temperature increases are generally greatest at higher latitudes, which results in some fish species increasing in abundance at the expense of others. In Wisconsin, the number of walleye-dominated lakes may decline as lakes with abundant largemouth bass populations continue to increase.[57] In Minnesota and Wisconsin, warm-water species like bluegill, pumpkinseed, black crappie, largemouth bass, and yellow bullhead have benefited from climate change, whereas, cold- and cool-water species like cisco, lake whitefish, walleye, yellow perch,

Rainwater runoff from lawns, streets, roofs, parking lots, and other impervious surfaces results in pollutants entering the water and degrading the lake and fish habitat. Better rainwater management is necessary to filter runoff and to get rainwater into the ground near where it falls. Courtesy of the Metropolitan Design Center Image Bank. Copyright Regents of the University of Minnesota.

smallmouth bass, and white sucker have suffered.[58] In Ontario, smallmouth bass will likely increase at the expense of walleye, and walleye will shift their range northward.[59] Changes in seasons are affecting the timing of walleye spawning and zooplankton production for young walleye and other fish.[60] Some lakes have gone from reliable ice cover for ice fishing to intermittent winter ice cover, thereby altering or eliminating walleye ice-fishing traditions, resulting in negative impacts to local communities.[61]

The last question our civilization asks should not be, How and why did our successes and excesses lead to our ruin?

IN A CLIMATE-ALTERED LATE SUMMER MORNING along the shore of a large lake, I catch a glimpse of an eastern tiger swallowtail butterfly fluttering above the tall bronze-green grass. I zero in on her movements. I'm bewitched as she dances to and fro in the still air.

She stalls and falls onto the side of a phlox's cluster of flowers, embracing the inflorescence with her dainty legs, sipping the nectar, clueless of the nearby underwater world where walleye are hunting young-of-the-year perch on the break. This butterfly species may be benefiting from the human-created climate change, perhaps extending its range farther north.[62] Walleye populations are decreasing in many lakes with warming water, and they are increasing in others up north. People are suffering from the consequences of our climate change sins. For some, it is easy to rationalize away our role in the pollution of the atmosphere; however, we must combat the environmental nightmares of our reality and pursue the sympathetic dreams of our imagination. Global warming is the tragedy of our time, and biosphere restoration is our project. It is true what Greta Thunberg said: "We can't just continue living as if there were no tomorrow, because there is a tomorrow."[63] Our project's successes hinge on growing affections—deep affections for lakes and rivers that we have experienced over time with family and friends.[64]

With our dreams there is hope. We dream of a healthy environment for our children and grandchildren, we dream of lakes with abundant walleye, and we dream of fish without contaminants to be eaten at the family table. With reverence and affection, we practice conservation and restoration on the places we love. Since no one single action will address the long emergency of our environmental crisis,[65] it will take top-down and bottom-up strategies, as well as side to side (across disciplines) and inside out (change that comes from within) approaches. While the work is hard, restoring fish habitat in your places, protecting water quality in the north, and working on reducing air pollution will allow walleye to flourish. Please lend a hand.

6

A SCIENCE OF QUESTIONS
Walleye Harvest Management

———•◦•———

The number of walleye in a waterbody is finite, so it is often necessary to limit walleye harvest. Governments and communities manage walleye fisheries in three general ways. The first and most common way is to regulate individual anglers with creel and fish length limits. In government speak, this is known as "passive" or "indirect" management. Second, especially where there is a commercial or subsistence fishery, walleye harvest is managed with an annual quota or total allowable catch (kill). The third approach is to explicitly manage the walleye exploitation rate through fishing regulation or, more rarely, with area or effort controls.

The term "exploitation rate" refers to the harvest rate. It is usually calculated for a year. The most common definition is based on the number of fish. Here, the exploitation rate is the ratio of the number of fish harvested in a year to the number of catchable fish at the beginning of the fishing year. For example, in a walleye sport fishery the annual exploitation rate may be calculated by dividing the number of walleye harvested in a year (usually estimated with a creel survey) by the number of walleye in the population (perhaps estimated with a spring mark-recapture study). A less common definition of exploitation rate, but an incredibly useful one, is based on a fish population's productivity.[1] It is often called the "production exploitation rate."[2] The annual production exploitation rate for walleye is the walleye biomass harvested in a year divided by the total annual walleye production. This latter definition may be used to detect overfishing where other assessment approaches might fail.[3] Annual production exploitation values greater than 1 mean that all of the annual production was harvested; however, surplus production from previous years can be harvested without concern.[4] For a fishery, a pattern of high exploitation rates is cause for concern.[5]

In this chapter, I'll provide some example walleye fisheries in each of these three buckets; yet, not all fisheries fit neatly into a single bucket. In addition, there is no best way to manage walleye harvest, but there are a lot of ways for harvest management to fail in ensuring a sustainable harvest or by allowing the taking of the harvestable surplus.

REGULATED BUT INDIRECT
HARVEST MANAGEMENT

For most fisheries dominated by sport fishing, walleye harvest is indirectly managed, most often with fishing seasons, creel limits, and fish length–based regulations. This management strategy is used on many of Minnesota's large lakes, including Leech Lake, Lake Winnibigoshish, Lake Vermilion, Lake Pepin, Rainy Lake, and all other Minnesota walleye waters besides Mille Lacs. In Wisconsin, most walleye waters outside of the treaty area use indirect harvest management. In Michigan, excluding the Great Lakes, walleye harvest is indirectly managed. In Canada, most walleye sport fisheries harvests are not directly managed.

There are several reasons for not directly managing walleye harvest.[6] Across hundreds or thousands of walleye lakes within a state or province, insufficient resources make it difficult to regulate the number of walleye killed or their exploitation rates within individual waters. Or, the regulatory or political will is inadequate, except in a few rare fisheries of substantial regional importance where there is enough political motivation for an agency to initiate such a bold move. Finally, for walleye fisheries, the demand for meaningful harvest management is often low.

The last reason is perhaps the most interesting. When anglers do request that fisheries managers improve a walleye fishery, their

requests tend to focus on enhancing walleye stocking or fiddling
with traditional regulations. In some areas, agencies have successfully maintained or improved walleye fisheries through the
development and implementation of objective management plans,
better stocking efforts in walleye-stocked lakes, and reductions in
creel limits and the imposition of length regulations. For example,
in Minnesota, biologists and statisticians have reported that walleye have had an increasing statewide trend in relative abundance.[7]
Since in these studies many of the walleye populations were sustained by stocking, it is possible that walleye stocking improvements
were responsible for a statistically significant trend. In Wisconsin,
biologists found that many walleye populations are not improving,
even with stocking, and instead are likely being jeopardized by declining productivity in combination with unchanging or declining
harvest, resulting in high harvest rates.[8] They stated that this high
harvest is likely due to multiple stressors affecting the number of
young walleye surviving to enter a fishery (recruitment), including
rising lake temperatures, reduced habitat due to lakeshore development, and greater competition with largemouth bass.

There may be another reason why anglers don't demand greater
action for harvest or exploitation control: we do not miss what we
have not experienced. For the average angler, there is little doubt
that walleye fishing is now worse due to the simple fact that more
people are attempting to harvest walleye and therefore less is available for each angler. People may perceive that their walleye fishery
has declined; however, the full extent of the decline may be under-
appreciated. A fishing trip to the past is not possible. Instead, the
baseline of good fishing shifts through time, with each generation
having a lower standard.[9] Shifting baselines result in humans' tolerance for an increasingly poorer and more polluted world. The air
is not as blue, the water not as clean, and the walleye not as pure.
We do not miss the passenger pigeon whose flocks washed over the
walleye mother-waters; we do not miss the continuous big woods
and giant white pines that protected those waters by holding soil

and filtering water; and we do not miss the sounds, smells, and sights of the lake free of industry. We do not miss what we did not or could not feel. This failing could be our downfall as we pollute the air and dominate ecosystems with consequences that we can't fathom or imagine.[10]

A creel limit is a daily or possession limit of the maximum number of fish by species or type (e.g., panfish) that an angler can keep. Along with fishing seasons, creel limits are often the principal fishing regulation for a state or province. Creel limits have been used to regulate angling for almost one hundred years in walleye mother-waters. In the beginning, agencies likely enacted creel limits to prevent large, but infrequent, harvests—to distribute the harvest among anglers. However, little evidence supports the assumption that today's creel limits conserve fisheries.[11] Nor is there enough evidence to support a purpose related to equity. As an individual angler's share decreases, the sharing of resources often becomes less equitable.[12] Agencies may not discourage or disparage these views.[13] In Minnesota, the creel limit remained at six walleye per day per angler from 1956 to 2022, while during that time the number of anglers approximately doubled. In Wisconsin and Minnesota walleye lakes, the average angler generally harvests about one walleye every four hours.[14] In good walleye waters, harvest is unequally distributed among anglers. In the last statewide evaluation of Minnesota creel statistics, about 80 percent of the angling trips resulted in no walleye harvested and only about 1 percent of walleye angling trips resulted in a limit of six fish.[15] Essentially, creel limits serve as checks on greed. Many anglers, however, generally believe that creel limits directly conserve fish populations.[16]

A simple analysis of angler walleye harvest statistics suggested that walleye creel limits would have to be reduced to two fish or less to realize a meaningful harvest reduction.[17] This conclusion is incomplete. Such an analysis assumes that fish "saved" by one angling party would not be caught by another and that anglers would not change their behavior to minimize any harvest losses.[18] Likely

MINNESOTA FISHING LAWS
1920

Open Season for Hook and Line Fishing:
(Open season includes both opening and closing dates.)
TROUT—(Except lake trout) April 15th to Sept. 1st.
LAKE TROUT, SALMON—Nov. 15th to Oct. 1st.
BLACK BASS—June 15th to March 1st.
ALL OTHER VARIETIES—May 1st to March 1st (Exception—Cities of the First Class, May 29th to November 1st).
UNLAWFUL—To use small game fish for bait, or to fish within 50 feet of a fishway.

Limits of Daily Catch; Limit of Possession:
BLACK BASS or WALL-EYED PIKE, 15 per day.
MUSKALLONGE, 5 per day.
CRAPPIES, PICKEREL, SAND PIKE, or TROUT, 25 per day.
MIXED VARIETIES, 25 per day.
Number of Black Bass allowed in possession, 25. Trout, 50 fish or 20 lbs. No limit on number in possession of other varieties. The taking of more than 25 fish in one day, of all varieties combined, or waste of fish, is unlawful.

Manner of Taking:
Any variety of fish may be taken by angling or trolling with one line and one bait.
Pickerel, Buffalo fish, whitefish, suckers, redhorse, carp , dogfish, eelpout, sheepshead, catfish, garfish and bullheads may be speared during the open season except in Hennepin and Ramsey counties and cities of the first class, but not more than 25 pickerel or 1 sturgeon in one day. Artificial lights allowed in spearing rough fish in streams only, April 30th to June 1st, inclusive.
All other methods unlawful except use of licensed nets for whitefish and herring in season, and commercial fishing in certain waters.
Spearing of pickerel unlawful during March and April, except that pickerel may be speared in licensed fish-houses until April 1st.

Sale of Fish:
Sale of Black Bass and Trout of all varieties from inland waters prohibited at all times.
Sale of Wall-Eyed Pike prohibited except from lakes opened to sale thereof by order of Commissioner.
Sale of other fish prohibited from lakes closed by order of the Game and Fish Commissioner.
Sale of fish prohibited from Lakes of Ramsey and Hennepin counties.

Size of Fish Allowed to be Taken:
TROUT (except Lake Trout), 7 inches in length.
WALL-EYED PIKE, 14 inches in length.
SAND PIKE, 10 inches in length.
PICKEREL, 14 inches in length.
BUFFALO FISH, 15 inches in length.
BLACK BASS, 9 inches in length.
MUSKALLONGE, 30 inches in length.
STURGEON, 15 pounds, dressed weight.
LAKE TROUT, 16 inches in length.
WHITEFISH, 16 inches in length.
SUNFISH, 5 inches in length.
Other varieties, except Yellow Perch and Bullheads, 6 inches in length.
(Measurement of fish is made from tip of nose to fork of tail.)

Licenses:
Non-Residents of State, over 16 years of age: License for angling, $1.00; may be procured of State Commissioner, County Auditors or Game Wardens—on sale at FISHING RESORTS.
License required for Fish-house, Whitefish Nets, Herring Nets and Commercial Fishing in certain waters.

CARLOS AVERY,
St. Paul, Minn.   Game and Fish Commissioner

Creel limits have been a part of Minnesota fishing laws since the 1920s. Courtesy of the Minnesota Historical Society.

result: a harvest reduction may not be realized. Creel limits may not directly control or limit total harvest. They regulate the individual or party, not the collective.

The primary purpose of creel limits is to regulate social issues,[19] and for more than fifty years most fisheries managers have generally accepted this fact. First and foremost, creel limits are a means for anglers to judge their fishing success.[20] For many anglers, getting the limit is the goal, and a successful angler is one who reaches that limit (and remember, anglers may exaggerate).[21] Anglers change their behavior with the imposition of reduced creel limits; some will increase the sorting of fish to harvest the largest sizes, and some may take more trips and accumulate fish at home or the cabin. Often anglers will avoid waters with low creel limits, so when there are several fisheries to choose from, they may select fisheries with the standard creel limit over those with reduced limits.[22] Agencies capitalize on the fact that anglers will react to creel limit reductions, and they use reduced creel limits to curtail angling effort on fisheries where they wish to see some harvest reduction.[23] Because creel limits are gauges of fishing success, agencies may set limits that cue reasonable expectations of good fishing. These limits provide a message to the angler about the vulnerability of walleye to overharvest and a reminder that walleye are finite. Sometimes the message goes unheard, and the angler keeps jigging until the catch becomes extreme, with the consequence of more dead walleye from hook and handling.

A length regulation is a requirement that a captured fish must be above or below a certain length to be legally harvested. In the past twenty years, length-based regulations have exploded across the continent.[24] There are now hundreds of lakes with these angling regulations, and they have been applied to most species, including walleye. Minimum length limits are biologically based on length at maturity, to allow a walleye to spawn at least once prior to being available for harvest; for example, a 15-inch (381 mm) minimum length limit is commonly used, as it often meets that biological criteria. Many walleye length regulations reflect anglers' current preference for protecting large fish, and common regulations include one fish over or two fish over a set length. There are many kinds of length-based regulations, including protected slots (which means that within a length range fish are protected and can't be harvested), harvest slots (within a length range fish can be harvested), minimum length limits, and maximum length limits.

Often length regulations are enacted to address quality overfishing issues, that is to say, to increase angler satisfaction by restricting harvest of large fish to increase the odds of larger fish being caught and released in the fishery.[25] Like with creel limits, length regulations may not directly control or limit total harvest. Length limits regulate the individual or party by prescribing the length of fish they can legally harvest; they do not dictate collective harvest because fishing effort is not regulated in typical sport fisheries. If the length limit is highly restrictive, then the harvest or the exploitation may be reduced.

A sign marks a lake management area in Vilas County, Wisconsin, 1946. See Sass et al. 2022a. Photograph by Reese W. Staber, Wisconsin Department of Natural Resources Collection, University of Wisconsin–Madison Library.

Fisheries managers have debated whether sport fisheries are self-regulating, that is, whether sport anglers would stop fishing when catch rates decline, thereby allowing the fishery to recover. For the controversy-averse, laissez-faire fish management is ideal. Some managers hoped that public sport fisheries could not be driven to collapse because anglers would quit fishing when fishing was poor, or they would shift to waters with better fishing. A debate ensued and scientific evidence was presented for and against this theory.[26] Shortly after, scientific consensus emerged. First, scientists agreed that low-productivity walleye waters were highly vulnerable to angling and that walleye overfishing in these waters may have occurred.[27] Second, they agreed that creel limit reductions may act as an indirect way of reducing angling effort but that their effects are likely to be temporary in nature.[28]

Fishing seasons, creel limits, and fish length–based regulations may not sufficiently reduce harvest in open access fisheries,[29] that is, where the access to the fishery by anglers is unrestricted within the fishing season. Most walleye sport fisheries are open access. And given angler opposition, many agencies are hesitant to impose limits on the number of anglers fishing in particular waters.[30]

QUOTA HARVEST MANAGEMENT

When you have a fishery that harvests a large number of walleye or where the harvest period occurs in a short period of time, such as a commercial or subsistence fishery, you can count and sum the number of walleye killed. From there, it is not a stretch to set a limit or quota on the number of walleye that can be harvested each year. Quotas are the most common approach to manage commercial fisheries.[31] Measure the kill (step 1), estimate the number of walleye in the lake (step 2), and multiply by a reasonable exploitation rate to compute a total harvest quota (step 3). Quota systems have resulted in the protection of many fisheries and have led to the rebuilding of many fish populations around the world. To many fisheries managers, this is the gold standard, and it might be. You might hope this has solved the world's overfishing problems, but unfortunately, this approach has its shortcomings. Nassim Nicholas Taleb said, "To understand how something works, figure out how to break it."[32] So, let's look at how quota harvest management sometimes breaks. Can you guess where things go wrong? Step 1, 2, or 3? If you guessed any one or all, then you are right.

Quota harvest management is a challenge to successfully implement. While the three steps appear simple, the workflow of each step is complicated with opportunity for problems at every turn.[33] Learning begins with questions. So, at each step, the fisheries biologist and quant[34] must ask a series of questions to challenge the shortcomings and assumptions of the data and models. I'll walk through the basics of the Mille Lacs walleye fishery workflow to demonstrate.

Step 1 requires the complete and unbiased estimates of the number of walleye killed by commercial or subsistence fishers and sport anglers. For Mille Lacs, angler creel surveys are conducted during the open water and ice-covered seasons. These surveys estimate the total harvest and fish catch. To obtain a representative sample of angler catch data, creel clerks are randomly assigned to locations to interview anglers about what they caught and harvested. The number of harvested and caught-and-released walleye are then calculated from these interviews and estimates. Since the number of walleye that are released wounded and then die may be significant, that number is included in the kill estimate (in recent years, estimates of hooking mortality accounted for most of the kill estimate). A hooking mortality rate is applied to the caught-and-released estimate to calculate the number of walleye that likely died after release. The estimated harvest plus the estimated released fish that died is the total angler walleye kill (elsewhere, the estimated deaths from hooking mortality are rarely used, and instead just the estimated harvest numbers are used). A fisheries biologist might ask the following questions at this point: Do anglers provide an accurate number of walleye caught, harvested, and released? If they do not, the angler kill estimate could be biased and the uncertainty of the estimate would be greater. Is a reasonable estimate of the release mortality rate available? A poor estimate of this mortality will inflate or deflate the total walleye kill estimate. For the subsistence harvest, censuses of fishers are conducted and fish harvests are enumerated. Do fishers avoid reporting their kill? Are there incentives to report inaccurately or to cheat? The goal should be to make it easy for fishers and anglers to do the right thing and hard to do wrong.

Step 2, estimating the walleye population, often starts with obtaining estimates of walleye relative abundance. For Mille Lacs, a fall gill-net assessment and periodic mark-recapture studies provide the principal measures of walleye abundance. The design of these assessments is important. A biologist might ask whether the management agency has a walleye survey protocol that provides unbiased estimates of walleye abundance by age with reasonable precision. Often, as is the case for the Mille Lacs fall gill-net assessment, these surveys have high uncertainty. Are biologists sampling the whole population, and are they correctly determining the age structure of the surveyed population? With any mark-recapture studies, were conditions necessary for an unbiased estimate met?[35] For Mille Lacs, since the time interval between mark and recapture has often been short, a reasonable estimate is only possible if all fish in the population have the equal chance of being recaptured. It's best to use multiple independent surveys, since each will be biased in some way.

This step also requires the use of mathematical fisheries models to estimate and reconstruct past walleye populations by age and year. For Mille Lacs, fisheries quants use statistical catch-at-age models. These Mille Lacs models are unreliable without recent mark-recapture studies that provide independent estimates of population size.[36] The assumptions of the models are important. For example, does the quant assume the correct natural mortality rate by age, and is that rate assumed to be static or dynamic?

For Mille Lacs, quants use a constant age-specific natural mortality. If the actual natural mortality is substantially different or fluctuates by year, estimates of the population size and exploitation rates would be biased. Are the assumptions about harvest selectivity by age and sex appropriate, and is the selectivity in the model allowed to change over time?[37] How bad is the model misspecified? How uncertain is the population estimate, and is it biased? Which population estimate of many should be used? Many of these model questions are unanswerable at the time the quota is set; you might have a better sense of the quality of a model only in hindsight. For this reason, using a set of models is often best (ranging from the simple to the complex). A complex model that includes the variability of the many interacting parts of the fishery is always better than reliance on a complicated model that fails to include such variability.[38] In addition, the quantitative rigor of these models depends on unbiased information. If, for example, the main walleye abundance survey is biased, say because of an environmental condition negatively or positively affecting the measure, then the estimated walleye population will be wrong. For these reasons, fisheries models often give the illusion of precision where little exists.

Step 3, computing a total harvest quota, requires appropriate harvest control rules that reflect the current condition of the walleye population. Is the estimated sustainable exploitation rate for the growth, mortality, and reproduction rate reasonable? For Mille Lacs, fisheries managers have used a 24 percent fixed exploitation rate and control rules specified in a consensus plan.[39] If step 2 produced an inaccurate estimate of the status of the population, then the wrong harvest control rule may be triggered. For quota harvest management fisheries, poor harvest data, survey data, models, or policies can lead to fishery collapse or forgone harvest (surplus production not harvested). These systems are fragile. It only takes one weak link in the chain for the system to fail.[40] The data, the calculations, and the harvest policies all must be reasonable or else serious problems could arise.

Quota harvest management is dependent on specialization. Fisheries biologists establish long-term fisheries surveys, and quants create multiple models, run computer simulations of the fishery, and complete periodic system evaluations. Fisheries managers administer the scientific work and effectively work with the public. But the fishery community and the manager may have incentives that lead to overfishing. Additionally, managers often are not fluent in the science of fisheries dynamics. Some time ago, in a walleye quota harvest fishery that I was heavily involved in, I was struck by the silos that quickly developed. Managers failed to understand basic issues of population model accuracy and precision, as well as concepts of sustainable harvest. They saw the fishery not as dynamic, vibrant populations of walleye and humans but as a bookkeeping endeavor with ad hoc harvest adjustment rules and no management plan. They were making important trade-off decisions that created hardships for others.[41] In this fishery, managers wasted much of their time on trivial matters, and their motivations did not allow them to effectively listen to their biologist and quant subordinates. I've also seen the reverse, where the biologists and quants got things wrong, the managers listened, and the fisheries went sideways.

Walleye sport fisheries have unique quota harvest management challenges. Traditional creel limits and length-based regulations are, at best, weak controls for harvest. Again, given open access, these traditional regulatory options may flatten the harvest curve, but they don't limit the collective harvest. Fisheries managers may be reluctant to close fishing seasons early when quotas are reached. In addition, it is expensive to monitor sport fishing harvest and to estimate catch-and-release mortality, so many agencies may only be able to afford one or a few quota harvest management systems applied to their largest sport fisheries.

Several walleye fisheries use quota harvest management. The largest walleye fishery, Lake Erie, uses a set of harvest control rules and age-structured population assessment models to assist in the determination of an annual walleye harvest quota (in number of fish).[42] The annual quota is allocated to Ohio, Ontario, and Michigan. Lake Erie is a mixed fishery, with both a commercial and a sport angling fishery. A commercial walleye gill-net fishery exists on the Ontario side of the lake, and in most years the harvest is close to the full Ontario allocation. The commercial fishery is closed when the harvest quota for Canadian waters is reached. The sport fisheries of Ohio and Michigan rarely approach or exceed their annual allocation; from 2000 to 2020, only one allocation was exceeded: Michigan in 2002. No in-season changes to sport fisheries regulations or controls to close them have been implemented. The quota harvest management approach on Mille Lacs is different. The Mille Lacs walleye fishery is managed with an annual kill quota (in pounds), which is allocated to Ojibwe subsistence fishers and sport anglers. Both groups are managed to stay within their allocations within the year, and if a group exceeds their allocation, a penalty is assessed. The Mille Lacs quota management system is unique in that it is a sport walleye fishery that has been aggressively managed with frequent in-season regulation changes.[43]

EXPLOITATION CONTROL

The final method of managing for sustainable harvest is to track the exploitation (harvest) rate and take steps to influence that rate or stop harvest when the established rate is reached. This approach requires that a known number of walleye in a population are marked or tagged and that these marked fish represent the harvestable population. Tracking the exploitation rate of the fishery then becomes a simple matter; the exploitation rate is the ratio of the number of recaptured marks in the harvest to the number of fish that were marked by biologists at the start of the season.[44] Like with quota harvest management, a reasonable exploitation rate needs to be determined based on the population parameters of fish growth, natural mortality, and reproduction (rates less than

20 percent have been suggested for many walleye populations).[45] Unlike quota harvest management, an estimate of the total number of walleye in the population is not required. Since fisheries models are not needed, there is no liability of model failure and no decision on which population estimate of many to use. This approach is less expensive to administer and less fragile than quota harvest management.

Exploitation control also has shortcomings. Biologists need to estimate tag loss, if possible, as well as the tag reporting rate, if the fishery is dependent on voluntary reporting. Implementation of tag loss studies and high-reward tags are often necessary to address these issues.[46] Alternatively, if walleye are marked with internal tags and a portion of the harvest is examined by biologists within a landing or creel survey, then tag loss and reporting rates are nonissues. The exploitation rate can be tracked and estimated for the time period associated with the survey. Direct control of the

Managing sustainable walleye harvests often involves tagging fish for estimating population size and tracking the exploitation rate. Photograph courtesy of the Minnesota Department of Natural Resources.

exploitation rate for sport fisheries still faces the same challenges noted earlier, specifically that traditional creel limits and length-based regulations don't limit the collective harvest, and fisheries managers can be reluctant to close fishing seasons early when the established exploitation rate is reached.

Commercial fisheries managed by exploitation control typically use time-area closures or limit fishing effort. For the former, fishing may be restricted to only part of the lake or to fishing grounds (zoning districts on the water for fishing);[47] for the latter, limits may include the number of fishers, gear used, and seasonal closures. To minimize sport fishing overharvest, limited-entry and time-area closures can be added to the traditional suite of sport regulations. For example, to reduce the probability of exceeding the established exploitation rate, only a portion of a large lake could be made available for sport fishing. In North America, there is a strong aversion to regulation of angler effort on public waters. Fishing and hunting culture in North America, with its open access to public lands and waters for all, was developed out of the revulsion to strict controls on the masses and the privatization of lands and waters for hunting and fishing in Europe. However, as angling pressure continues to grow, enforcing creel limits, limiting parking at public accesses, or limiting the number of lodging beds in far north resorts and camps will not be enough, and fisheries managers may need to confront this aversion to limits on angling effort in more direct and potentially unpopular ways.[48]

Some walleye fisheries are managed with some form of exploitation control. The Alberta government has implemented exploitation control via the use of special harvest licenses.[49] To keep walleye from certain Alberta lakes, an angler must successfully obtain a special harvest license through a draw system. Draws are limited to residents of Alberta, and the number of special licenses available is based on walleye population size. For waterbodies with these licenses, Alberta fisheries biologists estimate the number of walleye present and calculate how many walleye could be harvested. The special harvest license limits the number and the length of walleye harvested. Anglers without a special harvest license must follow catch-and-release regulations.

Of particular interest is Wisconsin's fish harvest management system, which applies to more than 900 walleye lakes within the ceded areas of the Treaty of St. Peters (1837) and Treaty of La Pointe (1842), encompassing approximately the northern third of the state. The system uses a hybrid approach—quota harvest management for the Ojibwe subsistence harvest and exploitation control for sport anglers. The management objectives are to allow a combined band subsistence and sport fishery and to prevent annual total exploitation rates from exceeding 35 percent in more than 1 in 40 lakes.[50] In lakes where Ojibwe spearing is likely to occur, lake-specific annual quotas are determined by estimating the walleye population with modeling or mark-recapture studies. The Ojibwe bands then declare an allocation of a lake's walleye quota (a percentage of the quota). So as not to exceed the band allocation on any lake, band members are issued permits nightly, with the number of permits and fish allowed for each permit set based on the remaining band allocation. For band members, compulsory harvest reporting is required at each lake.[51] For sport anglers, creel and length regulations are used (i.e., no quotas are directly applied to sport anglers). For sport anglers from 1990 to 2014, a creel limit ranging from one to five walleye per day and a minimum length regulation of 15 inches (381 mm) were used.[52] Since 2015, a three walleye per day creel limit and length regulations have been used.[53] Sport angling is monitored with creel surveys on a subsample of lakes to assess the effectiveness of this management system. The system appears to have worked.[54] From 2010 to 2019 for large lakes (greater than 1,000 acres [greater than 405 ha]) with creel surveys, the average total adult exploitation rate in the joint fishery was 14 percent, and only 4 percent of the surveys (2 of 46 surveys) had exploitation rates exceeding 35 percent (17 percent of the surveys had exploitation rates that exceeded 20 percent).

MANAGEMENT OF LARGE SYSTEMS
—◆—

Large rivers and lakes with walleye are a challenge to manage. There are many of these systems, including Lake Erie; the bays of Lake Huron, Lake Michigan, Lake Ontario, Lake Winnipeg, and Lake of the Woods; and the bays and estuaries of Lake Superior, Lake Athabasca, Lake Winnipegosis, and Lake Manitoba. These systems are complex in two ways. Let me use Lake Erie as an example. First, the biological communities may be complex and changing. Large systems are likely to have distinct walleye populations. The Lake Erie walleye management plan includes an objective of identifying and conserving walleye genetic diversity.[55] High spawning site fidelity, natal homing for spawning, and the large distance between spawning areas may reduce the mixing of distinct populations of spawners.[56] Fisheries biologists, using advanced genetic research, determined that there was a distinct difference between the Lake Erie spawning populations in the western and eastern basins.[57] The protection of this genetic diversity may provide the population with resiliency. As Aldo Leopold said, "To keep every cog and wheel is the first precaution of intelligent tinkering."[58] The challenge that fisheries managers face is how best to protect these distinct populations after they mix in Lake Erie and are harvested elsewhere (currently, the lake is divided into five management units). In addition, new aquatic species arrivals have changed the Lake Erie food web, which has influenced walleye population dynamics.

Second, the economic, social, and political dynamics are likely to be more complicated.[59] Lake Erie fisheries managers need to coordinate across five jurisdictions: the states of Michigan, Ohio, Pennsylvania, and New York, and the province of Ontario. Each jurisdiction has a different-sized portion of the lake, variable demands for walleye, unique governance structure, and local political pressures.[60] This makes for a difficult coordinating act. So, the overarching interjurisdictional organizational governance form needs to follow function, and it must be able to adapt with changing conditions and demands. And, importantly, fisheries managers must come to a consensus on the critical walleye harvest management decisions.

ECOSYSTEM-BASED
FISHERIES MANAGEMENT
——•◦•——

In the next chapter I'll discuss basic fisheries dynamic concepts. These concepts were initially used to manage just one species in isolation—a walleye population here, a lake trout population there. Single-species fisheries management, while easier to implement, often fails to achieve management goals because of a lack of concentration on anticipating consequences of species interactions, changing fisher and angler behavior, habitat impacts, pollution, climate change, and other forces.[61] Today, however, fisheries managers use these basic fisheries dynamic concepts within a larger and more holistic ecosystem-based fisheries management framework.[62] This framework is defined as a practice of scientific collecting, analyzing, and modeling of ecological, economic, and social dynamics to help make fisheries management decisions that protect and restore ecosystem and economic health as desired by society.[63] I will again use Lake Erie as an example.

The Lake Erie fisheries community has the scientific capacity to concentrate on multiple dynamics. It has a large school of the brightest biologists, quants, and ecologists working on walleye science in the world—these scientists work either at one of the five fisheries management agencies with jurisdiction, at a university, or in federal government. The Quantitative Fisheries Center at Michigan State University is an important partner, providing advanced quantitative science, assisting in the application of decision tools, and offering training opportunities. Lake Erie walleye science is expansive; a recent sample of research includes the effects of walleye predation on yellow perch, habitat issues, and the effects of land use and climate change on Lake Erie walleye.[64]

The walleye (Sander vitreus) *by artist Ellen Edmondson. Courtesy of the New York State Department of Environmental Conservation.*

The walleye's golden coloration acts as camouflage in the water and aids the fish in catching prey and evading predators. Photograph by Nathan Carruthers.

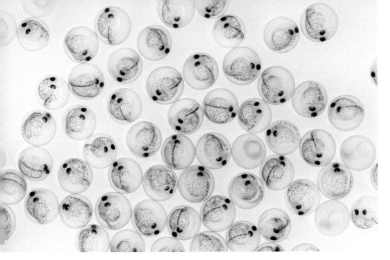

Walleye eggs a few days prior to hatching at Gavins Point National Fish Hatchery in Yankton, South Dakota. Photograph by Sam Stukel/ USFWS.

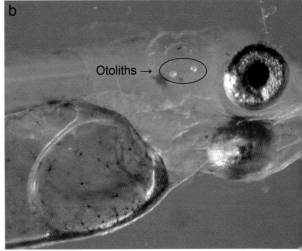

Otoliths →

Views of a newly hatched walleye fry. (a) The ventrolateral view shows the entire fish. (b) The view of the head identifies the calcified otoliths (ear bones), which researchers can extract to understand the fish's life history. Courtesy of Dale Logsdon.

Walleye fingerlings move from open water to vegetated shallow areas to hunt small fish. Photograph by Engbretson Underwater Photography.

An adult walleye displays beautiful coloration as it swims through lake vegetation. Photograph by Engbretson Underwater Photography.

A walleye waits on the lake bottom in anticipation of passing prey.
Photograph by Engbretson Underwater Photography.

A hungry walleye strikes at a young yellow perch.
Photograph by Bill Lindner Photography.

Red Lake tribal members during the walleye harvest at Red Lake, 1973.
Photographs by Jonas Dovydenas, Environmental Protection Agency
Records, U.S. National Archives.

A netted walleye caught using a jig on the Missouri River in South Dakota. Photograph by Sam Stukel/USFWS.

After being implanted with an acoustic transmitter, a walleye is released back into Lake Erie. The external red loop tag helps identify fish with transmitters. Photograph by Andrew Muir, Great Lakes Fishery Commission.

An adult walleye is carefully filleted by an angler with a sharp knife. Photograph by Nathan Carruthers.

A simple shore lunch of fried walleye. Photograph by Scott Gardner.

Freshly caught walleye from Round Lake, Ontario. Photograph by Andrew Muir, Great Lakes Fishery Commission.

The Lake Erie fisheries community has the governmental capacity to allow such expansive scientific advice to play a major role in policy decisions. The Great Lakes Fisheries Commission, composed of Canadian and U.S. representatives, facilitates cooperative fisheries management among state, provincial, tribal, and federal agencies. As early as 1981, the Great Lakes Fisheries Commission recognized the interconnected nature of the Lake Erie system and the impacts that one part could have on the whole lake, so they developed a strategic plan that incorporated an ecosystem approach. In 1997, they refined that approach to use an ecosystem-based management strategy. This strategy required agencies to "address the potential impacts of overlapping activities and decisions in an effort to coordinate and harmonize fishery and other environmental needs and objectives."[65] This included consideration of the biological, chemical, and physical needs of fish communities. On Lake Erie, the commission facilitates ecosystem-based fisheries management through the Lake Erie Committee, which organizes and governs the Walleye Task Group as well as other task groups. The job of the Walleye Task Group is to apply single-species management tools, such as age-structured population assessment models, and to manage walleye exploitation rates that will minimize negative ecosystem impacts, in particular to the forage fish abundance. In addition, it seeks to use the knowledge of genetic differences between spawning populations (western and eastern basins) to inform the allocation of total allowable catch.

FISHERIES MANAGEMENT AGENCIES are regulatory bodies, and they regulate walleye harvest sustainably in the public interest. Failure to do so is a dereliction of duty. Yet it is necessary to allow those interested in the fishery to have considerable say in which method should be used to manage walleye harvest and in the policies that have substantial embedded risk or reward. Dr. Carl J. Walters and Dr. Steven J. D. Martell, in their book on fisheries management, wrote something not often mentioned in heated public meetings on the status and management of a fishery: "Science cannot tell us what is right or wrong when there is a trade-off involving a hardship for people today versus a possible gain for people in the future."[66] Wise words from wise fisheries professionals. Together people need to create incentives for positive action, discuss a range of options, decide, and collaborate to manage walleye fisheries for today's benefits and tomorrow's needs.[67]

7

CROSSING THE RICKER

Walleye Fisheries Dynamics

———◦———

One of my favorite college classes was a fisheries dynamics course taught by Dr. Fred A. Copes, Biology 375. The class was affectionately called Ricker 101, because Dr. Copes used Dr. William E. Ricker's book *Computation and Interpretation of Biological Statistics of Fish Populations* as the main text. In its day, this book was the fisheries bible. One did not go into Dr. Copes's class without nature's rulebook as understood and written by Ricker. The course and textbook were eye-opening to a young biologist-in-training, as I learned how to apply statistical methods to the vital information needs of various fisheries: recruitment, mortality, and fish growth. Admittedly, the methods consisted of mostly independent analyses designed to be conducted in a piecemeal way. Today's textbooks combine the once separate fisheries analyses and provide guidance on how to build age-structured population assessment models.[1] These integrated models make concurrent estimates on multiple population statistics. These textbooks also outline how to develop ecosystem models that provide guidance on policies that will be robust to environmental variability.[2]

At this point we need to explore the work of Dr. Ricker, which is like a large walleye river that needs to be understood and ultimately traversed. This is the most difficult scientific part in understanding a walleye fishery—a river we must wade. Today on the Ricker, the river current is strong, the rocks are slippery, and the small mosquitoes of midsummer distract. Images of walleye appear in the current, but when I close my eyes I just see swaying strands of filamentous algae. A veery sings on the far shore under the beaked hazel, and tree swallows glide up and down the river harvesting emerging insects. The water swirls at our feet, and with each step the water pours away, refills, and reconstitutes an impulsive stream. We plod on—ensuring each step is understood before fully committing the next. Please stay with me.

We can study walleye and their relationships with other fish in wonderful detail, but in no way does it prepare us for what a fishery is and how to manage harvests sustainably. Walleye fisheries are harvest fisheries, unlike many bass fisheries, where the goal is to increase catch, not harvest. Remember, a fishery is made up of fish plus humans, specifically those people who fish and those who depend on the fishers. Some fisheries biologists forget the human part of a fishery, but that is the most important part.[3] For some fisheries quants, fisheries management science is the study of fisheries dynamics with all the interesting human variables set to zero. To manage a fishery sustainably, it is necessary to think about how most humans will act, not how they think or should act.[4] Think of it this way: what would your brother-in-law or your cousin do to sidestep a fishing rule? I'll interject the human element as I go, but first let's look at some important fish population dynamic principles. As we cross the Ricker, I'll review the details of a fish population's ability to produce enough progeny to sustain some level of harvest. Since it is important to know the mortality and growth rates to understand walleye population fluctuations and to manage harvests, I'll summarize these rates. Finally, our journey across the Ricker will help us understand the complex, but critical, concept of surplus production.

POPULATION DYNAMIC PRINCIPLES

Population dynamic principles are included within the framework of ecology, which itself can be explained with the science of physics. For example, the laws of thermodynamics constrain populations. Energy flows through lake food webs and up trophic levels, from primary producers (algae) to herbivores (zooplankton) to mid-tier predators (yellow perch, cisco) to apex predators (walleye, human). However, due to substantial energy dispersal into the environment at each trophic level, only about 10 percent of the energy transfers up a level in the food web. This limits a food web to a pyramid shape, with fewer predators than prey, that extends at most only five or six trophic levels. This principle is the reason why as our population size increases we will need to rely increasingly on a diet of plants.

Populations fluctuate following a set of basic principles.[5] First, a population will expand (or contract) exponentially in a stable environment experienced by all or most members of the population. "Exponential" means that the population grows or declines in an accelerating (nonlinear) fashion; that is, the number of individuals in the population over time will be expressed as a curve rather than as a straight line. "Environment" here means the physical and the interacting biological community. Second, a population cannot increase forever; there is always one or several limiting factors. The scarcest resource will ultimately reduce and limit population growth. Third, predator and prey (consumer and resource) populations will oscillate, and those oscillations can be small to large. When a prey population increases, the predator population will increase, often with a time lag. When a predator population is large in reference to prey, the prey population is impacted, and they decrease; a lower prey population ultimately results in a reduced predator population. Thus, predator and prey population numbers oscillate in space and time. Yet, simple rules of nature can also give rise to complexity and unpredictable outcomes. For instance, indirect species interactions can result in cascading changes up or down trophic levels within an ecosystem,[6] and population fluctuations can express chaotic behavior, leading to uncertainty in forecasting trends in population size.[7]

STOCK-RECRUITMENT

---◆◆---

The strength in number of young walleye added to a population is essential to a walleye future. Without young, life becomes
meaningless. Fisheries managers are therefore keenly interested
in the status of new recruits. Much scientific work has been done
to understand the relationship between the abundance of walleye (stock) and the recruitment of young fish to the population,
or stock-recruitment.[8] Since the rate of recruitment is usually
dependent on the stock size, biologists regularly use several mathematical formulations, called recruitment curves, to comprehend
this relationship.[9]

These curves have several characteristics: (1) when there are no
adults, there is no reproduction (naturally; also if stock size is very
low, reproduction is very low; there can be depensatory effects);[10]
(2) the number of juveniles exceeds the number of parents in some
part of the curve, or otherwise the population eventually perishes
(logical;[11] given compensatory effects, reproduction exceeds replacement levels and there is surplus production); and (3) the rate
of progeny production (recruits per stock) decreases with an increasing number of parents, creating either a curve that is dome
shaped or a curve where the number of recruits approaches an
asymptote[12] (reasonable; with the shape of the curve dependent on
the biology of the fish species). On this last point, which is confusing to many, it is the nature of fish populations for the survival rate
from egg to young fish to generally decrease with increasing adult
abundance due to density-dependent effects.

Walleye stock-recruitment curves are often assumed to be dome
shaped (Ricker curves, named for their inventor), because a large
population of adult walleye, through predation or competition, will
reduce the number of young walleye before they can recruit to the
fishery. In fisheries quant speak, this curve is the result of density-
dependent mortality: the survival of young walleye depends in part
on the density of the adults. Specifically, high numbers of adults

often result in low numbers of juvenile walleye or a weak year-class.[13] While these relationships are generally true, in reality there is great variability.[14]

Stock-recruitment analyses require multivariate statistics, and it is a challenging problem to forecast the number of future recruits. Many environmental conditions affect walleye recruitment, including yellow perch abundance, predator abundance, water temperature regimes, interannual variability, climate change, and female walleye condition.[15] There are immeasurable random interactions occurring, with a complex web of relationships creating unforeseen conditions. Certainty in the factors influencing recruitment is often low, and there may be lags in recruitment response. Cycles in walleye recruitment may occur for some populations, with peaks in recruitment occurring every two to five years or fluctuations with longer periods.[16] In the search for statistically significant environmental factors influencing fish recruitment, many false correlations are possible.[17] Walleye recruitment and spring water temperatures (or any other environmental variable) may only have an elusive statistically significant relationship. In addition, measurement errors in both the number of progeny produced and the number of spawners in the population may hide the true relationship.[18]

Determining the upper harvest limit is the main reason to assess the relationship between stock and recruitment. This knowledge may prevent recruitment overharvest, or the taking of too many adults.[19] This causes reductions in reproduction, thus influencing the number of future adults. Recruitment overfishing can quickly result in a downward spiral of the fish population, and many notable fisheries have collapsed due to recruitment overfishing, for example, the Atlantic cod fishery off Newfoundland and the Pacific bluefin tuna fishery.[20] There are strong reasons to protect some critical amount of adult fish in the population; the challenge for fisheries biologists and quants is to determine how much the adult population can be reduced before recruitment starts to decline.

The idea is not to define the relationship for short-term prediction but to better understand the consequences of fisheries management on recruitment.[21] Biologists have shared their wisdom on how to analyze these relationships. They encourage building many models of stock-recruitment that include environmental variables that might drive recruitment, thinking in probabilities and variances, and examining the kinds of patterns that the models are predicting across a range of spawner abundances.[22]

NATURAL MORTALITY

Fisheries biologists classify fish death into either natural mortality or fishing mortality, each with an instantaneous rate (a rate of change at a specific instant in time) and an annual rate (the percentage that die during the year).[23] Since fish often have high natural mortality rates, it is an important demographic rate to reckon. An assessment of natural mortality is necessary for estimating sustainable harvests, estimating population size by age using age-structured population assessment models, and predicting potential harvest yields at different levels of fishing mortality.[24]

The natural mortality rate is difficult to estimate for a population. Adding to the complexity is that natural mortality rates vary by age, sex, and year.[25] Natural mortality can be estimated using regression models within age-structured population assessment models; using mark-recapture studies; and indirectly via making estimates of total mortality and the exploitation rate.[26] But given the difficulty in obtaining reasonable estimates, fisheries biologists occasionally use assumed rates—they use rates that were estimated for fisheries with similar characteristics to those where the rates will be applied. Natural mortality is higher in fish that live in warmer waters, that don't get large (fish that have lower asymptotic length or mass), and that grow faster. Natural mortality is very high at young ages and generally decreases as fish age, but it may then increase as fish near the population's maximum age. Natural mortality can also be inversely related to fishing mortality, so when exploitation is high, death from natural causes may decline, and vice versa. This relationship may be due to a density-dependent decrease in natural mortality—a compensation for a reduced density due to harvest.

The magnitude of natural mortality constrains what is possible. Walleye populations with high natural mortality rates may be able to sustain higher exploitation rates,[27] but if you elect to only harvest this population at older ages or larger sizes, many fish will perish from natural causes before fishers or anglers can harvest them. In addition, density-dependent effects may occur; that is, with increasing population density, natural mortality may increase and growth may decrease.

GROWTH

I've mentioned growth dozens of times so far, believing that we all understand the concept since each of us has personally witnessed our own rate of growth from child to adult, which is often recorded by parents or grandparents with marks and dates on a door jamb or a wall. And we have also observed differences in growth rates between siblings or friends. Your parents or grandparents may have determined your absolute annual growth rate (inches or centimeters per year). Plotting your height by age produces a graph with a common pattern: from birth to age 3, you had what's called logarithmic growth, with fast growth initially and then slower growth; from age 3 to about sexually maturity, your growth was generally linear; and, finally, your growth in height eventually stopped. While your growth might have been tracked, it is unlikely that your family calculated the relative rate of growth or the instantaneous rate of growth for either you or the local human population, as a fisheries biologist would do to assess walleye growth.[28]

Walleye growth responds to physiological status (sex, health, stress, and reproductive status) and environmental conditions (prey quality, food quantity, and, most important, water temperature).

Given that walleye are wild animals, differing individual fish fates can greatly influence individual walleye growth rates, and variable environmental conditions highly influence average growth rates for walleye populations. Fish growth is dependent on age or size, and the walleye lifetime growth pattern has some similarities to our own: young walleye have rapid growth, often expressing exponential growth; juvenile walleye then have linear growth until maturity; at maturation, walleye growth slows. Males mature earlier and at smaller sizes than females, and females reach a larger maximum length and weight.[29] Both young fish and large fish have low absolute growth rates in total length or weight, and the instantaneous growth rates generally decrease with age. To represent the lifetime pattern of the average length- or weight-at-age for a population, fisheries biologists often model growth using various special cases of the generalized logistic function (S-shaped curve), including the Gompertz or, more commonly, the von Bertalanffy function.[30]

Like natural mortality, the growth rate constrains the possible. If walleye are growing slowly due to low prey availability, they may mature later and attain a smaller maximum length.[31] A change in the average lifetime growth pattern is observed after walleye populations experience high exploitation. Harvest reduces walleye relative densities, which reduces competition for prey, which then may result in higher survival of young fish, faster walleye growth, and earlier maturation (density-dependent effects on growth, survival, and maturity).[32]

PRODUCTION

—◆—

Recall that productivity is the rate of biomass creation in a population. Productivity is the total amount of biomass developed in a unit of time, even from fish that do not survive to the end of that time. It is measured in the number of pounds per acre per year (or kg/ha/year). Productivity integrates abundance, growth, mortality, and reproduction, and because of this integration, it is a useful measure for assessing exploitation and the vitality of the population. A walleye population with high abundance, good growth, and high survival will have high walleye productivity; however, since fish abundance is a major factor in productivity, low walleye density generally means low walleye productivity.

We can approximate walleye production by multiplying the instantaneous rate of growth by the mean biomass (size of the walleye population as measured in pounds or kilograms).[33] The calculation is often made for each age and sex and then summed to provide an estimate of total production. The rate of growth is estimated using the mean weights-at-age,[34] and the mean biomass-at-age is simply the arithmetic mean biomass between age classes. This method assumes an approximate steady-state population and exponential growth of walleye in each age class.[35] Rather than ideally compute the annual production for each cohort over time, total production is often calculated on a yearly basis for multiple cohorts by using population-at-age and mean weigh-at-age with no intervening population or growth data. These latter total annual production estimates generate a coarse approximation of production. In addition, population estimates for young fish may not be available, which is unfortunate, as young fish constitute a large portion of total annual production.

Walleye production estimates are uncommon. Most reported rates are below 5.4 pounds per acre per year (6 kg/ha/year), with a maximum rate at about 11 pounds per acre per year (12 kg/ha/year).[36] While the number of walleye production estimates is low, it appears that there is high production variability across lakes in a region and that production is generally higher in moderately dark water and low water clarity lakes.[37] For natural walleye lakes, walleye total annual production (for ages 3 and older) is often low and below 0.4 pounds per acre per year (0.5 kg/ha/year),[38] although some populations have high walleye productivity. For example, for Escanaba Lake, an extensively studied small Wisconsin lake

with natural reproducing walleye, the estimated total annual production (for ages 0 to 18) was high and variable (2.1–10.1 pounds/
acre/year [2.4–11.3 kg/ha/year]).[39] Investigators noted that on average the total annual production was harvested with about a 20
percent annual exploitation rate, and they suggested that a 20 percent exploitation rate may be a more appropriate upper threshold
rate (or limit reference point) than the 35 percent exploitation
rate used for walleye management in northern Wisconsin lakes.
For Mille Lacs, walleye total annual production (for ages 3 to 6)
was also high and variable (0.9–10.4 pounds/acre/year [1.0–11.6
kg/ha/year]).[40] It is interesting to compare these walleye production values with other wild fish or animal populations. In small
cold-water streams, brook trout production can be as much as ten
times higher than walleye production in lakes.[41] Let me just say, I'd
rather not be forced to choose an eating preference between brook
trout and walleye. As biologists estimate walleye productivity in
more places, it will likely provide additional insight into walleye
population dynamics and fisheries management.

SUSTAINABLE HARVEST

Determining the appropriate harvest (exploitation) amount is
also important for maintaining a sustainable walleye fishery. The
fundamental quantity at stake is called "sustainable harvest," or
in fisheries speak, "surplus production" or "harvestable surplus."
Measured in pounds or kilograms, surplus production is the new
weight of a fish population from growth and recruits minus what
is lost by natural mortality.[42] Fisheries managers usually estimate
annual surplus production as the change in the exploitable biomass between years plus the annual harvest.[43] Animals sustainably
kill (harvest) other animals all the time. For example, red-tailed
hawks kill squirrels and rabbits sustainably. Wolves hunt and kill
deer sustainably. Granted, in both examples the prey populations
may be diminished—but their productivity may not. Humans, too,

can harvest sustainably. How much of the walleye population's production can be harvested without altering the population biomass? What portion of the population can be harvested without jeopardizing its productivity? Walleye population biomass grows with reproduction and individual fish growth but is reduced by death from disease, starvation, and old age. Put simply, the annual sustainable harvest is the number of fish that can be taken in the year that will leave the fish population biomass unchanged. The annual sustainable exploitation rate is the portion of the population that can be harvested without harming that population. The key is to take just the harvestable surplus, that is, the amount that can be safely harvested.

Many people have a difficult time understanding harvestable surplus, so don't be hard on yourself. This seems like a good time to lean on the late Dr. John B. Moyle,[44] who wrote a wonderful illustrated article to describe harvestable surplus.[45] He used a barrel of rabbits (just to be clear, I would rather eat walleye than rabbit). I'll use a barrel of water. A barrel can only hold so much water; this is called the carrying capacity. As water is added to the barrel (analogous to walleye reproduction), the barrel fills to the top. However, as water continues to be added, there is a continuous loss of water as it overflows the brim (analogous to walleye losses from added disease and predation due to high abundance). The water lost on the ground next to the barrel is the surplus (analogous to surplus production). Managers of the barrel can increase the barrel size by adding a flange on the top so the barrel holds more water (analogous to increasing the carrying capacity by restoring habitat), or they can harvest the water that overflows to water the garden (analogous to the harvestable surplus).

Like a Ricker's recruitment curve with its dome shape, surplus production is expected to express a simple parabola or hill shape as population abundance changes. A walleye population likely produces its highest harvestable surplus at some intermediate level of abundance;[46] therefore, harvest in weight can be highest when the population is at a moderate level. Of course, when a walleye population is low, then the sustainable harvest is also low. If the walleye harvest is regulated and the population is low, then the regulatory agency may have a rule prohibiting harvest or a strategy to reduce exploitation. The harvestable surplus is also low if the walleye population is high, unfished, or lightly fished. This seems counterintuitive for three reasons. First, as previously discussed, walleye recruitment is low at high adult abundance due to cannibalism of young walleye and the likelihood of less forage available for young walleye, which results in higher death rates from starvation and disease (recall that these effects are called density-dependence effects by biologists in the population dynamic fellowship). Second, when the walleye population is high, the food supply becomes constrained. Each walleye gets fewer forage fish to eat, and then all walleye grow less. Third, old fish dominate an unfished or lightly fished walleye population, and old fish are inefficient at converting food into new growth (they divert energy primarily to reproductive tissues and not into muscle—old walleye grow slow, young walleye grow fast). If you harvested walleye from an unfished or lightly fished population, more forage becomes available, death rates decrease, reproduction increases, and individual walleye grow more, all of which result in a higher surplus production. Thus, the simple fisheries management principle: Don't save all of today's bounty for a tomorrow that does not come, and don't let yesterday use up too much of today. A walleye population consisting of high spawning biomass, which suppresses recruitment, means a considerable amount of forgone harvest and translates into an inefficient and unproductive fishery. On the flip side, a walleye population of low spawning biomass requires considerable care and caution in setting the amount of allowable harvest or the target exploitation rate for fear of depensatory effects.

The surplus production hill-shaped pattern where fish productivity is highest at intermediate abundance and lower at high and low abundance is analogous to another pattern that you may have already observed. Economists note that economic productivity declines when there is an abundance of elderly people, as individual productivity and innovation generally declines with age. I noted this economic pattern while hiking between Italian towns along the Mediterranean. The vitality of the towns appeared to be related to the population demographics. But you don't have to go to Italy to see differences in town vitality; we can see the same phenomena in woebegone Midwestern towns.

While fisheries biologists can estimate surplus production, only after fish have been harvested at various rates and at different population abundances can they truly comprehend the population's productivity. Walleye populations are in flux, and carrying capacities are not stationary. Carrying capacity and productivity can increase with environmental changes more favorable to walleye, for example, with more thermal-optical habitat at the walleye's preferred temperature and light intensity.[47] Understanding a population's surplus production in relation to the population's biomass is the key to sustainable harvest management.[48] The harvest is measured with landing surveys and estimated with sport angler creel surveys. But estimating relative or absolute walleye biomass in the dynamic environment of a lake—well, that's tricky.[49] To estimate walleye biomass, fisheries scientists use annual surveys of relative abundance, such as fall gill-net assessments. To estimate absolute abundance, they use mark-recapture studies and complicated fish population models that incorporate multiple population assessment datasets. Of course, a wild fish population can be statistically analyzed; however, an accurate and precise prediction or forecast of population size often remains elusive. Like an economist who studies plots of gross domestic product and employment to assess the quality of an economy, a fisheries scientist studies plots of stock-recruitment and surplus production biomass to assess the quality and resilience of the fishery.[50]

Determining sustainable harvest is a multilayered process. Fisheries quants must explore the depths of the data and use a variety of analytical approaches to come to some understanding of the fishery. They must then effectively relay this information and advice to the fisheries manager, for the truth is not always what we want to hear. It pays to do the hard work; learning something secondhand is the key to mediocrity. And, an anecdote or two may not be good data. It can be challenging work, and things can go wrong; remember, quants are human. An experience with a collapsed or near-collapsed fishery teaches many lessons. Models may not elucidate the complete truth, but they may provide insight into parts of reality, which is valuable.[51] Most quants are indispensable members of a fisheries management team; they are guided by good statistical science, and they have worked hard to understand the complexity of a fishery. The best advice often comes from those who wander the wild ranges of nature and number, swept up not in the importance of the work but in its adventure, humble to uncertainty but noble to doubt, confident in their views but open to other informed perspectives.[52]

LET'S RECAP. Walleye surplus production is related to walleye abundance (biomass). The relationship is hill shaped. From low to high walleye biomass, there is a low-yield collapse or near-collapse bottom, followed by a high-yield productive top, and ending at a low-yield high-spawner bottom. Fisheries managers want to stay on the hill and avoid the low ground. On the hill or the high-yield top, walleye biomass is substantial, yet not excessive, and the productivity sanctified. This is the management goal for a harvest-oriented fishery; plenty of walleye are available for people to eat, and there are periodic strong walleye year-classes. At the low-yield near-collapse bottom, there is a low abundance of walleye adults, and managers will substantially reduce harvest, as there may be too few adults to replenish the population. Fisheries managers do not want to collapse the walleye population. A collapsed fishery will anger fishers and anglers, and the local economy will suffer. At the low-yield high-spawner bottom, walleye spawning biomass is high, and managers will allow high harvest to reduce the preponderance of old fish. Fisheries managers do not want to forgo harvest unnecessarily. The fishery in this condition is diminished in quality—burdened with old fish that depress young walleye survival. This low-yield high-spawner condition has been observed for many fisheries, and it is well documented. Since it has happened, it may also be possible for your fishery.

When managers inadvertently keep a harvest-oriented fishery in the low-yield high-spawner bottom, the result will be high socioeconomic costs and lost opportunities, for example, commercial catch sacrifices, lost commercial fisher revenues, forfeited business and lost clients for fish processors, deprived tribal member and angler harvest for home and family meals, and decisions by anglers to abstain or choose to fish elsewhere, thereby impacting local business. When walleye fisheries managers are unduly conservative, they can create a paradox. It is created when an abundant adult fish population with a low death rate results in reduced young fish survival due to increased competition with and predation from adults. Ultimately, the number of new adults added to the population then decreases, which results in the population stabilizing at a lower population number. A shift away from this stable state occurs with increases in prey abundance or additional decreases in adult biomass. A fishery in the low-yield high-spawner bottom creates serious economic and social stress, but, in this condition, unlike being at the near-collapse bottom, it is unnecessary.

We've crossed the Ricker, and we are better for it.

PART III
WALLEYE FISHERIES

8

CONSERVATION GOALS
Lake Winnebago, Wisconsin

————◆————

The heart of the walleye mother-water currently consists of the waters of the Great Lakes region and of the northern latitudes of North America. In this area, a large walleye population lives in Lake Winnebago, located in east central Wisconsin. It is a lake from my past, and one with a long history. Lake Winnebago is a remnant of Glacial Lake Oshkosh, which was created at the end of the last glaciation by meltwater from the Green Bay Lobe of the Wisconsin Glaciation. About 13,000 years ago Glacial Lake Oshkosh was much larger than present-day Lake Winnebago, and unlike today, an outlet flowed southwest to the Wisconsin River. Walleye likely returned to this basin as soon as the water flow off the ice pack provided a sufficient place to swim and hunt, re-arriving and thriving thousands of years before humans. Several Native American peoples called Lake Winnebago home, including the Ho-Chunk and Menominee.

Lake Winnebago is the largest lake within Wisconsin (138,000 acres [55,700 ha]). It is a shallow, eutrophic (highly fertile) lake, with a mean depth of about 15.5 feet (4.7 m) and a maximum depth of 21 feet (6.4 m).[1] Summer water clarity is generally less than 4 feet (1.2 m), as measured by a Secchi disk, and with regular mixing the lake's water temperature is similar from lake surface to bottom. Today, Lake Winnebago is the largest inland walleye fishery in Wisconsin. Lake Winnebago is part of the Winnebago System, which includes the smaller, upriver lakes of Poygan, Winneconne, and Butte des Morts, which are fed by the Wolf and Upper Fox Rivers. The total surface area of the Winnebago pool is 166,000 acres (67,000 ha). Lake Winnebago has a large watershed that encompasses about 12 percent of the area of Wisconsin (5,500 square miles [14,300 km²]), and agricultural lands consisting of row crops and dairy dominate much of that landscape.² Lake Winnebago shoreland is heavily developed in many areas, with the cities of Fond du Lac, Oshkosh, Neenah, Menasha, Grand Chute, and Appleton on the shore or in the area (all but Fond du Lac obtain their drinking water from the lake). Treated wastewater is discharged into the Winnebago System.

Water levels are elevated from natural conditions by about 3 feet (0.9 m) due to two dams erected at the outlets 150 years ago: the Menasha dam, operated by the U.S. Army Corps of Engineers, and the Neenah dam, a private dam owned by Neenah Paper Incorporated. Water levels are regulated by a rule curve that operationally results in mostly stable levels during the open water navigation season and small late winter and spring drawdowns to reduce flooding potential. Annual fluctuations are generally about 2 feet (0.6 m).³ The Wolf River flows into the Winnebago System from the north, and the Upper Fox River from the southwest. These rivers provide critical spawning habitat for many fish species, especially for walleye. Agencies and sporting organizations are working hard on restoring, enhancing, and protecting spawning areas within these rivers, their tributaries, and floodplains.

The fish community in Lake Winnebago is stunning in its productivity. Freshwater drum are abundant in the lake; the population is estimated in the tens of millions, and this interesting fish likely constitutes much of the fish biomass in Winnebago. White bass, a popular sport fish, are also common.⁴ Sauger are present in the lake, but their abundance is generally low, with poor reproductive success apparently limiting the population size.⁵ The lake supports a lake sturgeon population, one of the largest self-sustaining populations of the species (approximately 40,000 adults).⁶ The sturgeon are supported by an incredible abundance of midges that live in the lake mud and emerge as nonbiting lake flies in early May to reproduce and then die. While the lake sturgeon may be the elephant of the Winnebago, the walleye is the lion of the lake.

An ice shanty on Lake Winnebago, 1946. Photograph by Reese W. Staber, Wisconsin Department of Natural Resources Collection, University of Wisconsin–Madison Library.

The walleye population for the Winnebago System has been estimated to average about 500,000 fish (greater than 15 inches [381 mm]; about 3 walleye/acre [7 walleye/ha] for the Winnebago pool).[7] Walleye are sustained by a diverse forage fish population consisting of gizzard shad, young-of-the year white bass, yellow perch, young-of-the-year freshwater drum, trout-perch, emerald shiner, and many other species. Winnebago walleye reach about 15 inches (381 mm) in length in three to four years. Males are usually sexually mature in three years, and females in four to six years. Spawning walleye move up the Wolf and Upper Fox Rivers seeking flowing water in floodplain marshes or old oxbows and deposit their eggs on the flooded grasses and sedges that provide a substrate for incubation.[8] Walleye year-class strength for the lake's population is influenced by spring water levels on the river; higher water flows are more favorable for egg survival and fry transport to Lake Winnebago.

Angling in the Winnebago System is as diverse as the fish community. In spring, walleye fishing in the lower Wolf River is popular. As the walleye move up to spawn, anglers fish the edges of the river channel and sandbars using jigs, Wolf River rigs, and slip bobber rigs. Adult walleye begin moving up the river in March, and the best walleye fishing generally occurs in April. As summer progresses, walleye anglers target the lake's nearshore reefs, probe the uncommon submerged aquatic plant stands along the shoreline, and then hunt for schooling walleye in the vast, shallow mid-lake waterscape. In the Winnebago System, angling for walleye is open all year and a daily harvest limit of walleye is imposed (currently three walleye with no length restrictions).[9]

The Wisconsin Department of Natural Resources (WDNR) manages the walleye fishery consistent with a written management plan that was formulated with extensive public consultation.[10] Management consists of standardized assessments, angler education, regulations, enforcement, and restoration and protection of walleye habitat and water quality. The assessment includes two surveys. First, an annual bottom trawl assessment is conducted in the late summer and through the fall, which samples established transects around the lake.[11] Local volunteers assist WDNR biologists in the field because the trawl captures a large number of young-of-the-year fish of many species that need to be sorted and counted. This survey, which has been conducted since 1986, provides estimates of walleye year-class strength and the relative abundances of forage fish in the lake. Second, annual spring electrofishing surveys are conducted in the spawning marshes of the Wolf and Upper Fox Rivers. Walleye are sexed, measured, and tagged with individually numbered tags. Anglers who harvest a tagged walleye are encouraged to report the tag and fish details to the WDNR, after which they receive a certificate with information on the fish caught. Since 1993, walleye annual exploitation (harvest) rates have been estimated as the fraction of the tags returned after adjustments for estimates of fish tag retention and angler tag reporting rate.[12] The WDNR uses tagging studies along with angler tag reporting because it is substantially less expensive than conducting annual creel surveys on a system with long rivers and multiple lakes. While the tagging misses estimates of the angler catch rate, angler effort, and some other angler statistics, it does capture the most critical piece of information necessary to manage the fishery—the exploitation rate. In 2020, based on recent estimates of walleye annual exploitation rates and extensive public feedback, the walleye daily creel limit was reduced from five to three fish.[13]

Unique to this fishery is the outstanding work on protection and restoration of walleye spawning marshes. This work began in the 1960s with science on walleye biology and life history that was specific to the Winnebago System.[14] Since then, advocates for walleye have successfully rallied people and organizations to work at a scale that is often difficult to sustain. These efforts involve collaboration with landowners, citizens, conservation clubs, and nonprofit organizations. This work demonstrates the endurance, perseverance, and dedication of biologists and citizens to ensure that walleye will flourish in Lake Winnebago.

Protection of the marshy habitat of the Wolf River upstream of Lake Winnebago has been critical to a thriving walleye population. Photograph by Wisconsin Department of Natural Resources.

I discussed the Lake Winnebago walleye work with Kendall Kamke, WDNR fisheries manager. Kendall grew up in Wausau, Wisconsin, just up the road from Stevens Point, my hometown, and he and I were graduate students together at the University of Wisconsin–Stevens Point. As an undergraduate student, I struggled with finding a purpose. I was still living at home and working morning and evenings at a family grocery. My parents encouraged college, but I was dubious of its job-producing opportunities in the field of natural resources management. At the time, I did not connect with other students. I usually did not look people in the eye, nor did I see any reason to. Kendall helped me with my work and would break down a tough fisheries lecture into easy-to-understand concepts. Without his help I probably would be in a different line of work. After graduating, Kendall began working for the WDNR in Hayward, Wisconsin, focusing on adjusting sport angler fisheries management with the return of Ojibwe walleye spearfishing.[15] Since 1990, he's been working on the Winnebago System, first as a biologist and more recently as a supervisor of fisheries personnel.

Kendall Kamke is an imposing figure—tall, with a broad, mustached face—but he is a jovial man, quick with an interesting story and a friendly smile. He is a thoughtful fisheries manager, well suited for the challenging task of working with passionate anglers. Through the years, I have heard often about the great work that he has been involved with on the Winnebago System. He is now in his early sixties, his hair gray, having dedicated a life and career to Winnebago fisheries management. Kendall reflected on this career while I listened intently. He told me that working with the public has been the key to the successes of walleye management for Lake Winnebago: "There is no way we could do this and all the work that needs to be done, even some of the survey work, without a huge volunteer army." The trawling on Lake Winnebago has been historically loaded with volunteers. Kendall noted that the volunteers enjoy getting intimately involved in fish data collection.

"We educate the public on what we do, and it helps quell the ridiculous rumors that have come up over the years."

Kendall explained the benefits of working with volunteers with a story involving a single day of electrofishing and tagging spawning walleye in the river marshes of the Winnebago. In the past, it took a big crew of people because they were tagging more walleye back then. The project required several boat teams, with three people per boat. The WDNR sought volunteers. Kendall recalled, "We would go meet somewhere at 6:00 a.m. and have breakfast and tell them what we would be doing. . . . They are like kids at Christmas. . . . You tell them what to expect, what we are going to do, run through the safety stuff." On this trip, he noted, "one guy was kind of standoffish. I said put that guy with me. We're going to show him some fish." After a long day of catching and tagging walleye in the marshes, they were wrapping things up and putting the gear away at the boat landing. Kendall noted that this man "was pacing around the back of the boat, kicking the gravel in the parking lot," and asked him what he thought of the day. Kendall relayed what the man then said: "'I got to tell you something,' he said. 'For many years I have complained about you guys and didn't believe anything that I was hearing, thought you were on these marshes collecting spawn and that was going up to stock the lakes up north with our fish. I cannot believe what I saw today.' He went on to say, 'I would have never in a million years believed that we were going to see these numbers of walleye and sizes of the walleye that we saw. I'll never bad-mouth you guys again.'" Kendall could tell this was hard for the man to say.

For Kendall, this was not a rare event. He has connected with hundreds of people interested in Winnebago walleye. "Over the years we've had enough people out who have helped us, saw what we did; we answered their questions, and you get that one-on-one time. . . . They find out that you are just another guy that's got a job just like they do, and all the foolishness that they heard in the bar . . . all the rumors and innuendo, and everything else, they find out that it is just that, bar talk," he said. "That is the kind of thing that I think we as resource professionals need to strive for; we're somebody they know, somebody they trust when they have a question." Kendall told me, "If you're willing to work with the public and they are willing to work with you, it has to be a mutual thing, and you get them to that point by being honest with them, going and talking to their clubs. But when you do that over a career or over several careers of different people, you start to build that rapport with the public. It is easy to hate an agency. It is easy to hate the DNR. But it is hard to hate a person when you know that person." He then emphasized this point: "My experiences as the biologist here led to all those really incredible relationships with the public and with our hook and bullet clubs in the area and around the system. I would have to say that those relationships with those groups and the amount of stuff that we have gotten done for the system really have been some of the highlights of my career."

Kendall stressed that the Walleyes for Tomorrow (WFT) organization and many other groups have contributed tremendously to the protection of the Winnebago walleye. A great deal of habitat work has been completed because of a unique collaboration between government and citizen organizations like Sturgeon for Tomorrow, Shadows on the Wolf, and Otter Street Fishing Club. Kendall explained that one large, well-functioning spawning marsh in the Winnebago System can produce more walleye fry than all the state hatcheries. "That is why habitat work is so absolutely critical, and that is the most effective thing we could do," he said. The collaboration draws together a broad and diverse group of people, including researchers, biologists, fisheries managers, college students, and, most important, passionate citizens, all working together, guided by science-based evaluations, to accomplish good walleye management with an emphasis on fish habitat restoration and protection. For many who get involved, it becomes an important part of their life.

Mike Arrowood, WFT chairman of the board, has been part of the organization since its inception in 1991. WFT is the most active fishing conservation organization in Wisconsin, with more than two thousand members. This nonprofit supports its activities through fundraising events across fourteen statewide chapters. On the Winnebago System, WFT has invested more than $1.5 million in privately funded fish habitat and walleye spawning habitat work. Arrowood has been responsible for organizing most of this work. He is a man of action, dedicated and laser-focused on walleye habitat projects and other activities to improve the quality of walleye fishing. He is also a man of science, having been trained in forest management. Yet he is clear with folks that he is not a fish biologist; he approaches this work as a citizen interested in helping with walleye management efforts to get results. Arrowood came to this work through a love of fishing. In the early 1970s, he was befriended by some WDNR fisheries biologists in Oshkosh because of his enthusiasm for walleye.

When we spoke, Arrowood reflected on WFT's early work. A drought in the late 1980s brought challenging times to a walleye population dependent on high spring river flows for successful spawning. Addressing a low-head dam and its scour or boil hole was the impetus for organizing anglers in the area (a boil hole is the turbulent area below the dam when under certain river flows and tailwater conditions organisms and objects can become trapped in a continuous eddy). Arrowood said: "When we started in 1991, we raised a whole $8,000 at our first banquet.... We went to Oshkosh and we said, 'Where can we get the biggest bang for our buck?' There is a dam on the Fox River called the Eureka Dam. They built these dams in the early 1800s for water transport up and down the rivers. They said, 'There is a dam at Eureka that has got a boil hole. Fill that boil hole in.' Gordon Priegel back in the 1960s had dropped 100,000 walleye larvae, above the dam, and then put fry or larval nets below, and never documented a single live larvae making it over that dam and out of that boil hole.[16] So we spent $154,000 filling in that boil hole. Like I said, we had $8,000. And that's what caused the start of the next eight chapters of Walleyes for Tomorrow to raise enough money to pay off that debt. . . . That got us going. Then we started with all the marsh projects. We've done twenty-seven marsh projects on the Wolf now and twenty-six on the Fox.[17] It is water in and water out; that's what counts. You have to have water flowing in the spring . . . (a) to have the eggs deposited and (b) to have the walleye washed down."

I asked Arrowood why the Winnebago System has attracted so much productive citizen involvement and he stated forthright, "The DNR, I give them all the credit in the world. Going back to 1972, the biologists up at Oshkosh were hands-on guys who brought the public into the fold; they formed committees." Arrowood was on one of the committees, and he got to know WDNR biologist Vern Hacker.[18] He explained, "They have an outreach here that was second to none. Kendall [Kamke] is part of it, Ron Bruch before him, Gordon Priegel before him, and Dan Folz before

A group of fishing boats congregates just below the Eureka Dam near Lake Winnebago during the walleye run in 1971. Photograph by Dean Tvedt, Wisconsin Department of Natural Resources Collection, University of Wisconsin–Madison Library.

him; all these guys have been people persons. . . . If you call Kendall and want some updates, he'll be there, you know he'll show up." Citizen involvement also includes participating in the science. For the bottom trawling crew, "every time it goes out, there's four volunteers, four different civilians in that boat; we get to handle the fish, count the fish. It is huge in keeping the public involved," Arrowood said.

As one might expect for an advocate as successful as he is, Arrowood has great people skills and considerable ability to communicate and organize the public into action. When asked how he engages the WFT membership to play the crucial long game with their walleye habitat work, he explained, "I was trained as a forester. You talk thirty- to fifty- or one-hundred-year rotations on your crop. And I bring that message to the people when I start chapters. Look, you're not going to have instantaneous results. . . . Up front tell them what to expect, and they buy in to that. Because it takes a while for a walleye to grow large enough to be able to keep; a four-year-old walleye here is about 15 inches. Arrowood documented each habitat project by taking many pictures, and during WFT meetings and banquets he displayed the images to show members how their money was spent.

The WFT's work reaches beyond that of population assessments and restoration of spawning habitat; it requires an understanding of wide-ranging concepts such as river dynamics and hydrology. For example, Arrowood stated that WFT local members got involved in public meetings a couple of years ago on the rebuilding of the Princeton Dam, about thirty miles upstream of the old Eureka Dam on the Fox River. He told me, "Our group went to three public hearings. While we don't pound on the table or jump up and down, we made it clear that there should be a fishway there." The WDNR finished the project in the spring of 2020. "So now the Fox River from Winnebago all the way to Portage, which is ninety-six miles of water, doesn't have a fish migration impediment on it. That is amazing. . . . If you build it they will come!" In addition, WFT funds walleye science, such as the reward tag study, which led to better estimates of Winnebago System walleye exploitation rates. The organization also supported the publication of a book titled *Biology, Management, and Culture of Walleye and Sauger,* published by the American Fisheries Society.[19] In 2018, WFT established an endowment for walleye research at the University of Wisconsin–Stevens Point, which will produce new information on walleye and walleye management for years to come.

Strong working relationships are also helpful when other issues come up. Kendall and I spoke about the recent reduction in the Winnebago System walleye creel limit from five to three fish, and he explained that the endeavor to get better estimates of walleye exploitation rates was the result of working with the public. First, after efforts to educate anglers about tag reporting, most anglers recognized the importance of reporting a tagged walleye and understood how those data were used. Over time, the WDNR made it easier for anglers to report a tag. Second, WFT and Battle on Bago, a group of Oshkosh-area Rotarians who support conservation efforts, funded reward tags that were used to quantify angler tag reporting rates. The estimates of exploitation rates were an important piece of science in discussions about reducing the creel limit. I asked Kendall if the three-walleye limit would reduce the number of anglers fishing the Winnebago System and if that was part of the calculus in reducing the limit. "No, I don't think we expect that we are going to see fewer angler-hours out there," he replied. Our conversation then wandered to other fisheries, to how fishing on Winnebago has changed through time, and to trolling and ice fishing, but I failed to get Kendall's thoughts on the mechanics of how their creel limit reduction would reduce exploitation. To find out, I asked Adam Nickel, the WDNR Winnebago gamefish biologist.

Adam Nickel has worked on the Winnebago System since 2014 and is heavily involved in the various walleye population assessments.[20] He did the science to improve the computation of the exploitation rate using high reward tags and is also working to

One of the collaborative restoration projects for Winnebago System walleye involved replacing small, perched culverts with a series of larger ones to allow more water flow into and out of the nearby floodplain marshes. Photograph by Mike Arrowood.

understand how to properly manage the walleye fishery for the future. Adam is an enthusiastic and dedicated biologist. In our discussion, he noted that some overfishing has occurred, especially in years with low abundance of gizzard shad and other forage fish. "What we've been noticing in the last number of years is that we get a good year-class in the system, but as immature females age 3 and 4 they're seeing annual exploitation rates as high as 60 percent." He specified that the high estimate of exploitation was observed in 2015, the first year that they tagged immature females, and that "as a result, a year-class can be substantially reduced after a year of fishing harvest." I asked about the proportion of anglers who harvest a limit of walleye. Creel surveys were conducted on the Winnebago System in the early 1990s, but there are no recent creel statistics for the system. Adam noted that most of the walleye harvest occurs in April, May, and June, with many anglers catching their limit. The main objective of the three-walleye creel limit is to reduce exploitation during those peak fishing months and to protect enough fish to sustain the population. Adam recognized there is always uncertainty with regulation change and explained, "We are planning to continue tagging fish each year and estimating exploitation annually so that five-plus years down the road we evaluate the regulation change and see if we are hitting a lower average exploitation rate or what might have changed."

I was curious about seasonal closures for Winnebago and whether that option was discussed with the public since reducing fishing effort or time-area closures is often part of exploitation control. Kendall noted that a spring spawning closure is a perennial topic with anglers. Some anglers only fish the rivers in the spring while others from the east side of Winnebago want to close the fishing during the spawning period. Kendall was clear: "We don't have an egg problem, we don't have a reproduction problem. . . . The fish are still laying the eggs, you're just harvesting them faster than we can grow them to the size you want to harvest them at. A big advantage of using individually numbered tags is that you know when and where fish are being taken, and since you were able to determine the sex of the fish at tagging, you can look at where and when your fish are being caught by sex. A lot of the times in the spring run they're catching males. The females don't really bite that good until after they've spawned. So, when you look at where and when your fish are caught, turns out if you're really concerned about saving adult and immature female walleye a case could be made to close the season in May and June on the Winnebago System." Kendall and Adam relay this science to anglers, and I suspect that well-informed anglers then focus their attention on other topics, such as creel limits and fish habitat.

Adam stressed the importance of working with the public to make decisions on how to maintain a healthy fishery. He referred to the recent development of an updated management plan, with its extensive public involvement, and the public consultation on regulation change. Each winter he and other WDNR staff meet with about twenty clubs around the Winnebago System. Adam was struck by that connection with anglers: "I've bounced around enough to know what is done in other states, other offices, agencies, that sort of thing, as far as typical field work and process. It is a good feeling when you go to a club meeting to provide an update and in some of those meetings you have over a hundred people there." Adam recalled that they talked to six hundred anglers in 2016 when they initiated the discussion about high exploitation. "I would say that was the most impressive thing that I've been able to experience is the number of people who are interested and passionate about the resource and are looking at making things better and preserving it for the future."

Finally, I wanted to know about the future of the walleye on the Winnebago System. Kendall replied, "I think we are in good shape, and I say that for a couple of reasons. We know the fundamentals of how the system works for walleye. I have to give credit going all the way back to Gordy Priegel in the 1960s doing a lot of the initial work on how the system works, where the walleye go, the spawning marshes and that. The anglers in our area have had the benefit of a succession of good biologists working on the system to collect the information and to increase the knowledge that we have of the system. . . . So, we know what we have to do to keep things going. Now it becomes a matter of being able to institute whether it is through our own agency, convincing them or convincing the politicians of the correct science, and that science is dictating our decisions. . . . We have spent decades working with the public on this system, helping them to understand, not keeping secrets from them and everything else. I've done my best to impart that on our new biologists who are working on the system so that they understand the value of that, and I believe they do." He continued, "Knowing the exploitation and that we are balancing on the knife's edge of it makes it all the more critical that we involve the angler component from the public and keep them on our side. So that we keep them informed so that they are willing to accept what the science tells us we need to do in the next few years or five years. . . . If we can stay true to that, I think that we're in good shape. . . . Are we going to have to make adjustments if exploitation continues to rise? Sure we would. But when we do it we will do it in a way that has involved the public so that we move in a direction together as opposed to us making that decision and then dragging them screaming and kicking through law enforcement to that point." Kendall concluded, "The habitat is the other critical component. Again we are working with the public. . . . The future looks good; it may be different, but it still looks good. Those marshes are critical, absolutely critical; we can manage the high exploitation if we can keep the productive recruitment going."

In a highly altered watershed, it takes a strong collaborative effort between citizens and all levels of government to ensure sufficient habitat for walleye to flourish. So, I was inspired to learn about Winnebago System anglers and biologists working together with the shared goal of restoring and maintaining fish habitat and water quality. They have sustained a long, productive partnership, and, importantly, anglers have been heavily involved in fisheries management decisions.

9
A FISHERY PREDICAMENT
Mille Lacs, Minnesota

———◆———

I often tell colleagues that the Mille Lacs walleye fishery is the most interesting of all walleye fisheries for us to study, understand, and manage. The waters and walleye of Mille Lacs have attracted and sustained anglers for generations. But in recent years, the management of this fishery has become highly charged. Fisheries biologists and managers who have worked on Mille Lacs have been challenged and unfairly disparaged. In 2014, a decline in walleye abundance led to an independent assessment of the walleye fishery. In 2015, for the first time in history the walleye sport fishery was closed midseason. In 2016, Minnesota politicians became more occupied with the fallout of low walleye quotas. And in 2017, I was asked to explore the status and management of the fishery, to develop theories to explain the recent past, and to provide advice about how to move forward. After a review of the data and discussions with others, I developed a professional opinion on the topic.[1] Walleye populations fluctuate and ecosystems change, and with notable changes, biologists conceive stories of cause and effect. Each biologist who has worked on Mille Lacs has a story to tell, and I do not judge their stories. I cannot do justice to the wide variety of these perspectives, but in this chapter I outline three common perspectives of the Mille Lacs fishery for the period from 2013 to 2022. The full, true story of this fishery is currently unknown; perhaps it can never be completely known.

Mille Lacs was formed by a glacial moraine.[2] About 15,000 years ago, a glacier in what is now central Minnesota deposited high ridges of sediment and rock. These ridges dammed the drainage to the south, creating an immense lake. About 10,000 years ago

Mille Lacs was larger than the present lake and was surrounded by tundra and spruce trees. Water forces cut outlets into the lake. Walleye moved in, coming up the rivers, always keen to explore and inhabitant new waters. About 9,000 years ago, humans hunted bison along the shores. About 8,000 years ago, the early Rum River began from a cut in the shore of Ogechie Bay. About 2,000 years ago, humans settled on the shore. A'aninin people built earth-covered wooden lodges near the waters. These lodges were later used by the Dakota. By 1700, the Dakota people had villages on the lake, and they called the lake Mdé Wakhán (or Bdé Wakán, Spirit Lake). The French explorers and fur traders called it Grand lac du pays des mille lacs (great lake in the land of a thousand lakes) or simply Lac des Mille Lacs. By 1750, the Dakota were pushed south and west by the Ojibwe, who were migrating west. The Ojibwe people settled along Mille Lacs (calling it Misi-zaaga'iganing, Grand Lake) and flourished on its shores, supported by a diet of deer, small mammals, turtles, fish, wild rice, berries, maple syrup, and other foods. In the Treaty of St. Peters (1837), they ceded their lands to the United States while reserving the right to continue to hunt, fish, and gather on them. Today, deciduous trees and human development encircle the lake, and many Minnesotans simply call it Mille Lacs.[3] Walleye are still flourishing here. Time creeps by, and in the long view, things change by degrees.

In the 1990s, after decades of charges against members of the Mille Lacs Band of Ojibwe for violating state fishing and hunting regulations while they exercised their rights in the ceded territory, the band sued the state of Minnesota. The federal district court split the case into two phases. Phase I would determine if the band retained any usufructuary rights under the Treaty of St. Peters, and Phase II would address the means of regulating any retained rights. In 1994, the court concluded that the band retained its usu-fructuary rights as guaranteed by the treaty. In addition, the court concluded that the state bore the burden to demonstrate that any regulation applied to the band must be reasonable and necessary for conservation, public health, or safety. In 1996, the court concluded that several Wisconsin bands also retained their hunting and fishing rights in the Minnesota portion of the ceded lands.

In the pre-trial period for Phase II, the bands and the state resolved many regulatory issues.[4] The state agreed to the bands' conservation code and management plans, and the bands and the state agreed to protocols to regulate and coordinate harvest management and resource assessment. However, the court identified several unresolved laws and regulations for summary judgment. In 1997, the court concluded that the bands and the state should attempt to determine harvestable surplus through consensus, in accordance with the protocols, and that either party could ask the court to resolve future disputes on the matter. Second, it concluded that the allocation of resources between the bands and the state was inappropriate at the time because need for allocation had not been shown.

The state appealed the court decisions. In 1997, a three-judge panel of the U.S. Circuit Court upheld the district court decisions. Two years later, the U.S. Supreme Court ruled on a five-to-four vote that the bands retained the hunting and fishing rights guaranteed them under the treaty. Today, the Mille Lacs walleye fishery is managed consistent with the protocols in the court's order, and both the bands and the state must agree on any changes to the harvest management and resource assessment provisions outlined in the protocols.

Mille Lacs is a large (128,250 acres [51,900 ha]), mesotrophic (moderately fertile) lake. It has a maximum depth of 42 feet (12.8 m), and about a fourth of the lake is less than 25 feet (7.2 m) in depth. Given that its average depth is 28.5 feet (8.7 m), the lake is generally mixed from surface to lake bottom during the ice-free period, so temperature and dissolved oxygen levels are similar with depth. Water clarity data for Mille Lacs are sparse and disjointed; before 1995 the summer Secchi disk readings averaged about 7.5 feet (2.3 m), while recently the average has been about

11 feet (3.4 m).[5] The fish community consists of yellow perch, walleye, northern pike, white sucker, cisco, smallmouth bass, rock bass, muskie, trout-perch, logperch, burbot, bluntnose minnow, golden shiner, spottail shiner, mimic shiner, and many other species. The walleye, as well as all other fish species present in the lake except perhaps muskie,[6] are self-sustaining. Those who called for walleye stocking to restore the fishery were ill advised, as the walleye population was large and has always had excellent reproduction. However, the population recently experienced a young walleye survival problem, and stocked walleye suffered the same fate.[7] The walleye population in Mille Lacs has been estimated to average about 650,000 fish (greater than 14 inches [356 mm]; 5.1 walleye/acre [12.5 walleye/ha]).[8] Walleye year-class strength is periodically high, with strong years in 1988, 2002, 2013, and 2017 and weak years between 2009 through 2012.

The Mille Lacs walleye fishery is a complex, dynamic socio-economic and biological system, and up until recently it was Minnesota's largest walleye fishery. It is a productive walleye fishery located a short distance from Minneapolis. The Mille Lacs Band of Ojibwe, with over four thousand members, has its main reservation on the southern end of the lake. Their community in Vineland (Neyaashiing) is home to one thousand people and houses the band's Government Center, the Minnesota Historical Society's Mille Lacs Indian Museum, and the band's Grand Casino Mille Lacs. The small cities of Garrison, Isle, and Wahkon are on the shore, as are Mille Lacs Kathio and Father Hennepin State Parks. Over two dozen large resorts and hotels and many small resorts are located around the lake, many of which cater to sport anglers and outdoor enthusiasts. Scattered around the lake are thirteen public boat accesses as well as numerous privately constructed harbors. Historically, walleye angling was most successful from the early May fishing opener until early June, with the median annual harvest about 280,000 fish.[9] Both open-water and ice fishing are popular on the lake (average angler effort: open water—1.4 million angler-hours, ice fishing—1.75 million angler-hours).[10] There have been some important recent changes to the lake. The food web has changed with the addition of zebra mussels (detected in 2005) and spiny water fleas (a species of zooplankton, detected in 2009).

MILLE LACS FISHERIES MANAGEMENT
—◆—

Mille Lacs biologists are diligent in the collection, compilation, and analysis of data on fish relative abundance, fish growth, angler creel statistics, and walleye population size. The walleye population is assessed yearly. In the fall, a standard Minnesota gill-net survey is conducted, which provides managers with estimates of fish abundance and size.[11] Winter and open-water angler surveys provide estimates of fish harvest, fish catch rates, and angler effort. Tribal spear and gill-net harvests are also monitored and enumerated. To assess walleye reproduction, biologists from the MDNR and the Great Lakes Indian Fish and Wildlife Commission (GLIFWC)[12] (respectively) complete fall and spring electrofishing surveys for juvenile walleye. A fall forage gill-net assessment is conducted to estimate relative abundance of walleye forage size, as well as cisco, yellow perch, and minnow populations. Finally, since 2002, mark-recapture studies to estimate the number of walleye (fish greater than 14 inches [356 mm]) have periodically been completed. These studies are necessary to pin the assessment models that are used to estimate population size to something likely; without these benchmarks, the models are free to wander into la-la land.

Since 1997 and consistent with the protocols in the court's order, the walleye fishery has been managed with kill quotas.[13] Annual quotas are determined by age-structured population assessment models, a 24 percent exploitation rate,[14] and the professional opinions of members of a fisheries technical committee.[15] The MDNR's population assessment model has evolved through time, and it is highly complicated. Like all models, it produces results that can't be fully trusted, so professional opinion and understanding of the fishery are critical. The annual quota is set by compromise and consensus between the MDNR and Ojibwe representatives. Annual quotas generally increased from 1997 to 2012.

From 1995 to 2004, I was one of several fisheries quants for the Mille Lacs walleye fishery. My job was to produce estimates of the number of walleye in the lake and to provide technical guidance on fisheries management, and at the time I was doing a terrible job on the former. When I look back at my previous estimates, they were often lower than my more recent estimates; that is, for any given past year, the most recent model estimated more fish than I had estimated years ago. This is called a retrospective problem. Retrospective patterns generally occur when the model inputs are wrong, for example, when assuming that the natural mortality rate was constant when it was likely changing with environmental conditions.[16] A retrospective problem can have either negative or positive bias. My modeling had a negative bias: my estimated number of walleye used for setting the quota

A walleye is captured in a gill net during a lake survey on Mille Lacs. Photograph by Paul Middlestaedt.

was generally lower than later population estimates. The consequence of this bias was likely conservative quotas in the early years of quota management.[17] My early modeling work suffered from a lack of mark-recapture studies to provide periodic independent estimates of the number of walleye.[18] As is the risk in these situations, my models wandered into la-la land.

After my departure as a quant, more mark-recapture studies were completed and the models got more complicated. However, it seemed to me that model reliability had not improved. Most alarming to me was that these models appeared to substantially underestimate the number of large, old walleye.[19] Retrospective analysis indicated that recent models were also indicating biases.[20] Most models used were similar in construction and assumptions.[21] Recent models gave high confidence to the estimates of the number of walleye in Mille Lacs, yet all the inherent uncertainties could not be included in the calculations. High precision is not possible when modeling nature, and precision pride can hinder work on real problems.

Seven of the eight years between 2005 and 2012 had quotas greater than the median historical walleye harvest (quota median for this time was 540,500 pounds [245,200 kg] compared to 475,000 pounds [215,000 kg] from the pre-quota harvest period). Harvests were generally high but under quota. During this period, the quotas may have been set too liberally. From 2010 to 2012, excessive exploitation of young and medium-sized walleye may have occurred. Those years had high quotas and length regulations that focused harvest on those smaller fish while protecting large fish.

Between 2013 and 2022, the quotas were set at low levels. This resulted in restrictive walleye harvest regulations. Most importantly, the walleye sport fishery was intermittently closed during this period out of an abundance of caution. These closures had large negative economic and trust-in-management consequences, and the local community bounced between frustration and exasperation. In 2014, resort owners and shoreland property owners sued the MDNR for managing the fishery with frequent angling regulation changes allegedly inconsistent with the preservation of the state's fishing heritage; however, the Minnesota Court of Appeals concluded that the imposition of strict fishing rules did not violate the state constitution. On August 3, 2015, after state anglers exceeded the low quota set, for in the first time in history the walleye sport fishery was closed midseason.

In early 2017, there was a consensus among Mille Lacs fisheries managers that the walleye population was overfished and standards were needed to gauge the status of the fishery. State and tribal natural resource management administrators approved and signed a consensus agreement[22] that had the goals of maintaining a mature walleye relative abundance of 20 pounds per net (9 kg/net)[23] and protecting the 2013 walleye year-class. Many citizens, as well as informed fisheries biologists, disagreed with the overfished assessment and the set standards outlined in the consensus agreement. So, from 2017 to 2022, Mille Lacs walleye fisheries management appeared to exist in an unsettled stasis.

THOUGHTS FROM A MILLE LACS INSIDER

I discussed Mille Lacs walleye fishing and fisheries management with Joe Fellegy, a longtime Mille Lacs walleye fishing expert. Fellegy breathes Mille Lacs, and I suspect he dreams Mille Lacs too. He grew up on the lake's north shore at a family resort that his parents built in the 1950s. When young, he was his father's bait boy on the family's fishing launch. By the age of fourteen, he was a fishing guide using a small boat with an Evinrude outboard motor. After graduating from St. John's University with an English degree, he started his own walleye launch business. Fellegy's schedule reflected the popularity of the fishery, and he guided daily trips from the beginning of the walleye fishing season opener in May until mid-October. As a fishing guide and launch captain, he experimented with all the latest fishing tackle innovations at the time, such as monofilament line, slip-sinker rigs, and jigs, and he pioneered spinner rigs for trolling. At the same time, Fellegy launched into writing about the outdoors. He authored a book titled *Walleyes and Walleye Fishing,* which was published in 1973. He assisted Al and Ron Lindner in starting the *In-Fisherman* magazine in the 1970s. Since terminating his fishing launch business in 1990, he has been writing for a living. From 1992 to 2007 he wrote and published the *Mille Lacs Fishing Digest,* a periodical about the lake with articles on walleye biology, walleye fishing, and the Mille Lacs community. As a result of his curiosity about walleye biology and management, he has befriended many fisheries biologists and managers over the years. Since 1988, Fellegy has been a regular contributor to *Minnesota Outdoor News,* a weekly publication on hunting, fishing, and natural resource management.

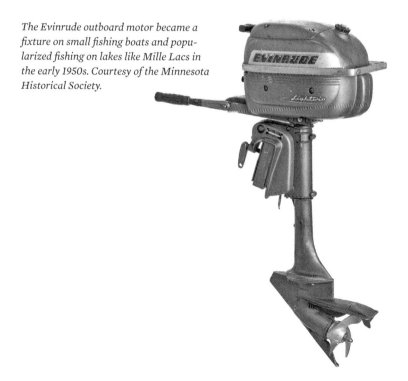

The Evinrude outboard motor became a fixture on small fishing boats and popularized fishing on lakes like Mille Lacs in the early 1950s. Courtesy of the Minnesota Historical Society.

I got to know Joe Fellegy through the late Dennis Schupp, my former supervisor at MDNR.[24] Schupp, while conducting creel surveys on Mille Lacs, visited the Fellegy family resort in the 1950s and 1960s. It was Dennis who got Joe interested in fisheries science. In 1970, Joe wrote an article about Dennis's Leech Lake walleye studies, and in the 1980s, Joe cajoled Dennis to attend some Mille Lacs Lake Advisory Association meetings. Fellegy was one of the founders of the association, an organization that provided feedback to the MDNR on fisheries management issues up until the early 1990s. At the time, Fellegy was highly respected by the MDNR for his objectivity and his ability to communicate to the public on walleye biology and management. With the advent of state and tribal fisheries co-management on the lake, Fellegy was appointed a member of the MDNR Mille Lacs Fisheries Input Group, which provided feedback to MDNR until 2015. Joe attended the meetings of a reboot of this input group (Mille Lacs Fisheries Advisory Committee), but he was not invited to be a member, possibly because the MDNR preferred people more amenable to the agency. Joe's dogged efforts for pragmatic fisheries management with accountability on the lake eventually resulted in efforts to discredit him.

Joe Fellegy is a lean man of average height. He is full of energy and tends to talk some with his hands. He is now in his late seventies, still quick in thought and clear in message. Given his lifelong commitment to Mille Lacs, it is easy to get him riled up about injustices of Mille Lacs fisheries management. Before our conversation veered to walleye quota management, we talked about Mille Lacs fishing. He shared some of his fondest memories: "In the fall of 1969, I bought a new 1970 Evinrude Bobcat snowmobile. Back then, ice fishing on Mille Lacs mudflats, often miles from shore, was still pretty rare. Having mental maps of the flats and knowing how they can produce walleyes in open water, I was super curious about ice-fishing success on those way-out spots. Locating mudflats and early ice fishing along the edges of curves, points, and tips that I had caught 'em on in summer was unforgettable for me." He recalled a long-ago launch trip. "On a calm afternoon either side of August 1 around 1980, my launch trip on the flats produced mediocre results, maybe fifteen walleyes with a big slowdown before 4:30. So, for the heck of it, I revved up the launch, cruised toward shore, and had my customers drop their lines—with my spinner minnow and spinner nightcrawler rigs—in about twenty-five feet of water over soft bottom outside harder-bottom, shallower water off the north shore. I had rarely seen walleye fishermen let alone launch captains fishing there in midsummer. Anyway, I started trolling and soon several customers yelled 'Fish on!' Wow, talk about fast action! The last hour of the trip produced phenomenal and surprising results."

I asked Fellegy to describe his launches. "I took a maximum of eight people on my launch trips. Hey, it wasn't how many people I could haul. For me it was how many I could fish, including forward trolling without tangles. One of my slogans was 'You gotta be ready for anything.' And I didn't want to spend precious fishing time retying lines for different spots, depths, and fishing methods. On my launch trips and when I did small-boat guide trips, even as a kid, I insisted that customers use my tackle. I banned customer tackle boxes and foreign rods on my boat. So, I carried about fifty rod-reels for eight people. On a given trip, half day or all day, I might be slip-bobber fishing with leeches on a shallow reef top; or drifting and dragging bottom on weedless shallow sand with slip-sinker/long-leader/plain-hook rigs; or trolling on an offshore mudflat with three-way rigs, heavy bell sinkers, and spinners baited with minnows or nightcrawlers. I used to joke about using my customers as guinea pigs." He mentioned a launch trip that he will always remember. "It was launch trip with mentally challenged adults from the Brainerd State Hospital. A guy sitting in a rear corner of the launch wound in a walleye. While I worked it out of the landing net, unhooked it, and rebaited his line, he told me about his fishing past on the Mississippi River. Okay. Fish talk goes on. But when I returned to the steering wheel, a hospital technician came up to me and remarked, 'Joe! That's the first time he's talked and conversed coherently in five years!' Quite the magical moment."

I was curious about his advice to walleye anglers fishing Mille Lacs. What kind of conditions were most and least productive? Fellegy said, "Waves are often a plus when fishing shallow water. That was true when bobber fishing with leeches, or casting jigs and crankbaits on shallow reef tops, and when drifting and trolling with live bait or with artificials along shallow sandy stretches. Calm water could sometimes bring maximum success over deeper water, like offshore mudflats and deep gravel bars, or on the deeper soft-bottom areas outside the shore breaks, slopes, and rocky points around Mille Lacs." He also noted, "Like other natural walleye lakes, Mille Lacs sees overall angler success rise when natural forage, especially young perch, is low. Historically, superabundance of tiny perch led to 'dead sea' years, when the bite got very tough and overall fishing success was labeled poor. At Mille Lacs, fishing success, or the bite, is not the same as the walleye population's status. The bite can vary a lot, even with the same walleye population. Sure, a fish population naturally varies from year to year, but Mille Lacs has always contained enough walleyes to provide excellent angling when conditions are favorable."

Fellegy's demeanor changed when I asked him about his current opinion of MDNR fisheries management. He rumbled, like a lake ice tsunami coming ashore with a strong wind at ice-out, "Years back, Mille Lacs locals worked with and mainly respected DNR fisheries managers. Surely the most noteworthy change—a real negative—came with the state-tribal co-management quota system. . . . Nothing in the big lake's biosphere has justified the recent extremist tight angling regs facing Mille Lacs state-licensed walleye anglers. . . . In 2020, the open-water regulations are that anglers cannot legally keep even one walleye and during July anglers can't even target walleye. DNR says it is to protect Mille Lacs walleye. Protect from what?" Fellegy believes, like many anglers,

Although this iconic building is now closed, guide services and bait shops are readily available around the shores of Mille Lacs, where the walleye population is a big draw for tourism in the area. Photograph by Glenn Allenspach.

that the Mille Lacs walleye population did not collapse. He questions why there have been so many years of low quota and the overprotective policies of a fish population with high numbers of mature fish.[25]

Much of Fellegy's unhappiness is directed at the system set up by the MDNR and tribal governments, which conducted meetings in private and developed harvest plans without public consultation. He suggested that there was little accountability when quotas were set conservatively or when management mistakes occurred. Of course, when the MDNR set up the management system for Mille Lacs walleye, it was their first experience in quota harvest management, and they made mistakes. For example, the agency created incentives to raise the quota to avoid penalties for any quota overruns. Fellegy is troubled by the apparent code of ethics for those involved. He shared his frustration: "With law and public policy, the good should outweigh anything bad. But with Mille Lacs co-management's extremism, the intolerable negatives and bad costs far outweigh anything positive. . . . Never-ending uncertainty regarding management decisions, changing regulations, and 'what comes next' for Mille Lacs, thanks to the co-management quota system. Negative economic impacts on Mille Lacs resorts and an array of fishing-related businesses." Over a dozen different angling regulations have been imposed since the enactment of the quota management system, often with angling regulations changing later within a summer. No economic study was conducted to estimate the losses to resorts and other businesses from the predicament. However, a $3.6 million Mille Lacs economic relief package was passed by the Minnesota legislature in 2016 and administered in 2017 to address some of the losses.

THREE PERSPECTIVES

The recent Mille Lacs walleye fishery predicament demonstrates the challenges of managing a walleye fishery with passionate interests in the outcomes. It appeared to me that the MDNR struggled to explain their quandary. First, the agency suggested that the Federal Clean Water Act of 1972, which reduced phosphorous pollution to the lake, lowered walleye productivity. Prior to 2015, the agency acknowledged that overharvest played a role in their management bind.[26] Next, in 2017, the blame shifted to a perfect storm of nonindigenous species, while fishing had been "a small player" in reducing the walleye population.[27] By 2020, the agency did not specify reasons for what was then a seven-year predicament.[28] Playing a role in the crisis was the lack of a comprehensive management plan. Fail to plan, plan to fail.

The question of what broke the most productive walleye fishery in the state was asked, and many answered.[29] Several biologists were asked to provide independent assessments.[30] Given the nature of this complex ecosystem and fishery, some answers were speculative.[31] Biologists have offered narratives for the Mille Lacs walleye fishery. People are natural storytellers—a trait spun into the strands of our DNA, woven in by hunting and fishing for hundreds of thousands of years. Scientists use storytelling along with mental models of reality to engage creative thought. Fisheries biologists formulate stories about a fishery to distill an overwhelming amount of data into a narrative that attempts to explain what might be happening. These stories always fail to capture the full complexity of what has happened and is still happening; however, sometimes they are correct and helpful. At other times they are wrong and misdirected. The responsibility of fisheries biologists is to evaluate these stories to see if they are supported by statistically credible cause-and-effect relationships.

By 2020, management of the Mille Lacs walleye fishery was struggling because the biologists involved could not agree on the condition of the walleye population. They were looking at the same data but coming to different conclusions. Under a co-management system, it is difficult to manage the fishery if there is no agreement on the population status. If agreement on the status is not possible, then management actions can't be agreed on as effectively: Should the quota be higher or lower? Should the harvest be higher or lower? Should the walleye population be higher or lower?

While there was a continuum of professional opinions on the status of the Mille Lacs walleye population, three stories or perspectives were common among the biologists. Perhaps, people saw what they were prepared to see. First, some biologists concluded that the fishery had been overfished and that they needed to provide greater protection of walleye from overharvest. Some with this perspective consistently believed overfishing had occurred over many years. Second, some biologists concluded that the lake ecology had changed, which lowered walleye population carrying capacity. Given this new dynamic, they believed that the walleye harvest needed to be reduced. Third, some biologists concluded that reduced carrying capacity plus high biomass levels in spawning stock brought down the walleye surplus production. They believed the consequences of these two changes depressed young walleye survival, and assuming a harvest-oriented fishery goal, future harvests needed to increase to reduce the excess spawning stock. Below, I outline each perspective, supporting data, and the independent biologists' assessments on the perspective.

Recovery Needed Perspective

Biologists with the perspective that recovery was needed believed that the Mille Lacs walleye fishery had been overfished. They believed that the recent (2011–2017) decline in walleye was the result of past overharvest of young fish. Sport fishing effort on Mille Lacs often exceeded 1 million angler-hours during the summer and 1.5 million angler-hours during the winter. When quotas were set high from 2009 to 2012, the high angler effort resulted in walleye harvests that diminished the population. Based on creel survey data, during this period the walleye harvest averaged about 330,000 pounds (150,000 kg), but for several years the harvest approached 400,000 pounds (181,000 kg).

Under this perspective, it was necessary to reduce walleye harvest. Near-term annual quotas needed to be much lower than the past quotas until the walleye population recovered to the agreed mature walleye benchmark. The 2017 consensus agreement to maintain a relative abundance of 20 pounds per net (9 kg/net) was reasonable, and management actions should have worked to achieve that goal. Biologists with this view believed that increasing the spawning stock biomass would increase the chance of future strong walleye year-classes. Given uncertainty, they argued that management should be conservative, believing that a recovered walleye population was one that had walleye abundance and spawning stock biomass at or near historical levels.

Independent biologists reviewed the data and acknowledged the recent decline in walleye biomass. However, they found no evidence that high fishing levels or low spawner abundance were responsible for a decline in Mille Lacs walleye. While they noted that sport fishing effort on Mille Lacs tended to be greater than other notable walleye fisheries, they found that the exploitation rates were not excessive nor were they the cause of a decline in the population. They found no evidence that walleye abundance declines were responsible for declines in walleye year-class strength. They noted that substantial numbers of fingerling walleye were observed in the fall, which suggested to them that spawning stock biomass was not the limiting factor. Young-of-the-year walleye survival had been low since 2000, leading them to conclude that these low survival rates were very likely contributing to a decline of walleye in Mille Lacs.

Changed Ecology Perspective

Biologists with the perspective that the lake ecology had changed believed that the consequence was a walleye population with a lower carrying capacity. Zebra mussels have reduced phytoplankton abundance and have increased water clarity, submerged aquatic plant abundance, and bottom-covering algae occurrences, all of which affect fish populations.[32] The increase in water clarity resulted in a possible reduction in walleye productivity.[33] The addition of spiny water fleas altered the zooplankton community, which may have also mitigated the zebra mussel effect on water clarity.[34] Zooplankton biomass and phytoplankton had substantially decreased with the addition of zebra mussels and spiny water fleas in the lake, and these ecosystem changes reduced resources available to walleye, which then impacted the population's carrying capacity.[35] The food web and energy flow changes occurring in Mille Lacs appeared to slightly reduce fingerling walleye growth.[36] In addition, climate change made the lake more suitable for warmwater fish species.[37] Whether from climate change or changes to the food web, smallmouth bass were now more abundant in the lake, and they competed with walleye for food.[38]

Under this perspective, the average long-term walleye harvest needed to be reduced. Biologists believed that the developed recovery metrics based on historical walleye population data were likely unachievable given the irreversible food web and environmental changes to the Mille Lacs ecosystem. Thus, the consensus agreement goals were viewed as unrealistic. The ecosystem had changed, but expectations and metrics had not. To these biologists, the 2017 agreement to obtain a relative abundance of 20 pounds per net (9 kg/net) was unreasonable; it was too high for a lake with lower walleye carrying capacity. What once was won't come back. Biologists with the "recovery needed" perspective viewed this perspective as giving up on the fishery, or they believed that the carrying capacity was not so reduced that the agreement requiring management action to meet the spawning stock biomass benchmark should be disregarded.

Independent biologists reviewed the data and concluded that zebra mussel and spiny water flea populations likely caused significant changes to the Mille Lacs ecosystem and that conditions to support the walleye production were no longer the same as they were twenty years earlier. Based on observations in other walleye lakes, they believed carrying capacity was lower than in the past. In 2020, MDNR biologists reported that Mille Lacs water clarity did not increase with increasing zebra mussel abundance.[39]

Lower Carrying Capacity + Perspective

Biologists with this perspective believed that the Mille Lacs walleye fishery had a reduced carrying capacity and was in the low-yield high-spawner bottom (recall the lessons of Ricker). While there was a decline in the walleye population, it did not collapse nor was it ever at risk of collapse. The walleye population was stuck in a low-productivity loop. There were high negative density-dependent effects on young walleye growth and survival, which resulted in poor walleye year-classes. Juvenile walleye faced low forage and high adult walleye competition and predation (high numbers of adults often result in low numbers of juveniles or weak year-classes due to competition and cannibalism).[40] Both young and adult walleye were generally slimmer and in poorer condition, suggesting less forage or greater competition for it. The yellow perch population had been depressed since 2013, indicating high predation by walleye or high exploitation by humans.[41] While the carrying capacity was diminished, the fishery was managed for low yield; that is, it was not on the high-yield productive hilltop. This is the key difference from the "changed ecology" perspective, and this makes all the difference in the world and in the judgment on the amount of walleye harvest that can be allowed.

There were many mature walleye in Mille Lacs, and biologists with this perspective thought the amount was high and even excessive at times. Since 1999 the exploitation rate on large walleye (greater than 20 inches [approximately 500 mm]) had been near zero, which, up until 2006, resulted in an increasing proportion of the population consisting of older, larger-sized fish. As the carrying capacity decreased, a high, relatively stable level of spawning stock biomass was maintained. There were plenty of eggs spawned and a superabundance of walleye fry naturally produced (an indicator of high mature female biomass). From 2016 through 2018, biologists marked the stocked walleye fry into Mille Lacs to estimate natural fry production. The estimates of natural fry production were 7,000, 13,000, and 18,000 fry per littoral acre (a range of 17,000 to 44,000 fry/littoral ha), which is seven to eighteen times greater than the typical MDNR walleye stocking rate used to produce a good walleye fishery in lakes without natural reproduction. By contrast, the Red Lake walleye population, which collapsed in the late 1990s, only produced an estimated 85 fry per littoral acre (210 fry/littoral ha) and 60 fry per littoral acre (150 fry/littoral ha) in 1999 and 2000. After the walleye population recovery, Red Lake biologists noted that high walleye fry densities (greater than 850 fry/littoral acre) were an indicator of an excessive buildup of the spawning population that negatively affected walleye recruitment.[42] In other Minnesota walleye lakes, biologists were using about 1,000 fry per littoral acre (2,500 fry/littoral ha) as a benchmark of possible excess spawning stock biomass.

Under this perspective, the biologists believed it was necessary to reconfigure the population's age and length distribution to a population with fewer old fish and more young fish. This required harvesting the excess old, large walleye. It was possible that temporary increases in harvest were necessary to complete this reconfiguration of the population. Biologists with this perspective also believed that the consensus agreement to maintain a relative abundance of 20 pounds per net (9 kg/net) was too high, and some believed that the use of a minimum benchmark of about 10 pounds per net (5 kg/net) was a more reasonable goal (they also advocated for use of a mature biomass surplus benchmark). Biologists with the "recovery needed" perspective noted that it didn't make sense to decrease spawning stock biomass or increase harvest, even with a diminished carrying capacity and lower productivity. Biologists with the "recovery needed" perspective and the "changed ecology" perspective viewed reconfiguring the walleye population's age and size distribution as reckless or a high-risk proposition with uncertain benefits. However, from 2013 to 2022, more Mille Lacs walleye died from natural causes than were harvested. Under this perspective, the biologists believed that the failure to harvest the doomed fish was unfortunate, unnecessary, and damaging to the fishery.

Independent biologists reviewed the data and concluded that the reduced variability of walleye year-class strength and recent low walleye recruitment were due to predation on juvenile walleye, mainly from adult walleye. They found evidence that there was ample egg and fingerling production, as fingerling abundance had been high since 2000. They stated that a reduction in adult walleye would lead to less cannibalism, higher recruitment, and an increase in young walleye. They also noted that the proportion of walleye 10 years and older generally increased after 1996. If density-dependent effects had occurred, they did not see any effects on walleye growth rates—growth rates had been constant over a long period. Contrary to the reductions in fish condition noted above, they found no trends in condition for walleye (ages 1 to 3).

In 2021, MDNR fisheries biologists provided clear evidence of recent declines in both the average walleye growth rate (for large fish) and fish condition (for all fish).[43]

BELOW DECK

In 2017, I was asked to provide my opinion on the condition of the Mille Lacs walleye fishery. I reviewed the data, interviewed many fisheries biologists and managers, and documented my conclusions and recommendations.[44] I articulated the "lower carrying capacity +" perspective. My informed professional opinion was that the carrying capacity was likely reduced and the overprotection of the large walleye had diminished surplus production—a feedback loop kept the fishery at a low productivity level. If you wanted a walleye harvest–oriented fishery, more tribal members to experience Mille Lacs, or more anglers to fish the lake to support your business, you might call this a negative feedback loop or a doom loop. The consequences of an unwritten fisheries management policy of overprotecting older fish likely resulted in substantial forgone harvest. Purposefully managing for excessive walleye spawning biomass begets lower vitality. I believed managers and administrators met their destiny on the road they took to avoid it. Stockpiling older walleye is reasonable if the goal is to create a catch-and-release fishery; however, if this was the goal, the potential downsides and trade-offs may not have been fully explained to anglers and the public.

In my 2017 assessment, I made a mistake on an important detail but today remain convinced on the main issue. I stated that the harvest of four-year-old walleye in the 2010–12 period appeared to have been very high, which likely resulted in reduced spawning stock biomass in the years following. First, even if the exploitation was high for those fish, any reduction in the spawning stock would have been insignificant given the ample abundance of spawners at the time. Second, I relied on a single model's prediction of exploitation.[45] It is not wise to rely on a single model, given model uncertainty, and the fact that some of the year-classes with predicted high exploitation were weak, those estimates would have been tenuous anyway. Therefore, I failed to be cautious with the data, and I made statements that were misleading or alarmist. I still believe that the Mille Lacs walleye fishery was stuck in a low-productivity loop. This remains my professional opinion, until additional data suggest otherwise. It is possible that my answer was wrong, and it is possible that my skepticism of authority clouded my judgment (suspicion and skepticism are not science). If my answer turns out to be incorrect, I will correct my mistakes. I may be maladapted for a government bureaucracy, but I am not a disgruntled old man.

There are two management options if you believed in the last perspective outlined. Option 1 was to change nothing. Retired MDNR fisheries manager Gary Barnard and I shared the same viewpoint on the Mille Lacs predicament. Gary made an interesting point: "There is no danger of walleye population collapse from harvesting significantly more fish. The high wild fry estimates, which provide independent adult population or spawning stock biomass estimates, confirm that spawning stock vastly exceeds what is necessary. . . . This is a climax-type fishery; they can persist forever in that state because there is always enough recruitment to replace the little bit of mortality that is occurring. . . . If you don't ever recognize the problem that needs fixing, there is no fix to it. You can wallow in it for decades and ruminate over what is causing it, and it'll never get fixed." Option 2 was to break the feedback loop. This feedback loop was breakable, of course, but it required acknowledgment of the causes.

Assuming that the Mille Lacs walleye fishery was managed primarily for perfect fillets, not for catch-and-release fishing, and that the fishery was in the "lower carrying capacity +" condition, fisheries managers would have attempted to break the feedback loop. Breaking a low-productivity loop of poor young walleye survival due to high abundance of large, old walleye is simple and intuitive, but it can be challenging. In this condition, since excessive spawning biomass is holding back young walleye recruitment, harvesting the excess portion of the larger, older fish is necessary. This can be tricky because angler catch rates are often high when in the low-yield high-spawner bottom. In May and June 2020, the average Mille Lacs walleye angler caught one walleye every 1.25 hours (0.8 walleye/angler-hour), compared to the pre-quota years on Mille Lacs when the summer average angler caught one walleye every 4.25 hours (0.24 walleye/angler-hour).

A CAUTIONARY TALE

Fisheries management is the selective modification of fish populations based on society's values. Almost all walleye fisheries are harvest-oriented fisheries. Humans desire walleye to catch and eat. It is a reasonable value for an omnivore. I'm not a speculator profiting on nature or life. I value life. I shed tears for the needless death of creatures large and small. And yet from 2013 to 2022, more Mille Lacs walleye died from natural causes than were harvested. Catching and eating some of these fish that were to die is not anti-conservation; it is advocating for a reasonable use of fish.[46] Tribal members catch fish to share with family and friends throughout the year. Anglers returning home from Mille Lacs have a fish dinner with their kids. When all is said and done, conservation is the sustainable use of nature's resources.

What lessons can fisheries managers and the public learn from this crisis and conflict? On some level, the governance structure on Mille Lacs struggled. Varying views of the Mille Lacs fishery by government representatives often resulted in a lot of unnecessary conflict. Misunderstandings or the failure to come to an agreement on the status of the fishery appeared to lead to excessive harvests from setting high quotas, as well as forgone harvest from implementing unduly conservative measures.[47] Both created hardships.

While the MDNR managed without a comprehensive plan and most agency representatives had little skin in the game, the families and communities experienced socioeconomic disruptions from lost walleye fishing and harvest opportunities.

Transparency and accountability of management decisions may have been an issue. It appeared to me that the Mille Lacs fisheries management approach consisted of a set of procedures that was heavily dependent on the flashy promise of complicated models, while it may have undervalued the basic fisheries principles of stock-recruitment and surplus production. In addition, the system seemed hard to explain, with its protocols, management procedures, consensus agreement, allowable overages, and overage caps. It also appeared to me that there were repeated difficulties in setting annual quotas. In my opinion, splitting the difference in quota proposals did not appear to address the root problem of the recent predicament. Besides quota harvest management, alternate approaches have been suggested.[48]

Quota harvest management is difficult work. The point is for all of us to learn from mistakes. Something that has happened once can happen again. Nassim Nicholas Taleb speaks of investigations of airplane crashes, where the application of science and the study of those tragedies make air travel safer.[49] If we have the courage to apply critical thinking to our fisheries assessment and governance challenges, then fisheries management will continue to improve.

During the period of no agreement on the population status, the Mille Lacs fisheries managers may have benefited from the wisdom of the Red Lake Nation and the biologists involved with the restoration of the Red Lake walleye fishery. The Red Lake Nation and the MDNR created a cooperative management system for this mixed walleye fishery that was both flexible and sustainable.[50] Notably, their system had mechanisms in place to avoid the trap of stockpiling excessive mature walleye biomass. It would have been reasonable for the Mille Lacs fisheries managers to have asked others for help, even when the facts are not always what we want to hear.

10

GETTING PEOPLE TOGETHER

Red Lake, Minnesota

———•◦•———

My first experience with Red Lake was ice fishing for walleye in
the upper basin during the winter of 1988/89. The fishing party
I was with traveled down from International Falls. I was assured
that fishing had been good and that we would likely catch plenty of
walleye. As we trucked across the great Minnesota bog, my mind
wandered. I recalled a presentation by a MDNR fisheries biologist
on the status of Red Lake walleye; the biologist noted the fishery's
productive, yet precarious, nature. Walleye here grew fast and matured early. As fast as the fish matured, they were harvested. Several
biologists and managers who were also listening to the presentation
expressed amazement that the fishery had not yet collapsed, as if a
series of lucky circumstances colluded to allow enough adult walleye to pass through the harvest gauntlet to reproduce. Recruitment
overharvest, or the taking of too many adults, was occurring, and a
walleye population collapse seemed imminent. I wondered aloud
why we were traveling to fish a troubled fishery. "Let's get it while
we can" was the message in the loaded truck as it rolled down one
of Minnesota's longest stretches of arrow-straight roads.

I was briefed on the Red Lake walleye fishery dynamics, but I
was ignorant of the sense of place. My wife, my newborn daughter, and I were recent migrants to northern Minnesota. The place
was foreign to us. We had no family in the state and no historical
understanding of the land, water, or people. Walleye fishing on Red
Lake was good that winter day. We gained access to the lake at one
of the small resorts, where we paid a small fee to drive out on their
ice road. It was a gray day, and the ice and sky blended together in
the far-off distance of the Red Lake Ojibwe Nation. We fished on

the ice without shelter, and while the air was cold, there was little wind to rob our heat. I drilled a hole by hand, but the others revved up their power ice augers and proceeded to drill more holes than could be fished. Soon our party caught several similar-sized walleye and added them to our buckets. The walleye were all about 14 inches (356 mm) in length, and I suspected they were all from the 1985 year-class (three-year-old fish). I don't recall any hot bite action, but several men of the fishing party harvested their limit. We stayed out on the ice until the last bites in the fading light and then packed up and jumped in the truck, hoping to get over the ice ridge without any serious incident.

To talk of the Red Lake walleye fishery is to talk of the Red Lake Ojibwe, who have an important past and community.[1] The Ojibwe people who fought the Dakota in 1760 in a battle to claim Red Lake were descendants of Ojibwe who traversed the north shore of Lake Superior. The Ojibwe call Red Lake Miskwaagamiiwizaaga'iganing, which translates to "the lake with the red body of water." The Ojibwe population at Red Lake grew fast, and the nearby lands of the Red River Valley were productive and bountiful. Other Ojibwe from the east joined the network of independent, self-governed communities around Red Lake. Buffalo, elk, moose, and woodland caribou were abundant. Wild game, wild rice, and berries could be readily harvested close to the villages. Fish were caught and sun-dried or smoked by families to sustain them through hard times.

Through the 1800s, some Red Lake Ojibwe continued the western migration, creating substantial villages far out into the prairie and the northern plains. During this time, white settler colonizers were moving west and north. To the south, other Ojibwe people ceded lands to the U.S. government. The Red Lake Ojibwe, under wise leaders, navigated rising rivers of settler colonizers. They became active in commerce and agriculture. They controlled a vast territory but came to realize that their harvesting far afield was to be constrained. They were not interested in relocation. The

U.S. government was keenly intent on obtaining additional land and advancing business interests by exploiting the white pine forests for needed wood. In 1863, with the Treaty of Old Crossing, the Red Lake Ojibwe ceded lands in the Red River Valley, and with the Nelson Act of 1889 they ceded additional lands.

In negotiating with the U.S. government over land ownership, the Red Lake Ojibwe took a principled approach to ensure the long-term success of their people. Their interests were to retain full and exclusive control of Red Lake (both the lower and upper basins), to preserve communal ownership of tribal lands (they wanted no allotments under the Nelson Act),[2] and to prohibit the sale or use of alcohol on their reservation. The U.S. government was uncharitable and often fraudulent in acquiring lands controlled by the Red Lake Ojibwe, and the Ojibwe made concessions in the various inequitable dealings. Ultimately, they were defrauded out of retaining full control of Red Lake—their primary negotiating goal. Today they control 83 percent of Red Lake, with the state of Minnesota controlling 40 percent of the upper lake basin. They were successful in keeping the land in communal ownership (referred to as a closed reservation, not opened to white settlement and private ownership), and they have maintained their traditional political structure of hereditary representative chiefs enhanced with a modernized tribal council.[3] They also retained their libertarian social culture and a love of nature. During the 1900s they fought to protect their interests and rights.[4] Through expansions, contractions, and conflicts, the Red Lake Ojibwe have flourished, and today they are known as the Red Lake Nation (place name: Miskwaagamiiwizaaga'igan).

Red Lake is one of many large lakes in central North America that are remnants of glacial Lake Agassiz. Much of Lake Agassiz has drained to the sea, but lake pearls, like Red Lake, remain. Red Lake is a large lake (284,260 acres [115,038 ha]) composed of a lower and upper basin. It is the sixteenth largest lake in the United States. Its dark, brownish-red water is the result of tannic acids draining from the surrounding bog lands. It is a mesotrophic lake (moderately fertile) with a maximum depth of 35 feet (10.7 m). Many tributaries enter the lake, and the lake discharges into the Red Lake River. The upper basin is more productive, shallower, and more bog-stained than the lower basin. In the upper basin, mean summer water clarity is 2.6 feet (0.8 m), as measured by a Secchi disk, and in the lower basin water clarity averages 3.9 feet (1.2 m). The recent walleye population for Red Lake has been estimated to average about 3.5 million fish (greater than 14 inches [356 mm]; 12.3 walleye/acre [30.4 walleye/ha]).[5] The fish community consists of many species, including black crappie, bluegill, brown bullhead, burbot, freshwater drum, goldeye, lake sturgeon, lake whitefish, northern pike, quillback, rock bass, shorthead redhorse, walleye, white sucker, and yellow perch. Minnow and small forage species include blacknose dace, common shiner, emerald shiner, fathead minnow, finescale dace, golden shiner, Iowa darter, Johnny darter, mimic shiner, river shiner, spottail shiner, and trout-perch. The Red Lake walleye consume a diet rich in yellow perch and various shiner species.

The Red Lake commercial fishery began in 1917 as a wartime effort under Minnesota law to address food shortages in the state.[6] Carlos Avery, director of the Minnesota Game and Fish Department, obtained federal approval for the state operation, since the state did not have jurisdiction over the fish within the reservation. The state only had the power to regulate the sale and transport of fish off-reservation. The Red Lake Ojibwe population was about fifteen hundred people at the time, and the fishery provided employment opportunities. In 1918, the fishery harvested 500,000 pounds (226,800 kg) of walleye and lake whitefish. The initial walleye harvested were said to average about 1 pound (0.5 kg) apiece. The larger walleye (greater than 3 pounds [1.4 kg]) brought the best price and were destined for the New York market. The fishers used pound nets (large trap nets) and gill nets (the state regulated gill-net mesh sizes). From 1920 to 1928, the state of Minnesota was the distributor and wholesaler of the fish harvested, while the tribal members fished under contract. The median walleye harvest during this time was 790,000 pounds per year (359,000 kg/year).

In 1929 the Red Lake Ojibwe were successful in obtaining exclusive control of the fishery.[7] The tribe formed a business co-operative, organized as the Red Lake Fisheries Association and regulated by the U.S. Secretary of the Interior. The tribal council required that all fish sales go through the Red Lake Fisheries Association. From 1929 to 1938, the median commercial walleye harvest was 925,000 pounds per year (420,000 kg/year). In 1943, the tribe obtained all Red Lake fishery buildings from the state of Minnesota, and the Red Lake commercial fishery became a wholly owned and operated tribal enterprise. In the 1950s, the association employed more than two hundred tribal members, and the fishery provided payments to cooperative members and tribal citizens.

Fish are processed and loaded for shipping at the Red Lake fishery, circa 1930s. Red Lake Agency Photographs, U.S. National Archives.

Until 1970, commercial fish harvest varied based on market demand and fish abundance. Static walleye harvest quotas were established, and harvest fluctuated around those quotas;[8] however, illegal commercial sales occurred and increased over time. In the 1970s, fishery harvests began to vary greatly as the walleye population became dependent on a single strong year-class.[9] Within just a few years, annual commercial harvests fluctuated between 200,000 pounds and 1 million pounds (91,000 to 454,000 kg/year). The sport angling walleye harvest in the eastern end of the upper basin was equally unstable and ranged from 13,000 to 122,000 pounds per year (5,900 to 55,000 kg/year). Overharvest was occurring, and the walleye population faced the likelihood of collapse. Tribal and state natural resource agencies began conducting standardized walleye population assessments in the 1980s,[10] and by 1990 the association peaked at about seven hundred fishers. The Red Lake Nation held numerous public meetings on the pending walleye collapse. The situation bottomed out in 1996, when the commercial walleye harvest was just 15,000 pounds (6,800 kg). It became obvious that action was needed, and in April 1997 the Red Lake Fisheries Association suspended commercial fishing.

GETTING PEOPLE TOGETHER

The restoration of the Red Lake fishery is a story of leadership and the application of state-of-the-art fisheries management science. To better understand the effort to restore the Red Lake walleye, and more importantly, how the restored walleye population is managed today, I spoke with Pat Brown, the Red Lake Nation's fisheries director, and Gary Barnard, former MDNR Bemidji area fisheries manager. Pat Brown is a serious fisheries biologist, and he has dedicated his career to making meaningful contributions to the Red Lake fishery for current and future generations. He received his formal education in fish biology and natural resource management at Northland College in Ashland, Wisconsin, and the University of

Minnesota–Duluth. Prior to his work on Red Lake, Pat conducted fish research on Lake Superior and the St. Louis River Estuary near Duluth and assisted in fisheries assessments related to tribal harvests in northern Wisconsin. Gary Barnard is a dedicated fisheries manager and a man of many talents. A pragmatic individual, he is often dressed in blue jeans and a rugged shirt. Gary worked at the MDNR Waterville fish hatchery for eighteen years before coming to Bemidji in the fall of 1994.

Pat Brown was hired by the Red Lake Department of Natural Resources (RLDNR) a month after the Red Lake Fisheries Association suspended fishing. He recalled the first day he cast his eyes on the expansive waters of Red Lake—the day of his interview for the job: "Number one, how are we ever going to recover this thing, and number two, how did they fish this thing out?" Pat reviewed the last convulsions of the Red Lake walleye population as it collapsed. He said, "The 1985 walleye year-class was the last major one before the collapse, and because the fish had been knocked down so far, they were growing very quickly. Within two to three years these fish were recruiting to the gill nets. It used to be that the average length of fish that were harvested were about 15 inches [381 mm], about four to five years old. There was a state angler boom, and the commercial fishery was going strong. We basically took that year-class out before it was able to replenish itself—it was gone. But we did not shut it down right then. We had a trickle year-class in 1989. But by the same time, the [yellow] perch population exploded because the walleye population was low, their main predator. The perch was as profitable as the walleye on the commercial market, and they grow extremely fast in Red Lake. In 1991, '92, '93, we took 1.7, 1.4, 1.1 million pounds of perch. So, there was a false sense of security. The fishers said, 'Well, if it's not a walleye fishery, let's go ahead and fish for yellow perch until the walleye can recover.' However, this did not happen, and once they fished out the perch and the walleye were also gone, then there was really nothing left. . . . Really in the end, the writing was on the wall, and they were going to have to shut it down and try to do something to bring this thing back. Sometimes that is what some fisheries take; you have to hit rock bottom before you can actually pull people together to do something."

Gary Barnard brought his experiences with fish stocking and his strong interest in evaluating stocking efforts to the Bemidji fisheries manager position. Interestingly, one of Gary's early assignments for the Waterville fish hatchery was going up north to work the walleye spawning station on the Tamarac River at Waskish in 1977 and 1978. This experience proved invaluable in the Red Lake recovery as he discussed changes in the fishery with the Waskish locals. I wondered if Gary's experience mirrored what I had noticed on Red Lake; that is, at the time there appeared to be a lack of urgency in addressing overfishing. It did, and he recalled the nonchalant attitude in response to the crazy walleye population fluctuations observed in the 1980s and into the 1990s: "That was kind of the message that was coming out quite a bit, not just on Red, but on a lot of lakes, that cycling of these walleye populations was a natural thing, and you just lived with the ups and downs and booms and busts."

As Gary began his work in Bemidji, he reviewed the Red Lake walleye population assessment data, and in 1997, after the Red Lake Fisheries Association suspended fishing, Dave Conner, Pat Brown's predecessor, approached him to begin a conversation about restoring the walleye population. Regarding that early dialogue, Gary said, "We were looking at what our options were, and there were not a lot of options on the table initially. We were talking about getting together a technical committee. . . . About the only plays on the table at that point were closing the sport fishery and closing the subsistence fishery. We were talking about those efforts, but we [the MDNR] were not ready to commit to those things obviously on our side until we could get a solid agreement. . . . It was a little bit uncomfortable for a while. It appeared that the state was dragging their feet a little in doing anything. . . . There was a lack of trust on both sides that everybody was serious about taking this on and following through on what needed to be done. Initially, it probably looked like we weren't being cooperative, but we certainly weren't going to close the fishery without having some formal long-term agreement." Gary noted the need to show some commitment to the RLDNR, so in 1998 the MDNR reduced the walleye creel limit from six to two. While the creel limit reduction made little difference in sport harvest, given the state of the walleye population, it did demonstrate the MDNR's commitment to a recovery effort.

The MDNR organized a citizen advisory committee that included concerned citizens and business interests. These were tough times for the resort owners and Waskish locals. Gary explained, "In meetings and town halls, people were genuinely upset about their livelihood and fearing they were going to lose it all, and some probably did. . . . Those early meetings were contentious for sure, and there were accusations being thrown out that you're putting our livelihoods on the line while you're still going to get paid. I remember that distinctly. What we tried to tell them was that this population is in a real dire situation and would not likely bounce back on its own any time soon."[11]

I was curious about what most surprised Pat as he began work for the RLDNR. Pat said that he expected little encouragement from the public but received strong support from the people of the Red Lake Nation. He elaborated, "We went to the tribal council meeting, and we basically made the recommendation that we should go in for a complete moratorium. I think I did this early on, in 1998. . . . I went in with this recommendation expecting the worse. I said, 'We are recommending that we basically shut everything down until we get a plan together.' . . . There was a little bit of discussion, but then Chairman Whitefeather was strong. He said, 'What do you think guys, do you want to take the last fish out of the lake?' And they all said, 'No. We're going to preserve the lake.' So that is what they did. We had great political leaders and the public was very supportive. . . . Fish are so central to the way of life for so many in the reservation, and not being able to eat fish for six or seven years was a huge culture shock. It was truly remarkable the support we received by most during this critical time."

Tribal council chair Bobby Whitefeather had taken decisive action previously—before the fisheries association suspended commercial fishing (before Pat was hired). The Red Lake walleye population supported three distinct fisheries—a tribal commercial fishery, a tribal subsistence fishery, and a state sport fishery. Whitefeather knew that all fisheries information needed to be shared and that there was strength in forging a relationship. He called MDNR commissioner Rod Sando, and in February 1997 the two leaders met to discuss the status of the fishery and to advance additional dialogue. Initially, in the fall of 1997 a core group of biologists from the RLDNR and the MDNR met regularly to review data and to discuss a recovery plan. The two parties negotiated, and each side made serious commitments. In 1998, the tribal council suspended subsistence fishing and the MDNR reduced the sport angler walleye creel from six to two fish, and in 1999 the MDNR closed walleye harvest in state-controlled waters. The outcome of Whitefeather's action was a formal agreement between the Red Lake Nation, the state of Minnesota, and the Bureau of Indian Affairs (BIA) that was signed in April 1999.[12] The memorandum of understanding formalized the Red Lake Fisheries Technical Committee, which was made up of representatives from the RLDNR, Red Lake Fisheries Association, MDNR, BIA, U.S. Fish and Wildlife Service, and University of Minnesota. The task of the committee was to implement the enforcement and recovery plans outlined in the agreement. The enforcement plan described a large, coordinated effort that would result in strict enforcement of fish harvest regulations. The moratorium's success depended on effective enforcement, and greater communication between jurisdictions was initiated. The recovery plan had two components: a recovery phase and a sustainable phase. The committee would also review the standardized walleye population assessment programs to make improvements and share data between agencies to provide science-based information.

RECOVERY PHASE

————◆◇◆————

I asked Pat about the initial biologists and committee meetings (1997 to 1999). Of those early interactions, he recalled, "One thing about coming into a new community, like I did here, is not only do you have to try to figure out how the different people operate, but at the same time you have to start earning people's trust so that they actually listen to you. Sometimes that can be extremely difficult. But, in two years we were able to get things together, not only here on the reservation, but as part of the committee. . . . One of the greatest things that happened with us is we got lucky that the small group of core biologists who were working on the recovery all worked extremely well together. We knew what we wanted to accomplish, and we respected each other. There were no personalities brought to the table; we basically wanted to help each other. And then we were able to go from that small group to build support for the whole committee between jurisdictions."

Pat then described how the early trials of the committee grew into a productive partnership: "The committee really did not work too well in the early years. I think we knew what we wanted to do, but there still was a lot of 'this is our side, this is your side,' a lot of turf wars. But eventually we came around in trusting each other. I really believe that the joint stocking actually helped to build teamwork between the different agencies." Pat noted that he brought a diverse group from Red Lake to the committee. The tribe's contingent included tribal members, including people from the board of the Red Lake Fisheries Association. These nonbiologists did invaluable work. Pat said, "The first thing they brought was a lot of insight into how the fishery was operated. Second, those individuals were usually voted into those positions by the commercial fishermen, so they knew how the fishers were going to see things that we recommended as a committee. These individuals were able to educate me very quickly, help convey our message to the general public, and prepare me when I needed to take my message to the public to gain their support. Without strong public support throughout the recovery stage of this program, it would have never worked. Tribal governmental support was handled by our natural resources director, who sat on both the technical committee and the tribal council. He was a very strong advocate for the recovery and would update the council regularly at the monthly council meetings. This helped to keep the politics out of the way for me and allowed me to focus on the job at hand. The beauty of working for the Red Lake Nation is, if I had a management recommendation that needed tribal council consideration, I could bring it to the council within several weeks, and we would have an answer. It did not happen this quickly on the other side."

One of the earliest decisions the committee faced was about the use of walleye stocking. It was clear that stocking a large waterbody such as Red Lake would face significant challenges. Pat agreed: "That was one of the tricky ones. In writing the recovery plan, that was one of the hardest ones we went through. The reason for that was the research that came out of the University of Minnesota right in the middle of this thing that concluded that walleyes should not be stocked in lakes where natural reproduction occurs.[13] . . . So, there was some heartburn surrounding this issue. . . . George Spangler [University of Minnesota fisheries professor] was on the committee at the time, and he wanted to make sure that we did not set back fisheries management. . . . If we were going to stock, we had to make sure that we were able to tell if the stocking brought the lake back or if it was natural reproduction." Before the stocking decision was made, the biologists estimated wild fry production based on the remaining walleye in the lake and on assumptions on female fecundity and egg hatching rates. They concluded that natural walleye fry densities were low but that the remaining walleye were likely insufficient in number for eventual recovery without intervention. However, the committee concluded that judicious stocking should proceed to greatly speed recovery, and they developed clear criteria for how to stock and when to stop stocking.[14]

Stocking Red Lake was a massive effort. The scale was large, and the number of fry needed was uncertain. The goal was to stock fry so that the total fry density (wild plus stocked fry) would be about 1,000 fry per littoral acre (2,500 fry/littoral ha). Gary recalled the calculations that occurred: "Ironically we were underestimating how dismal spawning stock and fry density really were because some of the parameters we used were optimistic. We thought we were using conservative parameters, but that wasn't the case.... We worked the numbers." Gary reminded me that I had helped with the calculations. My role was minor, but I recalled the work and the discussions. I was excited to be a small part of the effort. Gary continued, "We took our share of criticism over the years about how we did some of those calculations. There was a lot of back-of-the-envelope math going on, but we were working with what we knew and adapting as we learned. . . . It turned out that the population was in a dire situation, with even lower fry production than we predicted, making it fertile ground for fry stocking." Gary explained the challenges of stocking so many walleye fry into Red Lake: "We involved the locals in the fry stocking. That was pretty nice because it was a big event. We were way over capacity in our hatchery, and a six-hour marking procedure for every batch of fry added another layer of complexity. We had to haul out fry in the middle of the night because our fry tanks were loading up. So, having help on the other end wasn't just a feel-good thing, they were actually helping." The RLDNR contributed money to the fry stocking effort,[15] and they also distributed walleye fry across the lake.

The stocking effort also included cutting-edge science. Pat explained: "That was when oxytetracycline was just starting to be used." In the MDNR Bemidji hatchery, walleye fry and water containing a solution of oxytetracycline hydrochloride were poured into transport jugs. Oxytetracycline is absorbed into bony structures, resulting in a long-lasting fluorescent mark.[16] With this marking approach, biologists can examine walleye otoliths (ear bones) to determine both the age of the fish and whether the fish was stocked. Pat said, "We were some of the pioneers. . . . I give Gary Barnard a lot of the credit for this; I know Dale Logsdon [from the MDNR] followed through on this stuff, but it was Gary's hatchery experience and dedicated crew. If you're marking forty million walleye fry in ten days and transporting them without killing a whole bunch of fish, you are doing a really good job. . . . We were able to all come together to figure out this oxytetracycline thing, and you know what? It worked. . . . Not only did it tell us that the initial fry stocking did work, but it also gave us the ability to show people once we got natural reproduction."

The walleye fry stocking commenced, and it was a success. In 1999, walleye fry from the MDNR Pike River spawning-take operation were stocked into Red Lake. That summer RLDNR and MDNR biologists seined the lake to collect fingerling walleye. Back in the lab, otoliths were removed from those fish and inspected for oxytetracycline marks. Mark-recapture techniques were used to estimate the number of total and wild fry in Red Lake. Biologists determined that 86 percent of the fry were stocked fish and estimated that the total fry (stocked and wild fry) density was fairly abundant at about 600 fry per littoral acre (approximately 1,500 fry/littoral ha). When the 1999 walleye year-class reached maturity in 2004, there would be an abundance of walleye adults in Red Lake. And with a harvest moratorium, recovery of the population was assured. Stocking was repeated in 2001 and 2003, and the percentage of stocked fish was 70 percent and 97 percent, respectively. These stockings were insurance for the jump start.

In 2003, the biologists got a great idea to stock a small number of marked fry into Red Lake. Additional quantification of wild fry production would allow them to build out their walleye stock-recruitment curve for the lake, which would be necessary for future harvest management. Recall that fisheries managers need an understanding of the stock-recruitment relationship; otherwise they will be in the dark about the harvestable surplus. How many mature female walleye are needed to produce a strong year-class?

An otolith (ear bone) is extracted from a walleye. Otoliths are of great help to fisheries biologists in tracing the life histories of walleye. Photograph by Brian Borkholder.

How many adult walleye are too many? Will they reduce the number of young walleye, through predation or competition, before they can recruit to the fishery? Answers to these questions are critical, so the committee agreed to deviate from the recovery plan to obtain this information. In 2004 and 2005, mark-recapture studies were conducted using marked fry from an RLDNR spawn take on the Blackduck River, which flows into Red Lake.[17] The 2004 and 2005 stockings were at much lower levels than the production-level stockings in 1999, 2001, and 2003. In 2005, a small amount of stocking occurred, but natural reproduction produced large numbers of fry; most walleye (86 percent) were of wild origin. Since 2006, all walleye produced have been of wild origin. These data validated the fact that the Red Lake walleye had recovered.

Reflecting on the recovery phase, Pat said, "The big surprise was how lucky we got with the fry stocking. They were good years; we got good recruitment. Everything just worked out. Maybe it was just Red Lake itself; if you give it a chance it was going to take care of itself. All three of the stockings took [hold] great. . . . We got really lucky." Gary, responding to my question on the challenges through this phase, said, "The challenge was the lack of good quantitative data on wild fry production on any of these large walleye systems, the relationship between spawning stock biomass and wild fry, and how much walleye fry you can expect. . . . These facts did not exist, and we weren't aware of anyone who had done that. There was fry marking that was done prior to Red Lake, but the focus was always on determining how much fry stocking was contributing to a fishery. . . . We kind of turned the tables a little to look at the more interesting question to determine the amount of wild fry that are being produced and trying to establish that relationship between spawner biomass and wild fry production—every wild fry estimate we got was gold. That was the challenge, and it continues to be to this day. Knowing what we do now, I can't imagine trying to manage spawning stock on a naturally reproducing walleye population without knowing or caring how much fry is being produced."

SUSTAINABLE MANAGEMENT

—◆—

According to the recovery plan, the resumption of walleye harvest could proceed when the mature female biomass in the lake exceeded 1.5 pounds per acre (1.7 kg/ha) for three consecutive years. Setting a threshold level of walleye biomass was consistent with the need for an adequate abundance of mature walleye to have sufficient recruitment. In the fall of 2002 and 2003, the estimates of mature female biomass were 0.7 pounds per acre (0.8 kg/ha) and 8.3 pounds per acre (9.3 kg/ha), respectively. Therefore, the committee began in earnest to develop a harvest plan that would set a management framework for each of the fisheries (commercial, subsistence, and sport angling).

The initial harvest plan developed was simple.[18] With the walleye population having just recovered from collapse, the plan logically focused on avoiding overharvest. Since insufficient egg and fry production had led to the population collapse, the plan's goal was to maintain enough spawning stock to produce sufficient fry density for good recruitment. First, biologists determined that to maximize young walleye recruitment, the minimum amount of mature female biomass needed to be at least 2 pounds per acre (2.2 kg/ha), which was higher than the threshold in the recovery plan. Second, there was evidence that high adult walleye abundance reduced the probability of producing a strong walleye year-class. Mature female biomass over 3 pounds per acre (3.4 kg/ha) corresponded with weak walleye year-classes. Thus, biologists concluded that the optimal amount of mature female biomass ranged between 2 and 3 pounds per acre (2.2 to 3.4 kg/ha).[19]

The committee sought a harvest plan that would reduce the reliance on hard quotas. They settled on an approach where fisheries managers would use target harvest ranges. The goal was to obtain the target harvest range on an annual basis but required a three-year running average. Target harvest ranges were tiered based on mature female walleye abundance, which was determined by standardized gill-net surveys and a simple gill-net selectivity model. If the estimate of mature female biomass was well below the preferred range, no harvest would be allowed; if the estimate was well above the preferred range, there would be an opportunity to increase the harvest. The plan also provided harvest caps, which, if reached, required a cessation of walleye harvests. If the walleye spawning stock biomass was optimal, then the target harvest range was 1.75 to 3.5 pounds per acre (2.0 to 3.9 kg/ha). One shortcoming of this first harvest plan was that no increases in the target harvest were prescribed for a surplus population. Pat described the benefits of the straightforward harvest plan. He noted that with a well-structured plan, tribal members understand their potential earning opportunities and the degree of subsistence fishing that will likely be allowed, which can help address fears of arbitrary fisheries management.

Prior to reopening the fishery, each natural resource management agency reviewed various regulation and harvest monitoring options. The MDNR would impose a protected slot limit and a two-walleye creel limit and would monitor the harvest with creel surveys. The RLDNR held numerous public meetings and conducted a public survey. Red Lake tribal members wanted a cautious and prudent rollout of the walleye harvest. They sought a harvest-oriented fishery but were not keen on a fishery that was dependent on gill nets; they wanted to make sure that rules were strict and enforced so that a collapse would not happen again. They also advocated for regulations that would allow greater participation in the fishery. The tribal council deliberated and concluded that walleye harvest would proceed only with the hook-and-line method and that creel and length limits would be imposed for both commercial and subsistence fishing. The RLDNR would directly measure the harvest at the fish processing plant and conduct creel surveys. A hook-and-line commercial fishery was a dramatic change from the past dependence on gill nets, but the community benefits of having a greater number of tribal members participating and earning money were large and the public was supportive.

I explored this decision with Al Pemberton, RLDNR director. Al Pemberton is a Red Lake Ojibwe and is quick to start a conversation. He has served on the tribal council for twenty years and started his natural resources management career in forestry. He understands the importance of fish habitat and had long advocated for the restoration of the Red Lake outlet to provide fish passage and spawning habitat. He explained, "We decided to try hook-and-line fishing walleye. Some did not think that would work . . . but I knew it could work. I said, 'You got to change the mentality of what fishing is.' I think they did, for the most part now. The fishermen now, they are OK with that, and they want to keep doing it."

In 2006, walleye harvest was allowed on Red Lake. Walleye were growing fast and reproducing successfully. They were easily caught, especially in early winter and during May and June. Over time the population continued to grow, allowing each agency to gradually relax their regulations to promote greater harvests. In 2009, the Red Lake walleye population was declared fully recovered, having met spawning stock thresholds for both biomass and age diversity. The committee focused their efforts on future management issues and continued to be the mechanism for interagency sharing of population assessment and harvest data.

DEALING WITH A SURPLUS
—◆◦◆—

After 2009, the fishery appeared to be in a state of high abundance, and fisheries managers were beginning to see high walleye catch rates and troubling biological signs. Due to increasing popularity of the lake among sport anglers in state-controlled waters of the upper basin, walleye harvests were exceeding the target harvest range, and midseason regulation changes were needed to avoid reaching the closure cap. However, there was little indication that harvests were reducing the surplus spawning stock. The MDNR was forced to implement regulations more restrictive than biologically necessary to comply with the conservative target harvest range of the initial harvest plan. While the conservative framework of the initial harvest plan was a prudent approach for restoration, the negative effects of stockpiling excessive spawning stock were becoming apparent. The committee began working on a harvest plan revision.

I talked to Pat and Gary about going from low walleye abundance to recovery and then to a walleye population that was creating high negative density-dependent effects on young walleye growth and survival. The Red Lake walleye population was now on the opposite side of the hill from collapse and facing challenges associated with high spawner biomass. Pat explained that, as the walleye population grew and they collected more data, they needed to adapt. "When we put all this stuff together [for the first harvest plan], the system was broken and we didn't have a lot of good data at the time, and as we collected more data, of course we found out that we were on the conservative side because we didn't want to reopen the fishery and then collapse it right away."

Gary echoed Pat's thoughts: "We were coming off a collapsed fishery, so everybody was extremely conservative . . . and all we were really worried about was what we were going [to do] if spawning stock biomass declined below this level; how much we were going to restrict harvest; how much we were going to pull back; and when we would close the fishery. Our whole focus was what we would do if it started to slide back. We never anticipated when that first year-class matured that we were going to get catapulted into surplus condition." The consequences of the surplus walleye population were undeniable, however. Gary observed a near-collapse of the yellow perch population, slower walleye growth rates, high walleye natural mortality, a few large female walleye not producing eggs or reabsorbing their eggs before spawning, a parasite infestation, and high angler catch rates.

Pat's observations were similar: "The walleye had such great success early on that they basically ate themselves out of house and home. So, growth rates started to slow a lot; fitness levels started coming down, and we were not seeing enough shiners and perch. . . . The other big thing that we started seeing is when density gets too high, there is definitely some cannibalism that goes on. When the forage stocks were way down, walleye were eating a lot of young walleye—we would see those in the bigger walleye stomachs." Pat also shared what they learned about walleye mortality: "What really drives the system out here, we found, at least to this point, is natural mortality. We're barely touching mortality. Our mortality rates might be over 40 percent natural, and maybe only 10 percent might be from harvest mortality."

Based on this information and the new conditions, the committee decided to revise the harvest plan. Biologists reexamined the stock-recruitment curve with the additional data collected and target harvest ranges.[20] Operating in a surplus condition for several years was informative; it provided fisheries managers with valuable data points to populate the right side of the stock-recruitment relationship—they now had walleye density data ranging from collapse to surplus. While the stock-recruitment relationship was still dome shaped (high adult walleye abundance reduced the probability of a strong walleye year-class), the peak of the stock-recruitment relationship occurred at slightly greater densities than estimated earlier. The peak of the stock-recruitment relationship occurred at about 450 to 850 fry per littoral acre (1,100 to 2,100 fry/littoral ha), and the new optimal range of mature female biomass was 2.5 to 4.5 pounds per acre (2.8 to 5.0 kg/ha).[21] Most important, biologists increased and broadened the target harvest ranges. If spawner biomass was in the optimal range, fisheries managers could have target harvests between 2.5 to 5.0 pounds per acre (2.8 to 5.6 kg/ha) from a walleye population that may be over 30 pounds per acre (33.6 kg/ha). This was 1.4 times higher than the target harvest range in the previous harvest plan. The revised harvest plan, implemented in 2015, took an aggressive approach to harvest walleye when in surplus condition, not just to harvest the surplus production but to actively manage surplus spawning biomass back down into an optimal condition.

Pat and Gary were confident that they adapted well after the recovery. They were actively managing for the optimal amount of mature female biomass rather than stockpiling excessive spawner biomass. Pat noted that the fishery is no longer in the low-yield high-spawner status: "Here in the past three or four years now, it sure seems things are coming around. Number one, we are starting to harvest more fish. The density of the walleye population is coming down . . . and the perch, we're actually starting to see young-of-the-year perch that were making it through the predator gauntlet. . . . This lake used to be full of goldeye. During the whole recovery period we saw no goldeye. Now goldeye are popping up again."

The MDNR and RLDNR adjusted their fishing regulations to adapt as well. To allow harvest of larger walleye and to distribute the harvest across a range of fish lengths and year-classes, the MDNR replaced the protective slot with a "one over" regulation and increased the creel limit. The RLDNR adjusted hook-and-line regulations, and two or three summer net crews were used to supplement the commercial harvest. To increase the tribal harvest, it was also necessary to refurbish the Red Lake Nation fish processing plant, and the Shakopee Mdewakanton Sioux Community provided economic development grants totaling $2 million in assistance. The tribal walleye harvest is marketed through Red Lake Nation Foods.

I asked Pat and Gary if people had concerns about increasing harvest to take the surplus walleye. Perhaps a recent experience was on my mind—I had failed to convince the MDNR of the need to harvest more Mille Lacs walleye when that fishery was in surplus condition; I could not get them to move from a protective mindset to a sustainable mindset. Pat explained, "For us it wasn't too hard to convince. Basically, all we had to say was, 'Here is the deal: a dead walleye is a dead walleye. There's two places that thing is going. Number one, it is going to the bottom of the lake and it is going to recycle the nutrients into the system. Second place it can go is . . .

through the fishery—on your kitchen table. . . .' And that is the way I looked at it." Gary explained that the trust built over the years was key to the continued work with the public, even if they didn't totally agree on some regulations. He also found the angling public generally supportive of the change. "It's like trying to talk somebody into having an ice cream cone. They really don't think they should, but if you give all the reasons that they really wanted it in the first place, then 'Yeah, I guess we'll take a four-fish creel limit, we'll get rid of that protected slot and go with a one-over. Are you sure that it is going to be OK?' 'Yep. It is going to be ok.' 'Then let's do it.' But it was kind of neat to see them be cautious and to make sure that we don't go back to where we were. . . . They seemed to understand it."

Pat, Gary, and the other biologists had done the science—the fish population monitoring and assessment and the analysis of stock-recruitment relationships and surplus production. They shared the fishery statistics, and they effectively communicated the science and fishery goals to the public. They had a plan. And importantly, the biologists had proven themselves competent in managing the fishery. Good biologists know, however, that the one constant in the environment is change. Pat added, "One thing when you are starting to loosen regulations, especially up here, is that you have to remind them that we're adapting here. Now just because we are loosening things up today doesn't mean that in a couple years I might not have to come back and tell them that we going to have to ratchet this thing down."

I was interested in hearing one additional perspective: I wanted to talk to Henry Drewes, MDNR regional fisheries supervisor, who was also involved in the Red Lake restoration. Henry Drewes is as comfortable in a fishing boat as he is in an important business meeting. I've come to appreciate Henry's unique perspective on various fisheries, and I was curious about what he had to say about Red Lake. Henry is a systems thinker, always several steps ahead of me when we discussed fisheries matters. While Henry had similar opinions to those of Al Pemberton, Pat Brown, and Gary Barnard on the challenges and surprises they faced together, he provided some additional context on the history of the Red Lake fishery. He also shared his thoughts on where walleye fisheries management might be going in other Minnesota walleye lakes, given the surplus production lessons learned on Red Lake.

According to Henry, timing and the lack of politics were important in the Red Lake endeavor. "Things were bad. The Red Lake Fisheries Technical Committee was commissioned to put a plan together to recover the fishery. There were no politicians in that group—there were biologists, university faculty, people from the Red Lake commercial fishery, and they were allowed to work without political influence in drafting a recovery plan. . . . This was the best scientific plan put forward, which is very rare to get in fish and wildlife management. We were able to get this approved by the tribal government and also the DNR commissioner. That set the stage." Henry noted that the plan was signed without any changes from political officials. "The moon and the stars were aligned leadership-wise. They had the courage to deal with their respective pushback."

When the committee concluded that the walleye population was overfished and it had collapsed, Henry recalled, "they agreed very early that there was a lot of blame to go around. As a group, we did not want to be caught in the blame game. The common perspective was that the commercial fishery coupled with the black-market fishery crashed the system. The reality is when you peel the layers off that onion, for every illegally harvested and sold walleye, somebody bought it. And 99 percent of the time that was a non-band member who bought that fish. And it has always been illegal to buy or sell fish and game, as specified in the Lacey Act.[22] Pat Welle [Bemidji State University economics professor] did some work for the Red Lake Band helping them explore future management options. I will never forget how he characterized what happened on Red Lake; he called it 'the race to the bottom of the bucket.' That was the decades leading up to the collapse. . . . And so, when the bucket was empty and everybody realized that we had to do something, we focused on fixing the problem and not on fixing blame. . . . Al Pemberton and I did a lot of interviews approaching the reopening. Because there were tons of people who said that the tribe was just going to ruin it or the state was going to cheat. There was such a culture of noncompliance on that lake that it was a frequent discussion of our technical committee, and this is on top of the science. We needed to try to change the culture that existed and the mindset that 'you got to get them before the next guy does.' So, there was a very conscious focus on 'yes, we can do this; yes, we will adhere to the tenets of the harvest plan.' They have and we have. . . . We had a detailed enforcement plan, and we hit that lake hard and the tribe hit it hard. And in keeping with our desire to establish a new conservation ethic, we had zero tolerance for violations, and the tribe did as well . . . and with both jurisdictions doing the enforcement of their own users, it increased the confidence that both sides were going to do what it took."

While leadership and science were critical in the Red Lake effort, Henry noted that one other thing was invaluable—something that others often discount. He emphasized the importance of public consultation. Both the RLDNR and the MDNR made several significant efforts to get the public involved. He noted that Gary and he met with the public to get a consensus on the sport fisheries goals, so that those goals could be referred to when regulations were considered. The goals included a harvest-oriented fishery, no favoring of winter or summer, and an emphasis on high catch rates. These goals had a direct implication on how the fishery would be managed. Henry also emphasized the importance of bringing the nontribal public into the committee process to gain the trust and help of the local communities. The public became familiar with the memorandum of understanding and the tribe; two members of the citizen advisory committee sat in on the fisheries technical committee meetings. This gave the public a "behind the curtain" peck at the process and at the amount of heavy lifting involved. According to Henry, this was essential to show the commitment to the fishery on both sides: "They became familiar with all the dialogue; there was nothing going on in secret, and they then helped tap down all the anti-tribal buzz that was out there in the social media." Regarding inquires he still gets, Henry notes, "I say, 'The tribe lives up to every expectation that is articulated in the MOU [memorandum of understanding] and harvest plan and we're doing the same, and there is trust.' . . . Science was the foundation. . . . But with absence of supportive leadership, absence of bringing the public along with this, that science still might have failed, even if it was cutting-edge. It was all three legs of the stool— leadership, science, and strong public consultation."

I wanted to know what Henry had to say about the lessons learned after the recovery, specifically, how the fisheries managers adapted. Henry explained, "Adaptive management is paramount to our profession. One of the things that we've adopted in our large lake plans now is the three-year running average. . . . You don't react to a single year; however, you also don't wait for five or ten years before you adjust and react. I think we're learning about adaptive management. I won't say that it's universal throughout our profession in Minnesota, but I think we learned a lot here on Red Lake that we're exporting to other systems." According to Henry, the success of the Red Lake plan is because of the credibility and relationships built with the tribe and through the citizen advisory committee, which allowed for the flexible use of regulations as needed. Henry also mentioned that the science from Red Lake on optimal walleye fry densities, an index of adult walleye abundance, is now being used in managing other walleye lakes in his region.

Henry and I concluded our conversation talking about the importance of understanding stock-recruitment relationships and surplus production curves, since most walleye fisheries are harvest oriented. I told Henry that these population dynamic concepts often appear missing or lost in the context of sport fisheries management. Some fisheries managers want to create trophy wall-eye fisheries or to stockpile mature walleye, and they may not comprehend the negative consequences; that is, walleye harvest, recruitment, and growth will be reduced, and the yellow perch population and other forage fish populations may be altered. Regarding Red Lake, Henry stated, "We used the protected slot to build the spawner stock biomass, but it quickly became the wrong regulation, and we moved to other scenarios. It is also a rare lake that you can use a creel limit to make a difference . . . but even with a reduced creel limit now the winter fishery could overwhelm us, and that is the future challenge. . . . You don't react on a one-year basis, but if you average over three and you look at that and there are true trends, as blunt as our instruments are, then you adapt." Henry then shared a final piece of advice for those managing the fisheries in other Minnesota walleye lakes: "Being able to be nimble on these large, high-profile, high-participation walleye lakes has to be the future—not entrenching and wanting to wait five to ten years to see how our management is working; that game is over as far as I'm concerned."

RED LAKE WALLEYE FUTURE

Before the walleye restoration at Red Lake, there was mistrust between the community and the governments. Today, Pat says, when people at Waskish and the people of Red Lake understand what is happening and why, they stick up for one another. He reflected on the past twenty-three years: "It worked out well. . . . It is something that people saw as fairly important. We've had a lot of coverage on this thing over the years. I think it was the success and it was also the partnership that we had. Because you don't see a tribal and state agency working so well together. . . . And you know, that is really what it takes. We all know what the end goal is, and we need to push other things to the side and work on that one goal. . . . I really believe that the partnership is going to continue.

It is one waterbody, and we need to know what each other is doing. We showed that what we are doing works. So, there is no reason for either political party to give it up right now. . . . It is the best thing for the resource. Because if one hand knows what the other is doing, then we trust each other over time."

Al Pemberton agreed: "As the years went on, we began to trust one another. And I think that it fostered some cooperation and trust between the programs. And the Red Lake walleye recovery was a success because of the partnership. . . . We know what they're doing and they know what we're doing now. That is a positive part." As the committee evolves with new members, Pemberton was cautious: "They may not know about Red Lake, or what went on. . . . You have to have good people; if you don't, it's not going to work."

Pat is optimistic about the future: "Red Lake is only going to get better. I think we're going to start seeing larger walleye as long as we can start getting some bigger perch in the lake. It is a diverse fishery. I've been working on a cooperative lake sturgeon restocking program with Rainy River First Nations and the U.S. Fish and Wildlife Service since 2007, and the sturgeon are coming back strong. . . . We even have crappies that are starting to come back now. I'll almost guarantee that you'll hear a little more chatter on that. . . . It is an amazing resource. I'm happy to work on it and I hope to finish out my career doing this stuff. . . . If I could get a self-sustaining population of sturgeon in the lake before I retire, that would top off this amazing journey!"

Today, Red Lake could likely sustain an average annual walleye harvest of 1 million pounds (454,000 kg). Since the reopening of the Red Lake walleye fishery, millions of walleye have been harvested by Red Lake Nation members. Tribal members have fresh walleye to eat on a regular basis, and hundreds of members supplement their income by participating in the hook-and-line fishery each year. The fish processing plant pays out about $1 million annually to tribal fishers, and it currently retains up to fifty full-time employees. Nontribal sport anglers too have harvested millions of walleye from the eastern side of the upper basin. The sport fishery has been popular, and local businesses are prosperous. The Red Lake walleye fishery was restored, and it is a source of pride.

Late on a warm summer afternoon as Al Pemberton and I were wrapping up our conversation, he recalled a family memory. His grandmother had shared a question that his great-grandfather had asked:[23] "Why would you want to live anywhere else when you're living in paradise?" Red Lake is a sacred place with interesting people and beautiful fish. Paradise indeed.

EPILOGUE
Walleye Futures

Walleye have been around for a very long time. Nothing important comes into being quickly. Researchers have used two methods to understand the walleye's family tree and to make estimates of how long walleye and their relatives have existed in North America. Archeologists and geneticists provide the answers. In the first approach, differences in the structure of fossil skeletons of extinct and current species are used to understand family connections, and dating fossils or comparing a fossil to fossils and rocks with an estimated age provides an estimate of when they were alive. But, while fossils provide the best tangible record, up until recently few walleye family fossils have been found or described. But now, two recent discoveries in Canada shed light on the walleye family tree. The first is a fossil of a walleye-like species found on Ellesmere Island in the far north. It was believed to have come from an extinct walleye cousin, an Arctic walleye, that lived about four to five million years ago.[1] The other fossil was found in southern Saskatchewan. Estimates suggest it predates the Arctic walleye by about ten million years (i.e., this fish was living about twelve to sixteen million years ago).[2]

Using genetic evidence is the other approach to understanding the family tree. Genetics can determine the walleye's closest relatives, and the approximate time of genetic divergence between species can be estimated using the evolutionary mutation rate.[3] North America and Eurasia were once connected in a supercontinent. During the mid-Cretaceous period this supercontinent broke up, resulting in a split between North America and Eurasia. Since then, plant and animal species present in both have been drifting apart through the process of evolution. The walleye-like species' family tree now has two genetically distinct trunks: one in North America and the other in Eurasia.[4] Scientists estimate these trunks

separated about twenty-one million years ago.[5] Walleye and sauger
are distinct from zander, estuarine perch (or sea zander), and the
Volga pikeperch (or Volga zander). Walleye and sauger likely di-
verged about fifteen million years ago. The weight of evidence
therefore concludes that walleye and their ancestors have existed
in North America for millions of years—long, long before the Age
of Humans.

Through the recent ages, walleye lived alongside glaciers that
plowed south and retreated north. The waterscape changed with
the long rhythm of ice ages. Walleye lived, reproduced, and died in
the large glacial lakes and connected rivers that covered large parts
of North America. These bodies of water often exceeded the size
of the Great Lakes. Walleye also flourished in the non-glacial areas
far from the margins of the ice world.[6] Walleye did not ponder their
species' long-term fate, but they persevered. Walleye adapt. They
have little capacity to comprehend the physical dynamics of their
world beyond their senses of sight, sound, touch, and their limited
cognitive abilities.

Humans, with the gifted among them, have great capacity to understand their world and even their universe. But even today, with
the last glacial period having only ended fifteen thousand years
ago, many are challenged to visualize the scope and scale of time.
A millennium is difficult to grasp, and a million years that allow
species divergence is a bridge too far for some. If it is true that we
are traveling through time to a future that does not yet exist[7], we
can adjust the now to unfold our future. The nonmathematical perspectives of time also challenge us. What is now? It has been said
that a society with a long now is more likely to be anti-fragile—we
flourish by addressing the stresses in the now.[8] How important is
the unknown future? I've mentioned how economists discount the
future.[9] Our civilization cannot escape the future that it unfolds.[10]
Walleye school, but they do not organize to create a society or civilization. We humans do, and it is a huge advantage to our species.
We form a culture, and that culture matters.

To endure, a culture needs to foster the greater good more than individual self-interest. Rules, penalties, and incentives that target the greedy are often necessary, but these controls need to be well crafted to avoid negative consequences. Societies that flourish are the caring ones with high standards of behavior. These standards are not upheld through imposition but via the virtues expressed by family, neighborhood, tribe, and community that are accepted by all. For a society, the accepted and practiced ethics are more important than the law. A caring culture with an ethical motivation is the key to a good, healthy community. We have obligations to each other and to the rest of nature, on which we depend. We live on a planet with finite resources. Along with the calamity of extreme weather and forest fires from climate change, the tragedy of spoiled walleye lakes should bring us to the front lines in the effort to avert greater destruction to our environment. Our civil society depends on each of us working for the common good. Will our values evolve to reduce selfishness? Will we improve our justice to have equal justice for all? Will we expand our ethics to include the rest of nature? Sure we will, because we must, or both human and walleye will perish.

We can learn from the simple life of walleye, and we owe walleye respect. Walleye do not have prejudices. The brassy-yellow walleye do not discriminate against the olive-brown or gray-blue walleye. Walleye do not commit war or genocide. Human history can paint our species with a broad and evil brush. Walleye, while they eat other organisms, generally live in harmony with others. They excrete waste, but they do not poison the water or air as humans have. Our poisons seemingly propagate at the speed of light because as we create things we give more thought to convenience and profit than to the risks of future environmental contamination and ill health. Oy vey! Rachel Carson, the late marine biologist, environmental whistleblower, and author of *Silent Spring*, said: "I think we are challenged as mankind has never been challenged before to prove our maturity and mastery, not of nature, but of ourselves."[11] Humans adapt the world for themselves.[12] We have yet to master ourselves, and we don't share that world well with our undomesticated relatives. However, walleye also have rights to that world. Walleye are not property or just a resource, and it seems altogether fitting and proper that we fight to legalize those rights. While walleye are simple creatures, capable of little reason, shouldn't they have standing in this world?[13]

We are heating our lakes and rivers with our do-it-yourself solar cooker, and for a long time scientists have been asking and answering the question, What could possibly go wrong?[14] While I may like to warm my kielbasa at the campground this way, I, and most people, think it is a bad idea to do it on a global scale. We know that we are cooking the planet and mucking up the water in many places, and it is our responsibility to clean up our messes. Our environmental debt and burdens have been reckoned. Today, scientists are asking, How much are we going to save? We must work for ambitious systemwide pollution reductions while adapting to a world whose atmosphere and waters are laden with our past wrongs that are cooked into our future.[15] Given the global scale of our long emergency, a shared holistic view and an open mind help. Like the people who worked to restore the rivers and their floodplains of the Winnebago System, like the passionate Mille Lacs community members who challenged and demanded answers to a fisheries management crisis, like the people who worked to restore the Red Lake walleye population, we will accomplish good things together in an effort to protect our way of life.

With a deep affection for a lake or river that we have experienced with family and friends, we will become better kith and kin with the rest of nature, the land, and the water. Together we will protect walleye habitat through responsible management of our actions. We will practice a shared frugality of the Earth's finite bounty, while relying on the reusable and the renewable. We will restore walleye habitat in our part of the world and collaborate with others in solving our global pollution problems, as we are part of both a local community and this world. This work will re-quire the best of us. Each of us has a role, whether by planting, growing, connecting kids to nature in the backyard and at the lake, protesting, mentoring, litigating, defending, protecting, educating, funding, enforcing, regulating, or governing. Please lend your hand to help each other and this beautiful fish. Yes, it will take us all doing good work. As we increase our appreciation and ecological literacy, we will reduce our destructive environmental behaviors. Perhaps for some of us, the first step to restoring a healthy environment is introspection.

I've lost my way at several points in my life. The long periods of dark days frayed my spirit, so I would head out into nature. There are no shortcuts to things worth doing. Dressed for the cold and for protection from the splash of water, I would push out onto the lake. It is spring, and the walleye have spawned; they've placed a bet that tomorrow will be better. The waterlilies were dormant all winter, but now young leaves are forming near the lake bottom. The lilies too are betting that tomorrow will be better. The birds, spring migrants and summer nesters, are arriving and singing. They join in the bet. For walleye and the rest of nature, the will to survive is stronger than the desire to give up. I take solace that life moves forward and that tomorrow could be better. Near the shore, I see walleye fry struggling to rise up from the cobble-strewn lake bottom—free of the detritus. In communion with walleye, we too leave our past in the detritus. We're all betting that tomorrow will be better.

GLOSSARY

Age class: A group of individuals of the same age range in a population.

Annual total mortality: The ratio of the number of fish that die during a year divided by the number alive at the beginning of that year.

Area closure: The closure to fishing by particular gear(s) of an entire fishing ground, or a part of it, for the protection of a section of the population (e.g. spawners, juveniles), the whole population, or several populations. The closure is usually seasonal but it could be permanent.

Biomass: 1. Or standing stock. The total weight of a group (or stock) of living organisms (e.g. fish, plankton) or of some defined fraction of it (e.g. spawners) in an area, at a particular time. 2. Measure of the quantity, usually by weight in pounds or metric tons, of a stock at a given time.

Carrying capacity: The maximum population of a species that an area or specific ecosystem can support indefinitely without deterioration of the character and quality of the resource.

Catchability: The extent to which a stock is susceptible to fishing.

Cohort: A group of fish generated during the same spawning season and born during the same time period.

Commercial fishery: A term related to the whole process of catching and marketing fish and shellfish for sale. It refers to and includes fisheries resources, fishermen, and related businesses.

Compensatory growth: An increase in growth rate shown by fishes when their populations fall below a certain level; possibly caused by decreased competition between individuals for food or space.

Compensatory survival: A decrease in the rate of natural deaths that some fishes may show when their populations fall below a certain level; possibly caused by decreased competition between individuals for food or space.

Cost-benefit analysis: 1. A comparison of the economic benefits and costs of a project, policy, or regulation. 2. A comparison of the economic benefits of using a resource to the opportunity cost if the resource is used. Projects or regulations are typically evaluated based on how they change the cost-benefit ratio.

Creel (bag) limit: The number and/or size of a species that a person can legally take in a day or trip. This may or may not be the same as a possession limit.

Density dependence: The dependence of a factor influencing population dynamics (such as survival rate or reproductive success) on population density. The effect is usually in the direction that contributes to the regulative capacity of a stock.

Ecosystem: A geographically specified system of organisms, the environment, and the processes that control its dynamics. Humans are an integral part of an ecosystem.

Ecosystem-based [fisheries] management: An approach that takes major ecosystem components and services—both structural and functional—into account in managing fisheries. It values habitat, embraces a multispecies perspective, and is committed to understanding ecosystem processes. Its goal is to rebuild and sustain populations, species, biological communities, and marine ecosystems at high levels of productivity and biological diversity so as not to jeopardize a wide range of goods and services from marine ecosystems while providing food, revenue, and recreation for humans.

Ecosystem health: A measure of the stability and sustainability of ecosystem functioning or ecosystem services that depends on an ecosystem being active and maintaining its organization, autonomy, and resilience over time. Ecosystem health contributes to human well-being through sustainable ecosystem services and conditions for human health.

Eutrophication: Generally, the natural or human-induced process by which a body of water becomes enriched in dissolved mineral nutrients (particularly phosphorus and nitrogen) that stimulate the growth of aquatic plants and enhances organic production of the water body. Excessive enrichment may result in the depletion of dissolved oxygen and eventually to species mortality.

Exploitation rate: The proportion of a population at the beginning of a given time period that is caught during that time period (usually expressed on a yearly basis).

Fecundity: The potential reproductive capacity of an organism or population expressed in the number of eggs (or offspring) produced during each reproductive cycle. Fecundity usually increases with age and size. The information is used to compute spawning potential.

Fisher: A gender-neutral name for a person participating in a fishery.

Fisheries management: The integrated process of information gathering, analysis, planning, decision making, allocation of resources, and formulation and enforcement of fishery regulations by which the fisheries management authority controls the present and future behaviors of the interested parties in the fishery in order to ensure the continued productivity of the living resources.

Fishery: The combination of fish and fishers in a region, the latter fishing for similar or the same species with similar or the same gear types.

Fishing effort: The amount of fishing gear of a specific type used on the fishing grounds over a given unit of time (e.g. hours trawled per day, number of hooks set per day, or number of hauls of a beach seine per day).

Fishing mortality (F): 1. F stands for the fishing mortality rate in a particular stock. It is roughly the proportion of the fishable stock that is caught in a year. 2. A measurement of the rate of removal from a population by fishing. Fishing mortality can be reported as either annual or instantaneous. Annual mortality is the percentage of fish dying in one year. Instantaneous mortality is that percentage of fish dying at any one time.

Forage species: Species used as prey by a larger predator for its food.

Gill net: With this type of gear, the fish are gilled, entangled, or enmeshed in the netting. These nets can be used either alone or, as is more usual, in large numbers placed in line. According to their design, ballasting, and buoyancy, these nets may be used to fish on the surface, in midwater, or on the bottom.

Growth overfishing: When fishing pressure on smaller fish is too heavy to allow the fishery to produce its maximum poundage. Growth overfishing, by itself, does not affect the ability of a fish population to replace itself.

Growth rate (K): 1. Annual or seasonal. The increase in weight of a fish per year (or season), divided by the initial weight. 2. In fish this is often measured in terms of the parameter K of the von Bertalanffy curve for the mean weight as a function of age.

Habitat: 1. The environment in which the fish live, including everything that surrounds and affects them, e.g., water quality, bottom, vegetation, associated species (including food supplies). 2. The locality, site, and particular type of local environment occupied by an organism.

Harvest: The total number or weight of fish caught and kept from an area over a period of time. Note that landings, catch, and harvest are different.

Mark-recapture (study): The tagging and releasing of fish to be recaptured later in their life cycles. These studies are used to elucidate fish movement, migration, mortality, and growth to estimate population size.

Natural mortality (M): 1. Deaths of fish from all causes except fishing (e.g. aging, predation, cannibalism, disease, and perhaps increasingly pollution). It is often expressed as a rate that indicates the percentage of fish dying in a year; e.g. a natural mortality rate of 0.2 implies that approximately 20 percent of the population will die in a year from causes other than fishing. 2. The loss in numbers in a year class from one age group to the subsequent one, due to natural death.

Open access: Condition in which access to a fishery is not restricted (i.e. no license limitation, quotas, or other measures that would limit the amount of fish that an individual fisher can harvest).

Overfished (overharvested): A stock is considered "overfished" when exploited beyond an explicit limit beyond which its abundance is considered "too low" to ensure safe reproduction.

Population dynamics: The study of fish populations and how fishing mortality, growth, recruitment, and natural mortality affect them.

Population model: A component of a stock assessment model, made up of formulations that describe how the population changes from one time period to the next. The types of population models vary depending on the species life history and on data availability. Population models can roughly be classified as age/size structured or biomass- based, deterministic or stochastic, density-dependent or density-independent, spatially structured or spatially aggregated, equilibrium or nonequilibrium.

Production: The total elaboration of new body substance in a stock in a unit of time, irrespective of whether or not it survives to the end of that time.

Productivity: Relates to the birth, growth, and death rates of a stock. A highly productive stock is characterized by high birth, growth, and mortality rates, and as a consequence, a high turnover and production to biomass ratios (P/B). Such stocks can usually sustain higher exploitation rates and, if depleted, could recover more rapidly than comparatively less productive stocks.

Quota: A specified numerical harvest objective, the attainment (or expected attainment) of which causes closure of the fishery for that species or species group.

Recruitment: 1. The amount of fish added to the exploitable stock each year due to growth and/or migration into the fishing area. For example, the number of fish that grow to become vulnerable to the fishing gear in one year would be the recruitment to the fishable population that year. 2. This term is also used in referring to the number of fish from a year class reaching a certain age. For example, all fish reaching their second year would be age 2 recruits.

Recruitment curve: A graph of the progeny from an adult year-class at the time they reach a specified age (for example, the age at which half of the brood has become vulnerable to fishing), plotted against the abundance of the stock that produced them.

Recruitment overfishing: A situation in which the rate of fishing is (or has been) such that annual recruitment to the exploitable stock has become significantly reduced. The situation is characterized by a greatly reduced spawning stock, a decreasing proportion of older fish in the catch, and generally very low recruitment year after year. If prolonged, recruitment overfishing can lead to stock collapse, particularly under unfavorable environmental conditions.

Selectivity: In stock assessment, conventionally expressed as a relationship between retention and size (or age).

Spawning: Release of ova, fertilized or to be fertilized.

Spawning stock: 1. Mature part of a stock responsible for reproduction. 2. Strictly speaking, the part of an overall stock having reached sexual maturity and able to spawn. Often conventionally defined as the number or biomass of all individuals beyond "age at first maturity" or "size at first maturity"; that is, beyond the age or size class in which 50 percent of the individuals are mature.

Spawning stock biomass: 1. The total weight of all fish (both males and females) in the population that contribute to reproduction. Often conventionally defined as the biomass of all individuals beyond "age at first maturity" or "size at first maturity," that is, beyond the age or size class in which 50 percent of the individuals are mature. 2. The total biomass of fish of reproductive age during the breeding season of a stock.

Stock: A part of a fish population usually with a particular migration pattern, specific spawning grounds, and subject to a distinct fishery. A fish stock may be treated as a total or a spawning stock. Total stock refers to both juveniles and adults, either in numbers or by weight, while spawning stock refers to the numbers or weight of individuals that are old enough to reproduce.

Stock-recruitment relationship: The relationship between the level of parental biomass (e.g. spawning stock size) and subsequent recruitment level. Determination of this relationship is useful to analyze the sustainability of alternative harvesting regimes and the level of fishing beyond which stock collapse is likely. The relation is usually blurred by environmental variability and difficult to determine with any accuracy.

Stocking: The practice of putting artificially reared young fish into a sea, lake, or river. These are subsequently caught, preferably at a larger size.

Surplus production: 1. The amount of biomass produced by the stock (through growth and recruitment) over and above that which is required to maintain the total stock biomass at a constant level between consecutive time periods. 2. Production of new biomass by a fishable stock, plus recruits added to it, less what is removed by natural mortality. This is usually estimated as the catch in a given year plus the increase in stock size (or less the decrease).

Sustainability: Characteristic of resources that are managed so that the natural capital stock is non-declining through time, while production opportunities are maintained for the future.

Total length: The length of a fish defined as the straight-line distance from the tip of the snout to the tip of the tail (caudal fin) while the fish is lying on its side, normally extended.

Total morality rate: 1. A measurement of the rate of removal of fish from a population by both fishing and natural causes. Total mortality can be reported as either annual or instantaneous. Annual mortality is the percentage of fish dying in one year. Instantaneous mortality is that percentage of fish dying at any one time. 2. The sum of natural (M) and fishing (F) mortality rates.

Trophic level: 1. Classification of natural communities or organisms according to their place in the food chain. Green plants (producers) can be roughly distinguished from herbivores (consumers) and carnivores (secondary: Trophic group consumers). 2. Group of organisms eating resources from a similar level in the energy cycle. 3. Position in food chain determined by the number of energy-transfer steps to that level. Plant producers constitute the lowest level, followed by herbivores and a series of carnivores at the higher levels.

Vulnerability: A term equivalent to catchability (q) but usually applied to separate parts of a stock, for example those of a particular size, or those living in a particular part of the range.

Watershed: The area which supplies water by surface and subsurface flow from rain to a given point in the drainage system.

Year-class: Fish in a stock born in the same year.

NOTES

Preface

1. The word "walleye" is derived from "wall-eyed," which means an eye with a streaked or opaque white iris (*New Oxford American Dictionary*). Scandinavians may find it interesting that "wall-eyed" was adapted from the Old Norse word *valdeygðr* or *vagleygr*, meaning a beam in or film over the eye.
2. Kitchell et al. 1977a.
3. Sass and Allen 2014.

1. The World of Walleye

1. While the current walleye scientific name is *Sander vitreus*, it was formerly named *Stizostedion vitreum*. Several taxonomists believe that *Sander* is not appropriate and that *Stizostedion* should be reconsidered as the correct genus name (Nelson et al. 2016; Bruner 2021). Other common names for walleye include yellow walleye and yellow pickerel.
2. Kurlansky 1999.
3. A good example is bird art. Since 1976, the Leigh Yawkey Woodson Art Museum has had an annual *Birds in Art* exhibit.
4. Becker 1983.
5. Isermann et al. 2003.
6. Reverter et al. 2018.
7. Keylor 2018 used electroretinography to determine walleye light sensitivity, and he found that the peak sensitivity was at wavelengths from 500 to 550 nm; he also estimated that walleye may likely detect light when at a depth of about 256 feet (78 m) in a clear water lake (Lake Superior) and at 43 feet (13 m) for a turbid water lake (Lake Ontario). Walleye visual detection thresholds and reaction distance, measures of visual acuity, decrease with sediment and algal turbidity (Nieman et al. 2018; Nieman and Gray 2019).
8. Wetzel 2001.
9. This retroflector is called a tapetum lucidum, which is a layer of tissue in the eye behind the retina.
10. Braekevelt et al. 1989.
11. Ollivier et al. 2004.
12. The three different otolith bones from big to small are sagittae, lapilli, and asterisci. They are made of calcium carbonate extracted from the water, and as the fish grows so do these bones. Fish biologists use these facts to

assess the environment that the fish occupied by using chemical analysis and to determine the age of the fish by counting the layers that accumulate in the sagittae bone, much like counting tree rings (Carlson et al. 2016; Dembkowski et al. 2017).

13. Fish can make sounds. Notably, fish species from the cod family (Gadidae), the cod-like family (Lotidae), and the drum and croaker family (Sciaenidae) can create low-frequency drumming or grunting sounds by rapidly contracting and expanding the muscles associated with the swim bladder, which then vibrates. For example, male burbot and freshwater drum use these sonic muscles to produce sounds during their spawning seasons to attract females of their kind. Do walleye make sounds? Their sound creation may be limited to the sounds resulting from rapidly changing swim direction and bumping against things.

14. Rottiers and Lemm 1985; Kamaszewski and Ostaszewska 2015.

15. Valentinčič 2004.

16. Summerfelt et al. 2011.

17. More complex gas bladder systems exist for some fish, whereby the bladder is also connected with the ear, which allows greater sound detection. For walleye, the first fill of the gas bladder is accomplished by gulping air (Rieger and Summerfelt 1998).

18. Ali and Anctil 1977.

19. Ali et al. 1977.

20. Shepard 1998.

21. Fellegy 1973.

22. Scott and Crossman 1973.

23. Tingley et al. 2019.

24. Fishing, with its selective removal of large and aggressive fish, may reduce the ultimate size of fish and create less aggressive fish in highly exploited populations (Bowles et al. 2019; Monk et al. 2021).

25. Bogue 2000.

26. Through the 1700s and 1800s, the governments of Britain, Canada, and the United States crafted treaties for the Ojibwe whereby bands ceded large expanses of land for little money and supplies. The Ojibwe signed more than twenty treaties with Britain, twelve treaties with Canada, and more than forty with the United States. In many of the treaties, the Ojibwe also retained rights to hunt and fish on the ceded lands. In Canada, treaty rights are protected under the constitutional reforms of 1982, and with the Indian Act of 1985 those rights are protected against provincial legislation. In the United States, treaty rights are guaranteed under Article VI of the U.S. Constitution, which states that treaties are the supreme law of the land. This article also notes that U.S. state governments are bound

by the treaties. Fundamental to these treaties is the Ojibwe right of sovereignty or self-determination. In Canada, the existence of both historic and modern treaties adds to the complexity of resolving disputes between the Ojibwe and the federal government. In the United States, treaties have resulted in Ojibwe sovereign islands surrounded by an inland sea of U.S. law. Interpreting which system of laws pertains to a case has been a reoccurring issue for the U.S. court system—the courts of the victor. In both Canada and the United States, treaty promises have not been kept, which has forced the Ojibwe to challenge the federal governments to protect, retain, and exercise their treaty rights (Treuer 2010).

27. Nesper 2002.
28. Hmielewski 2019.
29. Michaels 2019.
30. Castañeda et al. 2020.
31. Schmalz et al. 2011.
32. Nesper 2002.
33. Mrnak et al. 2018.
34. Myers et al. 2014.
35. The blue-colored walleye was found to be genetically indistinguishable from the yellow-colored walleye (Haponski and Stepien 2014).
36. Lake Erie Walleye Task Group, March 2021.
37. Radomski 1999.
38. Lemm 2002.
39. Green and Derksen 1984.
40. Adam et al. 1996.
41. Zander (*Sander lucioperca*), a walleye relative, has been imported from Europe and is served at restaurants as "walleye."
42. These statistics from Department of Fisheries and Oceans Canada include sauger, which is a small proportion of the total.
43. Gaeta et al. 2013.
44. USDOI 2011, 2016.
45. Tingley et al. 2019.
46. Fisheries and Oceans Canada 2019.
47. In the United States, the federal Sport Fish Restoration Program also contributes substantial funds for state agency fisheries projects. Monies for this program come from taxes on sport fishing equipment, a portion of the gasoline tax attributed to motorboats, and import duties on tackle and boats. The program is administered by the U.S. Fish and Wildlife Service.
48. Radomski et al. 2001.
49. Tom Dickson, Has catch-and-release gone overboard? The case for harvesting trout, *Montana Outdoors Magazine*, May-June 2020; Tom Dickson,

Walleye start receiving the catch-and-release treatment, *Montana Outdoors Magazine*, May-June 2020.

50. Sass and Shaw 2019.

51. Walleye catch-and-release mortality increases with water temperature and depth of capture. In Mille Lacs, walleye hooking mortality was observed to be about 0 percent in May, when water temperatures were less than 68°F (20°C), and 12 percent in July and August, when water temperatures were higher (Reeves and Bruesewitz 2007). In Rainy Lake from July through September, walleye captured in 30 feet (9.1 m) of water had an 8 percent probability of death from hooking mortality, 40 feet (12.2 m) had 18 percent, and 50 feet (15.2 m) had 35 percent (Talmage and Staples 2011).

52. As Aldo Leopold (1949) writes in *A Sand County Almanac*: "A peculiar virtue in wildlife ethics is that the hunter ordinarily has no gallery to applaud or disprove of his conduct. Whatever his acts, they are dictated by his own conscience, rather than by a mob of onlookers. It is difficult to exaggerate the importance of this fact" (212).

2. Survival School

1. Matley et al. 2020; Jason Robinson's February 2019 presentation to the New York Chapter of the American Fisheries Society.

2. Hayden et al. 2018; Chen et al. 2020.

3. Walleye egg size averages about 2 mm (range: 1.3 to 2.1 mm) in diameter (Bozek et al. 2011a).

4. Baccante and Colby 1996; Bozek et al. 2011a.

5. Walleye egg characteristics related to energy content vary between and within populations (Moodie et al. 1989; Johnston 1997; Johnston et al. 2007; Wiegand et al. 2007). Walleye egg size generally increases with the size or age of the female (Johnston and Leggett 2002).

6. Johnston et al. 2021.

7. Malison et al. 1994.

8. Henderson et al. 2003.

9. Walleye in the southern part of their range may not spawn due to insufficient cool water temperature (Prentice and Clark 1978).

10. Bade et al. 2019.

11. Ellis and Giles 1965.

12. Raabe and Bozek 2015.

13. Since walleye appear to select specific spawning habitat (Raabe and Bozek 2012; Raabe et al. 2020; Zentner et al. 2022), perhaps it is a reasonable assumption that walleye are selecting habitats conducive to egg survival.

14. Priegel 1970.

15. Latif et al. 1999.

16. Raabe and Bozek 2015; Gatch et al. 2020.
17. Kamaszewski and Ostaswewska 2015.
18. The range in hatching times under natural conditions is 10 to 27 days (F. H. Johnson 1961; Priegel 1970; Engel et al. 2000). Water temperatures between 48°F and 59°F (9°C–15°C) are best for walleye eggs, and faster hatching times occur with warmer water (Koenst and Smith 1976). Walleye egg survival is higher at water oxygen concentrations above 5 mg/L (Oseid and Smith 1971).
19. Bozek et al. 2011a.
20. On Lake Erie, Bade et al. 2019 found that angler harvest during the walleye spawning season resulted in more males harvested than females, as males remain on the spawning shoals longer than females.
21. In rivers, walleye fry drift downstream, with numbers drifting greater during the night than during the day (Corbett and Powles 1986; Johnston et al. 1995).
22. Walleye fry feed on copepods and small cladocerans (Graham and Sprules 1992; Johnston and Mathias 1994; Hoxmeier et al. 2006).
23. Moodie et al. 1989.
24. Mathias and Li 1982; Engel et al. 2000; Galarowicz et al. 2006. For larval walleye, Gostiaux et al. 2022 estimated a 50 percent and 90 percent probability of piscivory at 0.4 inches (9 mm) and 0.6 inches (16 mm) in length, respectively, with yellow perch the most observed prey in their diet. These estimates of piscivory were higher than those previously reported.
25. The relationship between the larval growth rate and the probability of survival to a fall fingerling is complicated and not likely linear (May et al. 2020).
26. When they reach between 30 and 40 mm in total length, walleye shift to avoiding light (Bulkowski and Mead 1983).
27. Walleye at about 60 mm in total length begin to develop macroreceptors in the retina, which increase visual acuity in dim light (Vandenbyllaardt et al. 1991).
28. Maloney and Johnson 1957.
29. Colby et al. 1979; Forney 1980.
30. J. F. Hansen et al. 2012; G. J. A. Hansen 2015b; Boehm et al. 2020; Honsey et al. 2020.
31. Gleick 1987.
32. Forney 1974, 1976, 1977; Madenjian and Carpenter 1996; Schupp 2002.
33. Chevalier 1973; Swensen and Smith 1976; Forney 1976, 1980.
34. In some waters, walleye appear to select soft-rayed fish over spiny-rayed fish (Knight et al. 1984; Lyons 1987; J. C. Schneider et al. 1991).
35. Ryder 1977.

36. Aardema 1991.
37. Myers et al. 2014.
38. Henderson et al. 2003.
39. Kaufman et al. 2009.
40. Bozek et al. 2011a; Pedersen et al. 2018.
41. Massie et al. 2021.
42. Walleye feeding activity is reduced at water temperatures exceeding 72°F (22°C) (Hasnain et al. 2010), and in southern U.S. reservoirs, summer water temperatures are often higher and most walleye growth occurs in the fall (Quist et al. 2002).
43. Walleye age of maturity is related to climate (Bozek et al. 2011a). Growing degree days explains 96 percent of the total variation of immature walleye total length; males generally mature with 12,500 degree Fahrenheit days (6,900 °C days) and 13.8 inches (350 mm) in length, and females generally mature after 18,000 degree Fahrenheit days (10,000 °C days) and 17.7 inches (450 mm) in length (Venturelli et al. 2010a). Growing degree days appeared not to affect walleye length of maturity, and length at maturity seemed insensitive to large changes in walleye density (Venturelli et al. 2010a). For Lake Erie walleye, Gíslason et al. 2021 found that the length of maturity was more related to ecosystem changes than factors related to walleye harvest intensity.
44. Colby et al. 1979; Morgan et al. 2003.
45. Bozek et al. 2011a.
46. For a cohort, after maturity the maximum male total length is about 80 percent that of female (Bozek et al. 2011a).
47. Campbell 1998.
48. Gaeta et al. 2018.
49. Ryder and Kerr 1978; Henderson et al. 2004; Kaufman et al. 2009.
50. Henderson et al. 2004.
51. Jacobson et al. 2020.
52. Henderson et al. 2004; Herwig et al. 2022.
53. Tyler Ahrenstorff, personal communication.
54. Lantry et al. 2008.
55. Madenjian et al. 2010.
56. Kitchell et al. 1977b.
57. Tyler Ahrenstorff, personal communication.
58. Eddy and Underhill 1974.
59. This range of walleye swimming speeds is based on swimming for ten minutes (Peake et al. 2000).
60. The "balance of nature" concept alone is too simple of a mental model for ecosystems, so other models now include resilience, multiple-equilibrium

conditions or natural states, abrupt shifts in abundance and species composition, and unpredictable systems (Holling 1973; Berkes and Ross 2013). Resilience is not stability; it is the ability to recover from difficult conditions.

61. Rudstam et al. 2004; Schultz et al. 2013.
62. In the Lake Winnebago System, Koenigs et al. 2021 found cormorants to be opportunistic feeders, with gizzard shad and freshwater drum the most common prey in their diets.
63. Colby et al. 1987; Nate et al. 2003; Paul et al. 2021.
64. Johnson and Hale 1977; Inskip and Magnuson 1983; Van Zuiden and Sharma 2016.
65. Bellgraph et al. 2008.
66. Austin and Austin 1987.
67. Ryder 1961; Margenau et al. 1988.
68. Barton and Barry 2011.
69. More than eighty species of parasites have been found on walleye (Barton and Barry 2011, table 6.4).
70. Colby et al. 1979.
71. The female gill lice are parasitic on the gill filaments of their host fish (Hudson and Lesko 2003). These freshwater parasitic crustaceans, while commonly called gill lice, are not related to human head and body lice, which are insects.
72. Bozek et al. 2011a, table 7.1.
73. For Alberta lakes, Cahill et al. 2020 reported that high walleye population densities did not suppress walleye growth across all ages and the preponderance of small walleye caught by anglers was due to the excessive harvest of large walleye.
74. At low adult densities, reproduction often exceeds replacement levels, and this is an important factor in allowing sustainable harvests (Hilborn and Walters 2021). After increasing the exploitation rate for a northern Wisconsin walleye fishery, Sass et al. 2022b observed higher young survival, fish maturing at a smaller size, and higher and more variable young walleye abundance in the elevated-exploitation time period, thus demonstrating numerous compensatory responses that can offset the consequences of high exploitation rates on adult walleye abundance.
75. Post et al. 2002.
76. For northern Wisconsin walleye lakes, Sass et al. 2021 suspected that recruitment depensation might explain some walleye population declines.
77. Forney 1974; Ryder et al. 1974; M. G. Johnson et al. 1977; Baccante and Colby 1996; Lester et al. 2004; Chu et al. 2004.
78. Randall et al. 1995; Nash et al. 1999; Bozek et al. 2011b.

79. Rypel 2021.
80. Baccante and Colby 1996.
81. Parker and Nilon 2008.
82. For Escanaba Lake walleye, Rypel et al. 2015 found that adult densities were correlated with ages 4–6 production. Walleye densities did not appear correlated to fishing exploitation, but walleye production was correlated to exploitation. Thus, measuring production to track and management walleye fisheries likely has clear benefits. Walleye production estimates are rare, and Rypel and David 2017 found that those reported were almost all below 6 kg/ha/yr. Rypel et al. 2018 reported a mean walleye productivity of 1.2 kg/ha/yr for Wisconsin natural reproducing walleye lakes, with stocking-dependent lakes having a lower mean production of 0.5 kg/ha/yr.

    For northern pike, there appears to be a curvilinear relationship between density and production, where increases in production slowed at high pike densities. Northern pike production tended to decline with fish age (Pierce 2012).
83. Rypel et al. 2018.
84. The 25 percent natural mortality rate for walleye does not include deaths from humans; for some walleye populations the total mortality rate can exceed 40 percent (M. J. Hansen et al. 2011; Tsehaye et al. 2016). For comparison, the total mortality rate for humans in the United States is about 1 percent (Centers for Disease Control and Prevention, National Center for Health Statistics).
85. Nate et al. 2011.
86. Sass and Shaw 2018.
87. Olson and Scidmore 1962; Olson et al. 1978; G. C. Palmer et al. 2005; Carlson et al. 2016.
88. For lake-resident, river-spawning walleye, spawning river fidelity estimates have generally been high (greater than 70 percent) (Herbst et al. 2017; Dembkowski et al. 2018; Hayden et al. 2018; C. W. Elliot et al. 2022).
89. Bozek et al. 2011a.
90. Dan Isermann and Gregg Sass, personal communication.
91. Pauly 1980; Thorson et al. 2017.

3. The Thrill of the Chase

1. Kitchell et al. 1977b.
2. Schupp and Macins 1977. Oglesby et al. 1987 suggested that mean growing season chlorophyll a of 8 to 12 mg/m³ was optimal for walleye harvest. Chlorophyll a is a green pigment in plants used for photosynthesis, and the amount of this pigment in the water is a useful measure of algal

biomass, the base of the aquatic ecosystem food web pyramid. Walleye prefer medium productive lakes, which are called mesotrophic lakes by limnologists.

3. Sullivan 2003a; Rypel and David 2017.

4. Nate et al. 2000, 2001, 2003. While the total number of walleye is often greater in large walleye lakes, the walleye density may be higher in some smaller walleye lakes (Baccante and Colby 1996).

5. Fayram et al. 2005; Hoxmeier et al. 2006; Kerr 2008.

6. M. G. Johnson et al. 1977; Schupp 1992; Nate et al. 2003.

7. Marshall and Ryan 1987.

8. Wetzel 2001.

9. Kitchell et al. 1977b.

10. In Lake Erie, large walleye (greater than 15.75 inches [400 mm] in total length) were detected most frequently near the lake bottom during the day and night (Gorman et al. 2019).

11. Ryder 1977.

12. Walleye prefer light levels that would represent to us as illuminance between an overcast day and twilight.

13. Ryder 1977; Christie and Regier 1988; Lester et al. 2004.

14. The coldest water is just under the ice, and the warmer, denser 39°F (4°C) water is at the lake bottom (Wetzel 2001).

15. Deroba et al. 2007.

16. Cooke et al. 2012.

17. The Great Lakes Indian Fish and Wildlife Commission provides details on off-reservation harvest regulations for the eleven Ojibwe tribes in Minnesota, Wisconsin, and Michigan.

18. Prior to the 1950s, gill-net mesh was made of linen twine.

19. Hubert et al. 2012.

20. Bar measure of mesh is provided here.

21. For gill nets with meshes measuring between 0.75 and 2.0 inches (19 to 50.8 mm) bar measure, fishing intensity increased with mesh size (Radomski et al. 2020).

22. Anderson 1998; Grant et al. 2004a.

23. Reynolds and Dean 2020.

24. Reynolds and Kolz 2012.

25. Ricker 1975; MDNR 2017.

26. Cook et al. 2001.

27. Mrnak et al. 2018; Cichosz 2021.

28. Baccante 1995. Often angler catch rates are modeled assuming a zero-inflated negative binomial distribution or Poisson distribution (Su and He 2013).

29. Cook et al. 2001.
30. Ryder 1977.
31. Bailey et al. 2019.
32. Shaw et al. 2021.
33. Norton 2003 (28).
34. Quoted in Meine 2019 (76).
35. To tie the fishing line to a hook or lure, I tend to use the Improved Clink Knot (and its deviations, such as the Trilene Knot) or the Palomar Knot.
36. Lead (Pb) is used extensively in fishing tackle. It is highly toxic to fish, wildlife, and humans. There is no established safe level of lead exposure. Lead should not be added to lakes and rivers. In lakes with high angling effort, annual tackle loss from sport anglers translates to many metric tons of lead deposition (Radomski et al. 2006). A single lead sinker or lead jig can kill a loon. In Minnesota, lead poisoning from lead fishing tackle is responsible for 14 percent of the adult loon deaths (100 to 200 loons per year). Effective solutions to lead tackle pollution require a sociopolitical response (Grade et al. 2019). To limit lead exposure and its detrimental effects on wildlife and human health, lead was banned in gasoline, paint, and waterfowl ammunition. Six U.S. states (Maine, Massachusetts, New Hampshire, New York, Vermont, and Washington) have enacted regulations banning the sale and/or use of lead in fishing tackle of specific sizes.
37. In a study of Lake Erie charters fishing for walleye, investigators found that white lures were most effective in clear water, yellow in turbid conditions, and black during algal blooms (Nieman et al. 2020).
38. Walleye's sensitivity to light comes at the expense of visual acuity. The greater the ratio of ganglion cells to photoreceptors, the better the visual acuity. Humans have about one hundred rods and cones to each ganglion cell, a 100:1 ratio, and walleye have about a 140:1 ratio (Ali and Anctil 1977). Human eyes have a high density of cones in the center of the retina (fovea), with a high ganglion cell to cone ratio (less than 5:1 ratio).
39. Please dispose of unwanted bait in the trash and use only indigenous bait species. Many bait worms are of European origin, so remember to use worms and crawlers with care and do not release them into the wild, as they will change northern forest ecosystems that have existed without worms (Hale et al. 2005; Frelich and Reich 2010).
40. Fathead minnow, scientific name: *Pimephales promelas*. Other common names include saddleback, blackhead, tuffy, or tuffies. An orange-colored variety of the species is also called the rosy-red or ruby-red minnow. Young fathead minnows are often sold as "crappie minnows," but this marketing label is also applied to other small minnow species.

41. Creek chub, scientific name: *Semotilus atromaculatus*. In Minnesota, the fish is sometimes called red tail.
42. Common shiner, scientific name: *Notropis cornnutus*. Other common names include silver shiner, eastern shiner, or redfin shiner.
43. Golden shiner, scientific name: *Notemigonus crysoleucas*. They are used in winter rather than summer because they usually perish in the summer bait bucket.
44. Common minnow and minnow-like species that can be found in walleye lakes: banded killifish *(Fundulus diaphanous)*, blackchin shiner *(Notropis heterod)*, blacknose shiner *(Notropis heterolepis)*, bluntnose minnow *(Pimphales notatus)*, brook stickleback *(Culea inconstans)*, central mudminnow *(Umbra limi)*, emerald shiner *(Notropis atherinoides)*, finescale dace *(Chrosomus neogaeus)*, hornyhead chub *(Nocomis biguttatus)*, Iowa darter *(Etheostoma exile)*, Johnny darter *(Etheostoma nigrum)*, logperch *(Percina caprodes)*, mimic shiner *(Notropis volucellus)*, northern redbelly dace *(Chrosomus eos)*, spotfin shiner *(Notropis spilopterus)*, and spottail shiner *(Notropis hudsonius)*.
45. Grant et al. 2004a.
46. Cooke and Schramm 2007; Arlinghaus et al. 2007.
47. Reeves and Bruesewitz 2007; Talmage and Staples 2011; Twardek et al. 2018. Talmage and Staples 2011 accounted for the experimental handling time (i.e., the time from hook removal to placement in holding cages for study), which had a significant but small negative effect. The other two studies cited here did not account for experimental handling time, so it is likely that their hooking mortality estimates may be biased high.
48. Two techniques are currently deemed to humanely kill a fish: producing a swift blow to the head (percussive stunning) and inserting a sharp spike to the brain (spiking).

4. Fish In, Fish Out

1. In a trout stocking study conducted in the 1960s and 1970s, Vincent 1987 found adverse effects of stocking hatchery trout on wild trout in sections of the Madison River and O'Dell Creek in Montana. For Madison River, discontinuing stocking resulted in higher wild trout populations and larger trout. For a previously unstocked section of O'Dell Creek, trout stocking reduced the trout population. This study led the state of Montana in the 1970s to discontinue all trout stockings in streams with wild trout, which resulted in better trout fishing in Montana. This study also triggered other states to evaluate their trout stocking activities and outcomes.
2. See G. J. A. Hansen et al. 2015b for a northern Wisconsin walleye management example. See van Poorten and MacKenzie 2020 for the importance

of fisheries management objectives and the use of decision analysis to communicate trade-offs of different objectives. MDNR has excellent fisheries management plans on many lakes. I encourage the reader to review a number of these plans, many of which have a clear goal and specific objectives.

3. Arlinghaus and Mehner 2003; Jackson et al. 2004; Sass et al. 2017.

4. Walleye are the most stocked fish as measured by the number of fish, and rainbow trout are the most stocked fish as measured by weight (Halverson 2008).

5. Logsdon and Schultz 2017; Lawson et al. 2022.

6. Edwin Pister, a fishery biologist who worked for the California Department Fish and Game and saved the Owens pupfish from extinction, when reflecting on the common angler of the high mountain lakes of California, said, "If fishing is good, they will generally attribute it to a successful stocking program; if it is poor, their feeling will likely be that the water 'needs stocking.' For whatever reason, there remains a common assumption that equates good angling with regular stocking, even though in fact there may be little (or no) relationship between the two" (2001, 283). Pister (1987) stated that stocking programs can be detrimental, as they often distract and divert agency resources from meaningful efforts of maintaining or restoring healthy ecosystems.

7. Lawson et al. 2022.

8. The increase in walleye stocking resulted in 51 percent of the lakes having no change in the walleye abundance, 21 percent having an increase in walleye abundance, 19 percent having declines, and 9 percent requiring further evaluation (Logsdon and Schultz 2017).

9. Rainy Lake and Namakan Reservoir Water Level International Steering Committee 1993.

10. International Rainy and Namakan Lakes Rule Curves Study Board 2017. In 2018, the rule curves were again revised based on additional biological and hydrological study.

11. MDNR and Ontario Ministry of Natural Resources 1992.

12. In 1991, Jeff Eibler, Dave Friedl, and I drafted a regulation proposal to address Rainy Lake walleye overharvest. Jeff Eibler pursued what was a long process that ultimately led to the first biologically based walleye angling length-based regulation in Minnesota—a protected slot limit from 17 to 25 inches total length (432 to 635 mm) that was implemented in 1994.

13. Neven 1900.

14. Fenton et al. 1996; Kerr 2008.

15. MDNR 2020.

16. Cobb 1923.

17. MDNR 1996.
18. Smith and Moyle 1945; Dobie 1956; Daily 1996.
19. Laarman 1978; Nate et al. 2000; Jacobson 2004; Raabe et al. 2020.
20. Jacobson 2004.
21. Dave Orrick, The cost of Minnesota's walleye-industrial complex, *Pioneer Press,* May 7, 2014. Walleye from my local fish market, Morey's Seafood Markets, cost about $12 per fish.
22. Summerfelt et al. 2011.
23. In the past some might have used an eagle feather to stir the concocted life mixture.
24. Thompson 1996.
25. Malison et al. 1994.
26. Logsdon et al. 2004.
27. Peter Jacobson, personal communication.
28. Hatchery walleye egg fertilization rates are dependent on sperm density, and rates can be as high as 91 percent with high sperm density (Casselman et al. 2006).
29. Summerfelt et al. 2011.
30. Colby et al. 1979.
31. It is common for fishery hatcheries to report walleye egg survival rates above 70 percent.
32. A standard weight is assumed: an average walleye fry weighs about 4.5 mg, which computes to 220,000 fry per kilogram, about 100,000 fry to the pound.
33. MDNR 2016.
34. Lilienthal 1996.
35. Lilienthal 1996.
36. Parsons and Pereira 1997; Weber et al. 2020.
37. Jacobson and Anderson 2007.
38. Kampa and Hatzenbeler 2009; Grausgruber and Weber 2020; Lawson et al. 2022.
39. Li et al. 1996a, 1996b; Jacobson and Anderson 2007 (the latter notes that the law of diminishing returns is consistent with the concept of carrying capacity).
40. Jacobson and Anderson 2007.
41. In northern Wisconsin lakes, Lawson et al. 2022 estimated that 21 percent of the walleye stockings failed to such a degree that no stocked walleye were found in electrofishing surveys in the following year.
42. MDNR 2016.
43. Kahneman 2011.
44. H. Zhao et al. 2020; Bootsma et al. 2021.

45. Radomski and Goeman 1995; McMahon and Bennett 1996; Kerr 2011.
46. Sagoff 2018. Scientists are humans, and sometimes the easiest thing to find is what they are looking for. They speak of "damage" when an objective scientist would use terms such as "change." Value judgment and labels (good/bad, native/nonnative, invasive/noninvasive) appear to limit pragmatic natural resource management (Davis et al. 2011). With regard to the application of the "first, do no harm" ethical principle for aquatic plant management and nonindigenous species, see Radomski and Perleberg 2019.

5. The Long Emergency

1. Klein 2014.
2. Sternberg 2017.
3. WMO 2019.
4. Sternberg 2015.
5. Vitousek et al. 1986, 1997; Haberl et al. 2007, 2012.
6. The carrying capacity is the limit to population size determined by the availability of resources (Pulliam and Haddad 1994). With regard to humans, carrying capacity is, in part, contingent on our technology and culture, and it is dynamic, as environmental and social conditions are dynamic.
7. Callicott et al. 1999.
8. Di Guilio and Hinton 2008; Bozek et al. 2011b.
9. Joseph et al. 2009; Radomski and Carlson 2018.
10. A lakes's watershed is an extent of land from which water drains downhill into the lake, and it also includes the streams and lakes upstream.
11. Ackerman and Heinzerling 2002 and Ackerman 2008 discuss the shortcomings of cost-benefit analysis and why it should not be used for environmental policy decision-making. They note that not all people think like investment bankers; the future does matter to many in a caring society. In addition, future generations matter, and shifting environmental degradation to future generations is unjust. These analyses create illusions that the costs are too high and that environmental degradation is not worth fixing—the selfish justifying their selfishness.
12. Taleb 2007.
13. Specifically, the conventional use of exponential discounting is computed as the $P = F / (1 + r)^t$, where P is the present value, F is the future value, r is the discount rate, and t is year; whereas conventional compounding is $F = P (1 + r)^t$, where r is the interest rate. Ramsey 1928 wrote that discounting the future like this was "ethically indefensible and arises merely from the weakness of the imagination" (543). As a way to allow intergen-

erational justice or equality, Ramsey provided an equation to estimate a discount rate by inclusion of a time preference variable. In addition, Weitzman 1998 suggested use of low discount rates for events in the distant future.

14. The calculations were estimated using the formation of a cost-benefit analysis from Pennell 2015.

15. Besides the conventional approach to discounting, other functions include hyperbolic discounting and discount rates that decline over the time period.

16. See the Stern Report (Stern et al. 2006), which is an economic analysis of climate change. Also see Weitzman's 2007 review of the report, where he notes that the uncertainties and risks are likely more serious than outlined and that those risks are hard to calculate. I think of risk as a function of the probability that something bad will happen and the consequences of that bad thing. Applying this definition of risk to climate change, which has a high probability of occurrence (it is happening now) with epic negative consequences, means that climate change is a societal risk of monumental proportions.

17. Wetzel 2001; Carpenter et al. 2011; Jenny et al. 2020.

18. See Radomski and Carlson 2018 for a prioritization example applied to Minnesota lakes.

19. Leopold 1949.

20. "A thing is right when it tends to preserve the integrity, stability, and beauty of the biotic community" (Leopold 1949, 262). Leopold provided five second-order principles for conserving nature: our conduct should not result in the loss of ecosystem elements, our actions should be moderate and gentle in consequence, we should care more for ecological health and beauty than economic benefits, we need to stabilize human population, and we need to stabilize soil and maintain/restore natural hydrology (Callicott and Freyfogle 1999; see also Radomski and Van Assche 2014 for a listing of Aldo Leopold writings that support his second-order principles).

21. Loew 2014.

22. We are indeed relatives to all other life on the planet. All life on Earth is related, which can be expressed as a phylogenetic or evolutionary tree (Darwin 1859). The great tree of life appears to consist of two trunks or domains—one consisting of the bacteria and the other consisting of archaea (single-celled organisms lacking a defined nucleus) from which emerged the eukaryotes (e.g., fungi, plants, and animals) (Hug et al. 2016; Williams et al. 2020).

23. K. P. Whyte 2015.

24. Cialdini 2006.
25. Vaugeois et al. 2021 explored site-specific and watershed-based contaminant mitigation in the effectiveness to protect walleye reproduction, and they suggested that single-site contaminant mitigation may be more effective when focusing on spawning sites that are substantially polluted and impaired. In other pollution cases, like runoff nutrient pollution, prioritizing locations within a watershed may be most effective.
26. Clair et al. 2011.
27. Hoffman and Hitting 2017; Brahney et al. 2020.
28. Ramstack et al. 2004; Sanzo and Hecnar 2006; Novotney et al. 2008; M. E. Palmer et al. 2011; Dugan et al. 2017.
29. Writer et al. 2010; S. M. Elliott et al. 2017.
30. Barber et al. 2015; Thomas et al. 2017.
31. Walleye prefer waters with dissolved oxygen levels above 5 mg/L (Bozek et al. 2011b).
32. Wetzel 2001; Reinl et al. 2021.
33. Gatch et al. 2020.
34. Carpenter et al. 1998; Carpenter 2008; Schindler et al. 2008.
35. Blann et al. 2009; J. A. Foley et al. 2011.
36. Given the challenges that farmers face, they often ask for public assistance to not pollute their neighbors. There are farmer incentives to increase their operations and incentives to stop farming sensitive lands; however, the magnitude of intensive ag is immense. The large scale of our agriculture likely requires radical change to produce significant positive benefits for both farming families and the environment. For more information, read the articles from Alan Guebert, an agricultural journalist who writes the syndicated agriculture column "The Farm and Food File."
37. About 15 percent of Minnesota forestlands have been converted to agriculture (Pete Jacobson, personal communication).
38. W. H. Whyte 1988 stated an important principle for cities: "Open space, like development, needs the discipline of function. Use it or lose it" (305). In our society, I suspect this is also true for forests, in that they need to be working forests. For the private landowner, forest harvest provides a way to live on the land, pay the property taxes, or retain the property.
39. Jacobson et al. 2017.
40. Chu et al. 2018; Lamothe et al. 2019.
41. Jacobson et al. 2016.
42. I've come to believe that we don't own a piece of land, but rather we hold a relationship with a place. In Minnesota, the Minnesota Land Trust works with property owners to provide perpetual habitat protection with conservation easements. In Wisconsin, a wealth of organizations

protect land, water, and habitat with conservation easements (for more information, contact Gathering Waters: Wisconsin's Alliance for Land Trusts).

43. Bozek et al. 2011b, table 5.4.
44. Bellmore et al. 2017.
45. Aadland 2010.
46. M. M. Foley et al. 2017a, 2017b.
47. Raabe et al. 2020.
48. For lakes, the duration of ice cover is decreasing (Magnuson et al. 2000; Magnuson 2002; Lopez et al. 2019; Sharma et al. 2019). Sharma et al. 2021b found that ice cover duration for a group of sixty Northern Hemisphere lakes had decreased more than two weeks per century. Climate change has altered habitats and many fish communities (Stefan et al. 1996; Schindler 2001; Kling et al. 2003; Ficke et al. 2007; Woolway et al. 2020). During this phase of climate change, lakes are experiencing a phenological whiplash, as the variability in the ice-out times has increased in the last two decades, which means ice-out dates have been more unpredictable (Hilary Dugan, personal communication).

    Fish ranges are shifting with fish movement and with human-assisted migration. Sunfish and largemouth bass are expanding their range north; walleye are declining at their southern range and will likely increase in the north; and cold-water species such as burbot, lake trout, lake whitefish, and cisco are likely to increase in parts of the Great Lakes, are declining in small lakes, and will continue to be eliminated in many lakes at the southern end of their range. Research studies on cisco declines due to global warming include Jacobson et al. 2010; Fang et al. 2012; Jiang et al. 2012; Jacobson et al. 2012; and Lyons et al. 2018.

49. Climate change pollution is also changing areas of suitable human habitat, and the continued failure to address air pollution will accelerate human migrations (Xu et al. 2020).
50. Millennium Ecosystem Assessment 2005; Jimenez Cisneros et al. 2014; Pryor et al. 2014; Masson-Delmotte et al. 2021; G. J. A. Hansen et al. 2022.
51. Woolway and Merchant 2019; Bachmann et al. 2020; Woolway et al. 2020, 2021a, 2021b; Jane et al. 2021.
52. Williamson et al. 2016; Mahdiyan et al. 2021.
53. For example, Gutowsky et al. 2019 found that the velocity of climate change along with decreasing forest cover interacted to negatively affect Ontario walleye populations.
54. For example, Ozersky et al. 2021 noted the difficulty in predicting the consequences of climate change on the Great Lakes.
55. Venturelli et al. 2010a; Lynch et al. 2016b.

56. G. J. A. Hansen et al. 2015a, 2017a, 2017b, 2019; Winslow et al. 2015; Rose et al. 2016; Bunnell et al. 2021.

57. G. J. A. Hansen et al. 2015b show that bass abundance has increased in Wisconsin. G. J. A. Hansen et al. 2017b predicted that the number of walleye-dominated lakes in Wisconsin would decline due to climate change from 184 lakes (9 percent) to 17 lakes (1 percent) by late century, as the number of lakes with abundant largemouth bass populations increase.

58. Rypel et al. 2016; Jacobson et al. 2017; Renik et al. 2020.

59. Van Zuiden et al. 2016; Van Zuiden and Sharma 2016; Paukert et al. 2021; Staudinger et al. 2021.

60. In Minnesota, climate change is shifting walleye spawning earlier in the spring (K. N. Schneider et al. 2010). In northern Wisconsin, walleye recruitment has declined (G. J. A. Hansen et al. 2015b).

61. Sharma et al. 2019; Filazzola et al. 2020; Sharma et al. 2021a, 2021b.

62. Ryan et al. 2018.

63. Charlotte Alter, Suyin Haynes, and Justin Worland, TIME 2019 Person of the Year, *Time Magazine*, December 23–30, 2019.

64. Berry 2012.

65. Masson-Delmotte et al. 2021; Seibert and Rees 2021.

6. A Science of Questions

1. For the Escanaba Lake walleye fishery, Rypel et al. 2015 found that there was a significant relationship between the two measures of exploitation.

2. Ricker 1946 conceived a methodology to estimate fish productivity based on instantaneous growth rates and mean biomass, and he referred to the production exploitation rate as the "ecotrophic coefficient."

3. Embke et al. 2019.

4. Rypel et al. 2015.

5. Embke et al. 2019 found that about 40 percent of the northern Wisconsin walleye populations were production overharvested—not from rising harvests but rather from declining productivity in combination with constant harvest.

6. Pereira and Hansen 2003.

7. Grant et al. 2004b; Bethke and Staples 2015.

8. Rypel et al. 2016, 2018; Embke et al. 2019.

9. McHarg 1969; Pauly 1995; Pitcher 2001; L. P. Jones et al. 2020.

10. Berry 2012.

11. A creel limit of one walleye may not conserve a fishery, but the consequences of a low creel limit that reduces angler effort may (Fayram and Schmalz 2006). It should be noted that Minnesota's creel limit of six

walleye did not result in the collapse of its many productive large lake walleye populations.

12. C. L. Smith 1990.
13. Radomski et al. 2001; Radomski 2003.
14. Beard et al. 2003a; Isermann 2007; Haglund et al. 2016; Mrnak et al. 2018.
15. Cook et al. 2001.
16. Currie and Fulton 2001.
17. Cook et al. 2001.
18. Truncate the negative binomial distributions from complete trip angler survey data (see Radomski et al. 2001).
19. Scalet et al. 1996.
20. Noble and Jones 1993; Cook et al. 2001.
21. Sullivan 2003b.
22. Beard et al. 2003a.
23. For Minnesota anglers, Carlin et al. 2012 found that walleye creel limits had a large influence in the lakes selected for angling.
24. Radomski et al. 2001.
25. Isermann 2007.
26. See M. J. Hansen et al. 2000 for the case for self-regulating and Post et al. 2002 and Sullivan 2003a for the case that angling-based fisheries are not self-regulating. The types of lakes in these latter two studies were lower in productivity, which may be an important factor (however, see Cahill et al. 2022).
27. Cahill et al. 2022 reevaluated the walleye fisheries studied in Post et al. 2002 and concluded that forgone harvest had occurred in many of those fisheries, which contradicted the earlier assertion that many Alberta walleye populations were overexploited.
28. Post et al. 2002; Cox et al. 2002.
29. Cox et al. 2002.
30. Radomski 2003.
31. Walters and Martell 2004.
32. Taleb 2010 (98).
33. Walters and Martell 2004.
34. A fisheries quant is an expert in the branch of science concerning fisheries dynamics and analyses of fish populations and fisheries assessments.
35. For mark-recapture studies, Ricker 1975 lists six conditions that should mostly be met.
36. Bence 2003.
37. Radomski et al. 2005.
38. Hilborn and Walters 1992, figure 3.14; Walters and Martell 2004.

39. Venturelli et al. 2014 recommended that the fixed exploitation policy of 24 percent be revised. Kumar et al. 2017 used an ecosystem model to estimate reference points for a dozen fish species in a step to ecosystem-based fisheries management. For Alberta walleye sport fisheries, Cahill et al. 2022 stated that fisheries managers should be wary when exploitation rates are at or above 0.17 to 0.25 (instantaneous fishing mortalities of 0.2 to 0.3).

40. Taleb 2012.

41. A good explanation of why this occurs can be found in Walters and Martell 2004, box 2.1 and the quotation from Ray Hilborn on page 31.

42. Lake Erie Walleye Task Group, March 2021.

43. Schmalz et al. 2011.

44. Martell and Walters 2002.

45. Baccante and Colby 1996; Lester et al. 2014; Rypel et al. 2015; Tsehaye et al. 2016; Sass and Shaw 2018.

46. Examples include Sackett and Catalano 2017; Sackett et al. 2018.

47. Pauly et al. 2002.

48. Radomski 2003; Carpenter et al. 2017.

49. Schmalz et al. 2011.

50. M. J. Hansen 1989; M. J. Hansen et al. 1991.

51. Mrnak et al. 2018.

52. Beard et al. 2003c.

53. Cichosz 2021.

54. There has been an observed decline in abundance of young walleye in northern Wisconsin lakes (G. J. A. Hansen et al. 2015b) and an observed increase in the proportion of large walleye in these lakes (Cichosz 2021). Several reasons may explain this apparent reduction in walleye recruitment. First, it could be due to sampling bias, with only the best walleye lakes sampled early in the time series and a more representative sampling later (G. J. A. Hansen et al. 2015c). Second, it could be due to increases in water temperatures and largemouth bass competition (G. J. A. Hansen et al. 2017a, 2017b; Sass and Shaw 2019). Climate change is a likely reason for the reduction in walleye recruitment for many of these lakes (Brandt et al. 2022). Third, it is possible that walleye surplus production could have been reduced due to a reduction in walleye harvest and the protection of large walleye, which through predation or competition could have reduced the number of young walleye before they could recruit to the fishery. To support the latter theory, I note that walleye harvest may have decreased (the mean harvest was 1.92 walleye/acre for the period 1980–1987, and it was 0.97 walleye/acre for the period 2010–2019 [Staggs et al. 1989; Cichosz 2021]); recently there has been a greater protection of large walleye with protective slot regulations (Cichosz 2021); and the mean size of walleye in

these lakes has been increasing (Cichosz 2021), suggesting a shift to walleye populations with higher abundances of large, old fish.

55. Kayle et al. 2015. In 2018, the Lake Erie Committee extended this plan to 2024.
56. Y. Zhao et al. 2011; Hayden et al. 2018.
57. Chen et al. 2020.
58. Leopold 1949 (190).
59. Cooke et al. 2016.
60. Roseman et al. 2012.
61. Hilborn 2011.
62. Trochta et al. 2018.
63. Lackey 1998 defined ecosystem management as "the application of ecological and social information, options, and constraints to achieve desired social benefits within a defined geographic area and over a specified period" (29).
64. Zhang et al. 2018; J. P. Stone et al. 2020; Dippold et al. 2020.
65. GLFC 2007 (10).
66. Walters and Martell 2004 (12).
67. Taleb 2018.

7. Crossing the Ricker

1. Age-structured population assessment modeling is a common standard for estimating fish population abundance from the past to the present. These models integrate information about a population (Quinn and Deriso 1999). There are two families of models: virtual population analysis model and statistical catch-at-age assessment model (Walters and Martell 2004; Radomski et al. 2005). The population estimates for the most recent years are often the most unreliable, which is unfortunate given that the estimates of current stock size and age composition may be used to set a quota.
2. Quinn and Deriso 1999; Zar 1999; Walters and Martell 2004; Zurr et al. 2009.
3. Arlinghaus et al. 2017.
4. For studies on regulation compliance, see Page et al. 2004, 2012; Page and Radomski 2006.
5. Turchin 2001; Knapp and D'Avanzo 2010.
6. Carpenter and Kitchell 1993.
7. Gleick 1987.
8. The stock of fish is measured in number of spawners, weight of spawners (spawning stock biomass), or egg production. If there are changes in the size structure of the population through time, it is best to use egg

production as the measure for the spawning stock size because the abundance of adult female fish (in number or biomass) may be a poor measure of reproduction potential through time (C. T. Marshall et al. 2006). Alternatively, to address this issue it is possible to use the age composition of the spawning biomass within a stock-recruitment analysis (Shelton et al. 2012). For recruitment, the measure is often the number of young fish that will enter the fishery.

9. Beverton and Holt 1957; Ricker 1975; Beverton 2002.
10. Walters and Martell 2004.
11. Hilborn and Walters 2021 found substantial compensatory increases in egg to young fish survival rates as adult densities decline.
12. This is a characteristic of Beverton-Holt recruitment curves (Beverton and Holt 1957), named for Dr. Raymond Beverton and Dr. Sidney Holt. While recruits per stock decreases, these curves are not dome shaped. Progeny production may also become relatively constant or stable at some threshold of parental stock size.
13. Forney 1980; M. J. Hansen et al. 1998; Beard et al. 2003b; Madenjian et al. 1996; Shaw et al. 2018.
14. Quinn and Deriso 1999.
15. Baccante and Colby 1996; M. J. Hansen et al. 1998; Beard et al. 2003b; Cohen and Radomski 1993; G. J. A. Hansen 2015a. Biotic factors: Chevalier 1977. Competition and predation: Forney 1977; Madenjian et al. 1996; Fielder et al. 2007. Female walleye: Venturelli et al. 2010b; Feiner et al. 2018; Shaw et al. 2018. Abiotic factors: Nate et al. 2000; Serns 1982; Quist et al. 2003, 2004; Honsey et al. 2020; Brandt et al. 2022.
16. Cohen and Radomski 1993; Nate et al. 2011; Cahill et al. 2022.
17. Hilborn and Walters 1992; Walters and Martell 2004.
18. Quinn and Deriso 1999; Nate et al. 2011.
19. Growth overfishing is the other way to overfish. This type of overfishing is the result of harvesting too many small fish rather than harvesting too many adult fish (recruitment overfishing). Growth overfishing is taking too many fish when they are too small and when they are still growing fast, thus giving up potential future biomass.
20. Hilborn and Walters 1992 (page 241 lists the fisheries).
21. Walters and Martell 2004.
22. Hilborn and Walters 1992; Walters and Martell 2004.
23. The sum of the instantaneous rates (natural + fishing; M + F) equals the instantaneous total mortality rate (Z) (Ricker 1975, equation 1.3).
24. Ricker 1975, chapter 10, yield per recruit.
25. Ricker 1975; Bozek et al. 2011a. Ahti et al. 2021 discussed the consequences of age-dependent increases in natural mortality on fisheries management.

26. Instantaneous total mortality may be estimated in the sequential decline of number of fish by age or decline of a cohort with time (catch curve analysis; Ricker 1975, chapter 2), and the exploitation rate from estimates of harvest and starting fish population numbers. Then, natural mortality can be computed from relationship between parameters (Ricker 1975, section 1.5.2).
27. Lester et al. 2014.
28. Ricker 1975, sections 1.6 and 9.2.
29. Bozek et al. 2011a.
30. Ricker 1975, chapter 9. Bozek et al. 2011a described the use of the biphasic growth model for walleye.
31. Bozek et al. 2011a.
32. Lester et al. 2014.
33. Ricker 1975, equation 1.42.
34. Ricker 1975, equation 1.36.
35. Rigler and Downing 1984; Rypel et al. 2018.
36. Rypel and David 2017.
37. Jarvis et al. 2020.
38. Rypel et al. 2018 reported a mean walleye productivity (for ages 3 and greater) of 1.2 kg/ha/year for Wisconsin natural reproducing walleye lakes, and stocking dependent lakes had a lower mean production of 0.5 kg/ha/year.
39. Rypel et al. 2015.
40. Heidi Rantala's presentation at the Eighty-first Annual Midwest Fish and Wildlife Conference, February 1, 2021.
41. In a central Wisconsin stream, brook trout production was estimated to be about 90 pounds/acre/year (100 kg/ha/year) or greater (Hunt 1966).
42. Another way to define surplus production is the increase in population biomass that would have occurred if there was no harvest.
43. An estimate of annual surplus production can be calculated as the biomass at the start of year 2 minus the biomass at the start of year 1 plus the harvest in year 1 (Walters et al. 2008). The biomass estimates often come from population models. If using relative biomass indices from population assessment surveys, a catchability coefficient is needed, and it may be necessary to adjust biomasses to the start of the year (Quinn and Deriso 1999).
44. Dr. John Briggs Moyle (1909–1977) was Minnesota's preeminent aquatic biologist and botanist. He worked for the Minnesota Department of Natural Resources (Department of Conservation at the time) for thirty-six years as a biologist and research supervisor. He published several books on Minnesota's wildflowers, and he completed about two dozen

peer-reviewed scientific publications and many more agency investigations. Perhaps most astonishing were his writings to educate the public on fish, plants, lakes, and other natural resources. He authored about one hundred articles in the *Minnesota Conservation Volunteer*.

45. Moyle 1957.
46. Ricker 1975.
47. For a lake, the optimum water clarity for walleye productivity increases with maximum depth (Lester et al. 2004). For a 33-feet (10 m) deep lake, the optimum Secchi depth for walleye is about 5 feet (1.5 m), and for a 66-feet (20 m) deep lake, it is about 10 feet (3 m). The Lester et al. 2004 rule states that the optimum Secchi depth in meters for walleye is about 17 percent of the effective maximum depth, where effective maximum depth is the thermocline in stratified lakes and the lake bottom in nonstratified lakes.
48. Walters et al. 2008.
49. The concept of safe operating space that recognized changes in thermal and water clarity was proposed and demonstrated for the Mille Lacs walleye fishery (G. J. A. Hansen et al. 2019).
50. For some example surplus production plots, see Hilborn and Litzinger 2009.
51. NCR 1998; Babyak 2004; Shmueli 2010.
52. System thinkers generally have strong views that are weakly held (Meadows 2007, 2008; Jacobson 2014).

8. Conservation Goals

1. Winnebago Waterways Lake Management Plan 2020 (www.winnebago waterways.org).
2. All four lakes of the system are on the impaired waters list from high phosphorus concentrations as a result of high phosphorus loads delivered by the tributaries and subsequent release from lake bottom sediments (Robertson et al. 2018; Robertson and Diebel 2020).
3. U.S. Army Corps of Engineers 2010.
4. WDNR 2004.
5. Nickel 2020.
6. Kline et al. 2009.
7. Koenigs et al. 2013.
8. Priegel 1968 and Czajkowski 1993 proved that most walleye returned to the same river to spawn year after year (i.e., high spawning river fidelity for both the Wolf and Upper Fox Rivers).
9. There was no closed season for walleye on the Winnebago System, and a year-round open season was allowed for a long time on this fishery. Refer to the WDNR for the current fishing regulations.
10. WDNR 2018.

11. Nickel 2020.
12. The tag reporting rate is estimated as the relative recovery rate of standard tags to the recovery rate of high-reward tags (Henny and Burnham 1976; Pollock et al. 1991). Overestimating the tag reporting rate results in underestimating the exploitation rate. For Winnebago walleye, annual exploitation rates, μ, were estimated using the following equation: $\mu = (R/T) / (M \times [1 - L])$, where R represents the number of tagged fish reported by anglers as harvested, T represents the tag reporting rate, M represents the number of fish tagged in the population, and L is the probability of tag loss (Koenigs et al. 2013).

    Winnebago biologists acknowledge that angler tag reporting rates may vary among angling groups and across time. The tag reporting rate was determined by use of 200 reward tags ($100 a tag), with the assumption that all reward tags collected are reported. The four-year average of the annual estimates of the tag reporting rate was 33 percent (2016–2019), which is lower than the 50 percent rate previously used by the WDNR (Adam Nickel, personal communication).

    Greg Sass (personal communication) noted that female walleye are more vulnerable to angling (Myers et al. 2014) and are often marked disproportionately lower compared to males. So, this calculation exploitation rate may underestimate the true exploitation. I suspect that it may be necessary to calculate exploitation by sex and then add the male and female exploitation to get a total annual exploitation rate.

    Also see Miranda et al. 2002 for estimating the exploitation rate and confidence intervals using tag returns.
13. WDNR press release, April 1, 2002. The stated goal of the reduced creel limit was to reduce the walleye exploitation rate.
14. Priegel 1963, 1966, 1968, 1969a, 1969b, 1970.
15. WDNR 1997; GLIFWC 2007; Schmalz et al. 2011.
16. Gordon Priegel, WDNR fisheries research biologist, worked on Winnebago from 1959 to 1970, and he conducted important investigations on Winnebago System walleye reproduction and recruitment (Priegel 1970). Regarding the boil hole, Bruch 2008 described the history of the low-head Eureka Dam and how the addition of a fishway in 1988 and the conversion of the dam to rock rapids in 1993 aided in fish migration in the Upper Fox River.
17. The restoration projects varied from breaching roads that bisect a floodplain to replacing small culverts with a series of larger culverts to allow more water flow into the floodplain marshes.
18. See Vern Hacker's *A Fine Kettle of Fish* for some fish recipes (1982).
19. Barton 2011. This book is a compilation of walleye and sauger science, which updated a 1979 walleye synopsis (Colby et al. 1979).

20. Adam Nickel, Walleye management on the Winnebago, *Badger Sportsman Magazine*, July 10, 2015.

9. A Fishery Predicament

1. Radomski 2017.
2. Dengler 2017.
3. In 1843, the U.S. government published a map that labeled the lake as "Mille Lacs" as well as "Minsi Sagaigoning," which appears to be a misspelling of the Ojibwe place name Misi-zaaga'iganing (Nicollet 1843).
4. In 1995 for the U.S. District Court, fisheries biologists for both the bands and the state wrote expert reports on critical fisheries management issues. In addition, the state produced a rebuttal report to the bands' court report on tribal fisheries, which documented the state's major areas of concern and potential means to address those concerns. I was one of several state biologists involved in these efforts. In March 1996, I and a few other biologists were deposed to give testimony on the disputed fisheries areas of concern.
5. This water clarity increase implies a reduction in walleye productivity. Using the Lester et al. 2004 rule, the optimum Secchi depth for Mille Lac walleye is estimated to be about 7.1 feet (2.2 m).
6. Muskie have been recently stocked into Mille Lacs on an every-other-year basis. Muskie are reproducing in the lake; however, without the stocking, the current amount of natural reproduction likely would not support the current fishery (Tom Heinrich, personal communication).
7. MDNR stocked 10 million walleye fry into Mille Lacs annually from 2016 through 2018; however, the walleye population was sufficiently large and self-sustaining at the time.
8. Mille Lacs walleye population estimates came from the seven mark-recapture studies conducted from 2002 to 2018 (2002–2004, 2008, 2013, 2014, 2018). The median walleye population estimate was 650,000 fish (at the time of spawning, range was: 200,000 to 1,100,000 fish greater than 14 inches [356 mm] in length).
9. This walleye harvest statistic is for the time period 1983–1996.
10. Van Assche et al. 2014.
11. Moyle and Burrows 1954; MDNR 2017.
12. GLIFWC's mission is to assist eleven Ojibwe bands in Minnesota, Wisconsin, and Michigan in the implementation of treaty rights consistent with the Ojibwe way of life. The organization uses biological science and indigenous values, perspectives, and local knowledge to guide natural resource management decisions (Reid et al. 2020).
13. In the early days of Minnesota's Mille Lacs walleye treaty management work (1995–96), two approaches were promoted within the MDNR. The

first approach (the one I preferred) was what I call a "target harvest approach." With this approach, biologists would develop a harvest goal and use population metrics to manage the Mille Lacs walleye fishery so that the age and size distributions would resemble those observed in the past or consistent with well-managed comparable walleye fisheries. The harvest goal was to be a sustainable harvest range to target, with a set of operational rules to trigger management actions (this approach and some of the methods developed for Mille Lacs were later applied to and expanded on for Red Lake; see Barnard et al. 2019). Of course, the other approach—the one that prevailed—was the use of strict hard quotas with penalties for overages ("safe allowable harvests").

14. The 24 percent exploitation rate was initially conceived as a target reference point, not as a limit reference point (MDNR 1995a, 1995b).

15. In recent years, the 24 percent exploitation rate stipulated in the protocols has not been used; rather, the quotas have been set based on professional opinion (Tom Heinrich, personal communication).

16. Radomski et al. 2005.

17. If a superabundant year-class isn't harvested, a considerable surplus production may be forgone. In addition, if walleye prey become limited, vulnerability to angling and natural mortality will increase; that is, young walleye will die at a faster rate due to stresses of competition (disease, infections, starvation, etc.). A case in point was the early Mille Lacs attempts to meet quotas (2001–2002). During that time, an abundant walleye population was overly protected from harvest, which resulted in low forage fish abundance that then created very thin walleye and high walleye mortality rates due to starvation and disease. In hindsight, if a higher sustainable harvest had been allowed, the walleye population could have been in better shape in the following years.

18. Bence and Quinn 2001; Bence 2003.

19. Radomski et al. 2020.

20. Radomski 2017. Figure 2 in this document shows an example of one of the Mille Lacs walleye age-structured population assessment models used, the MDNR's statistical kill-at-age model. This model had large retrospective errors.

21. The assumption of static natural mortality is a common modeling assumption, but when density-dependence effects are evident, this is a significant shortcoming.

22. Consensus: Mille Lacs Fishery Harvest Plan, 2017–2020, dated March 31, 2017.

23. The relative abundance of mature walleye was based on the fall gill-net assessment survey of fifty-two gill nets. This index has been quite variable through the years. In the fall of 2016, this index was about 13 pounds per

net (6 kg/net), and in 2017 it was about 19 pounds per net (9 kg/net). From 1998 to 2019, the range was 11 to 31 pounds per net (5 to 14 kg/net) with a coefficient of variation of 27 percent.

24. Dennis Schupp was often called Mr. Walleye: Tom Dickson, Mr. Walleye, *Minnesota Conservation Volunteer Magazine,* May–June 2007; Tim Post, Mr. Walleye's work is a legacy for the lakes, *MPR News,* September 19, 2007; Joe Fellegy, Remembering Dennis Schupp, *Outdoor News—Minnesota,* December 9, 2016.

25. MDNR press release, January 30, 2020, announced a total quota of 150,000 pounds.

26. Radomski 2017.

27. MDNR official on July 18, 2017; American Fisheries Society Walleye Technical Committee, Mille Lacs workshop, McQuoid Inn, Isle, Minnesota.

28. MDNR press release, March 17, 2020.

29. Bence et al. 2014; Venturelli et al. 2014.

30. Chris Vandergoot, personal communication, 2017.

31. The MDNR has received excellent external reviews; for example, see Mille Lacs Lake Walleye Blue Ribbon Panel (Venturelli et al. 2014). Several peer-reviewed scientific articles on the Mille Lacs fishery have been published, but these articles focus on specific elements of the fishery and do not fully address the predicament discussed here.

32. Higgins and Vander Zanden 2010; Nienhuis et al. 2014; Gutowsky et al. 2019; G. J. A. Hansen et al. 2020, 2022; Whitinger et al. 2022.

33. Lester et al. 2004; G. J. A. Hansen et al. 2019.

34. Jodie Hirsch and Heidi Rantala, personal communication.

35. Kumar et al. 2016.

36. G. J. A. Hansen et al. 2020.

37. G. J. A. Hansen et al. 2017b.

38. A 2017 mark-recapture population estimate put the smallmouth bass population at about 67,000 fish.

39. Biologists found no significant trend in water clarity during the period from 2007 to 2015, and they suggested that the concurrent increase in the spiny water flea population reduced zooplankton populations, which allowed typical algae abundances and water clarities in the lake (Jones and Montz 2020).

40. After the elimination of walleye harvest in Escanaba Lake, investigators noted an increase in adult female walleye, an increase in the mean size of adult males, and less variability in fingerling (age 0) walleye (Haglund et al. 2016).

41. Holbrook et al. 2022.

42. Barnard et al. 2019.

43. Presentations by MDNR biologists at the Eighty-first Annual Midwest Fish and Wildlife Conference, February 1, 2021, titled "A Brief History of Mille Lacs Walleye Management."
44. Radomski 2017.
45. "To derive the most useful information from multiple sources of evidence, you should always try to make these sources independent of each other" (Kahneman 2011, 84).
46. Lynch et al. 2016a determined that inland fisheries provide 40 percent of the world's fish production and these fisheries are important for individual food security and well-being. Embke et al. 2020 estimated that anglers in Wisconsin annually harvest about 9 million pounds (4,200 t) of fish from lakes, or about 2.4 pounds per angler (1.1 kg/angler/year). Walleye constituted about 30 percent of the harvest.
47. Sunstein and Hastie 2015.
48. "Given the extensive experience the parties have with this fishery they may want to consider agreements on regulations rather than on actual yield, with careful monitoring that the regulations are not regularly exceeding their intended impact on the walleye population" (Bence et al. 2014, 33).
49. Taleb 2012. In addition, the concept of crew resource management is a system that promotes aviation safety through better communication, and with this system any crew member can question a decision and offer input.
50. Barnard et al. 2019.

10. Getting People Together

1. Treuer 2015.
2. The Dawes Act (1887), along with the Nelson Act (1889) for Minnesota, allotted tribal lands to nontribal members. The consequence was that many reservations experienced large land losses and many parcels were no longer tribal controlled. The policy of allotment ended with the Indian Reorganization Act of 1934 (Treuer 2010).
3. In 1918, Peter Graves and Paul H. Beaulieu modernized the tribal council by drafting a constitution, which enabled greater self-governance (Treuer 2015).
4. Red Lake Ojibwe became U.S. citizens with the Indian Citizenship Act of 1924.
5. Tony Kennedy, personal communication.
6. VanOosten and Deason 1957.
7. Under the leadership of Peter Graves, secretary-treasurer for the Red Lake Tribal Council, a phased transfer of the commercial fishery from state to tribal control was completed on March 27, 1929 (Treuer 2015).

8. The Bureau of Indian Affairs set the annual quota at 650,000 pounds (294,800 kg).

9. Barnard et al. 2019.

10. In 1987, the Red Lake Nation created a natural resource management department, and Dave Conner was the first fisheries biologist employed.

11. In 1996, the standardized RLDNR and MDNR fall gill-net assessment surveys on Red Lake had dramatically low values of relative walleye abundance: 0.1 walleye/net on the lower basin and about 3 walleye/net on the upper basin. Recently, these surveys have often seen 30 walleye/net or greater.

12. Memorandum of Understanding between the Red Lake Band of Chippewa Indians, the Minnesota Department of Natural Resources, and the United States Department of the Interior, Bureau of Indian Affairs, April 1999.

13. Li et al. 1996a.

14. From the 1999 Memorandum of Understanding (Attachment A–Recovery Plan for Red Lakes Walleye Stocks): "An aggressive, short term stocking effort will be made to assist recovery of walleye stocks. . . . Target levels for total fry production (natural + stocked) should be near 1,000 per littoral acre (79 million fry). Stocking of walleye fry will only occur in years when natural fry production is projected to be less than 500 fry per littoral acre. Stocking will be stopped permanently as a restoration tool if either of the following conditions are met: either projected natural reproduction exceeds 1,000 fry per littoral acre (i.e. restoration has sufficiently progressed and stocking is no longer needed); or after five attempts where stocking fails to produce a strong year class (i.e. restoration is still underway, but stocking is not assisting the rate of natural recovery)."

15. The Red Lake Nation contributed $40,000 per year of the total $68,000 annual cost for the walleye fry stocking (the MDNR paid the remaining $28,000 per year using money from fishing license sales).

16. Logsdon et al. 2004, 2016.

17. Barnard et al. 2019.

18. Harvest Plan for Red Lake Walleye—2006.

19. The mature female biomass was estimated with a gill-net selectivity model (Anderson 1998), which may underestimate this value. If they use a different fish population model, they will need to reconstruct the stock-recruitment relationship and compute new optimal level thresholds.

20. Harvest Plan for Red Lake Walleye—2015 revision.

21. Again, if they use a different fish population model, they will need to reconstruct the stock-recruitment relationship and compute new optimal level thresholds.

22. The Lacey Act protects wild animals and plants from trafficking. Under

this law, illegally taken wild organisms cannot be traded, and it is enforced by several federal agencies.

23. Al Pemberton (Ojibwe name: Coming Down to Earth Thunderbird) is a great-grandson of Peter Graves, who in 1929 was responsible for obtaining tribal control of the Red Lake commercial fishery.

Epilogue

1. Murray et al. 2009; they named the fish *Sander teneri*.
2. Murray and Divay 2011; Divay and Murray 2013.
3. This approach is commonly referred to as the molecular clock technique.
4. Haponski and Stepien 2013.
5. To put this in context, 66 million years ago the non-avian dinosaurs became extinct after an asteroid impact, and Kauaʻi, one of the main Hawaiian Islands, formed 5 million years ago over the Hawaii volcanic hotspot.
6. Stepien et al. 2015.
7. Nature proceeds by cause and effect and apparently chance. On the latter, nature itself produces uncertain randomness, from the random variation in our genes to the timing of our death and many things in between.
8. This theory was cited by Brian Eno, in a conversation recalled by Stewart Brand (Brand 1999).
9. Downing et al. 2021 note that economists often project only a narrow range of potential benefits. Using Lake Erie and reasonable discount rates to illustrate, they estimated that the value of reducing pollution to the lake for the purpose of reducing methane production even exceeded the value of those pollution abatements to beach use.
10. Nor should a civilization deny its past, for acceptance and reuse of the past generate innovation (Brand 1999).
11. Eric Sevareid and Jay McMullen, The Silent Spring of Rachel Carson, *CBS Reports*, April 3, 1963 (transcript 31).
12. Diamond 1999, 2005; Harari 2015, 2017.
13. C. D. Stone 1972.
14. The first quantitative study of the effect of carbon dioxide air pollution on global surface temperature was conducted in 1896 by Svante Arrhenius, a Swedish scientist.
15. Polasky et al. 2020 suggested making the direct connection from climate change to land use change. To maintain and enhance walleye and the water quality that they depend on, within critical watersheds we can protect and restore wetlands, ensure forest cover remains by advocating for working forests, and implement many other strategies that minimize land use changes that increase runoff pollution and flooding.

BIBLIOGRAPHY

Aadland, L. P. 2010. *Reconnecting rivers: natural channel design in dam removals and fish passage.* Minnesota Department of Natural Resources, St. Paul.

Aardema, V. 1991. *A Nandi tale: bringing the rain to Kapiti Plain.* Pictures by Beatriz Vidal. Puffin Books, New York.

Ackerman, F. 2008. Critique of cost-benefit analysis, and alternative approaches to decision-making: a report to Friends of the Earth England, Wales, and Northern Ireland. Global Development and Environment Institute, Tufts University, Medford, Massachusetts.

Ackerman, F., and L. Heinzerling. 2002. Pricing the priceless: cost-benefit analysis of environmental protections. *University of Pennsylvania Law Review* 150:1553–1584.

Adam, A., J. Bogard, J. Carriere, M. Hewison, T. Maher, G. Morin, A. Pahlke, C. Sigurdson, and R. Visvanathan. 1996. The Saskatchewan commercial fishery: final report. Commercial Fishing Working Group, Regina, Canada.

Ahti, P. A., S. Uusi-Heikkilä, T. J. Marjomäki, and A. Kuparinen. 2021. Age is not just a number—mathematical model suggests senescence affects how fish populations respond to different fishing regimes. *Ecology and Evolution* 11:13363–13378.

Ali, M. A., and M. Anctil. 1977. Retinal structure in walleye (*Stizostedion vitreum vitreum*) and sauger (*Stizostedion canadense*). *Journal of the Fisheries Research Board of Canada* 34.1467–1474.

Ali, M. R., R. A. Ryder, and M. Anctil. 1977. Photoreceptors and visual pigments as related to behavioral responses and preferred habitat of perches (*Perca* spp.) and pike perches (*Stizostedion* spp.). *Journal of the Fisheries Research Board of Canada* 34:1475–1480.

Anderson, C. S. 1998. Partitioning total size selectivity of gill nets for walleye (*Stizostedion vitreum*) into encounter, contact, and retention components. *Canadian Journal of Fisheries and Aquatic Sciences* 55:1854–1863.

Arlinghaus, R., and T. Mehner. 2003. Management preferences of urban anglers: habitat rehabilitation versus other options. *Fisheries* 28(10): 10–17.

Arlinghaus, R., S. J. Cooke, J. Lyman, D. Policansky, A. Schwab, C. Suski, S. G. Sutton, and E. B. Thorstad. 2007. Understanding the complexity of catch-and-release in recreational fishing: an integrative synthesis of global knowledge from historical, ethical, social, and biological perspectives. *Reviews in Fisheries Science* 15:75–167.

Arlinghaus, R., J. Alós, B. Beardmore, K. Daedlow, M. Dorow, M. Fujitani, D. Hühn, W. Haider, L. Hunt, and B. Johnson. 2017. Understanding and managing freshwater recreational fisheries as complex adaptive social-ecological systems. *Reviews in Fisheries Science and Aquaculture* 25:1–41.

Austin, B., and D. A. Austin. 1987. *Bacterial fish pathogens: disease in farmed and wild fish.* Springer, New York.

Babyak, M. A. 2004. What you see may not be what you get: a brief, nontechnical introduction to overfitting in regression-type models. *Psychosomatic Medicine* 66:411–421.

Baccante, D. A. 1995. Assessing catch inequality in walleye angling fisheries. *North American Journal of Fisheries Management* 15:661–665.

Baccante, D. A., and P. J. Colby. 1996. Harvest, density, and reproductive characteristics of North American walleye populations. *Annales Zoologici Fennici* 33:601–615.

Bachmann R. W., D. E. Canfield Jr., S. Sharma, and V. Lecours. 2020. Warming of near-surface summer water temperatures in lakes of the conterminous United States. *Water* 12(12): 3381.

Bade, A. P., T. R. Binder, M. D. Faust, C. S. Vandergoot, T. J. Hartman, R. T. Kraus, C. C. Krueger, and S. A. Ludsin. 2019. Sex-based differences in spawning behavior account for male-biased harvest in Lake Erie walleye *(Sander vitreus)*. *Canadian Journal of Fisheries and Aquatic Sciences* 76:2003–2012.

Bailey, C. T., A. M. Noring, S. L. Shaw, G. G. Sass. 2019. Live versus artificial bait influences on walleye *(Sander vitreus)* angler effort and catch rates on Escanaba Lake, Wisconsin, 1993–2015. *Fisheries Research* 219:105330.

Barber, L. B., J. E. Loyo-Rosales, C. P. Rice, T. A. Minarik, and A. K. Oskouie. 2015. Endocrine disrupting alkylphenolic chemicals and other contaminants in wastewater treatment plant effluents, urban streams, and fish in the Great Lakes and Upper Mississippi River regions. *Science of the Total Environment* 517:195–206.

Barnard, G. C., A. J. Kennedy, W. P. Brown, and D. L. Pereira. 2019. Walleye management in the Red Lakes, Minnesota: collapse, recovery, and cooperative management. Pages 323–352 *in* C. C. Krueger, W. W. Taylor, and S.-J. Youn, editors. *From catastrophe to recovery: stories of fisheries management success.* American Fisheries Society, Bethesda, Maryland.

Barton, B. A., editor. 2011. *Biology, management, and culture of walleye and sauger.* American Fisheries Society, Bethesda, Maryland.

Barton, B. A., and T. P. Barry. 2011. Reproduction and environmental biology. Pages 199–231 *in* B. A. Barton, editor. *Biology, management, and culture of walleye and sauger.* American Fisheries Society, Bethesda, Maryland.

Beard, T. D., Jr., S. P. Cox, and S. R. Carpenter. 2003a. Impacts of daily bag limit reductions on angler effort in Wisconsin lakes. *North American Journal of Fisheries Management* 23:1283–1293.

Beard, T. D., Jr., M. J. Hansen, and S. R. Carpenter. 2003b. Development of a regional stock-recruitment model for understanding factors affecting walleye recruitment in northern Wisconsin lakes. *Transactions of the American Fisheries Society* 132:382–391.

Beard, T. D., Jr., P. W. Rasmussen, S. Cox and S. R. Carpenter. 2003c. Evaluation of a management system for a mixed walleye spearing and angling fishery in northern Wisconsin. *North American Journal of Fisheries Management* 23:481–491.

Becker, G. C. 1983. *Fishes of Wisconsin*. University of Wisconsin Press, Madison.

Bellgraph, B. J., C. S. Guy, W. M. Gardner, and S. A. Leathe. 2008. Competition potential between saugers and walleyes in nonnative sympatry. *Transactions of the American Fisheries Society* 137:790–800.

Bellmore, J. R., J. J. Duda, L. S. Craig, S. L. Greene, C. E. Torgersen, M. J. Collins, and K. Vittum. 2017. Status and trends of dam removal and research in the United States. *WIREs Water* 4:e1164.

Bence, J. R. 2003. An evaluation of retrospective patterns and use of tagging estimates of abundance in age-structured walleye assessment models for Mille Lacs Lake. Report submitted to the Minnesota Department of Natural Resources and the Great Lakes Indian Fish and Wildlife Commission, St. Paul, Minnesota, and Odanah, Wisconsin.

Bence, J. R., and T. J. Quinn II. 2001. Review of the Minnesota DNR's Mille Lacs Lake walleye assessment. Report submitted to the Minnesota Department of Natural Resources, St. Paul.

Bence, J., T. Brenden, and R. Reilly. 2014. Quantitative Fisheries Center review of walleye population management on Mille Lacs Lake, Minnesota— Final Report. Report submitted to the Minnesota Department of Natural Resources, St. Paul.

Berkes, F., and H. Ross. 2013. Community resilience: toward an integrated approach. *Society and Natural Resources* 26:5–20.

Berry, W. 2012. It all turns on affection. Jefferson Lecture, National Endowment for the Humanities, Washington, D.C.

Bethke, B. J., and D. F. Staples. 2015. Changes in relative abundance of several Minnesota fishes from 1970 to 2013. *Transactions of the American Fisheries Society* 144:68–80.

Beverton, R. J. H. 2002. Man or nature in fisheries dynamics: who calls the tune? Pages 9–59 *in* E. D. Anderson, editor. The Raymond J. H. Beverton lectures at Woods Hole, Massachusetts: three lectures on fisheries science given May 2–3, 1994. U.S. Department of Commerce, NOAA Technical Memorandum NMFS-F/SPO-54, Washington, D.C.

Beverton, R. J. H., and S. J. Holt. 1957. On the dynamics of exploited fish populations. Great Britain, Fishery Investigations, Series 2, Volume 19. Reissued in 2004 by Blackburn Press, Caldwell, New Jersey.

Blackhart, K., D. G. Stanton, and A. M. Shimada. 2006. NOAA fisheries glossary. U.S. Department of Commerce, NOAA, Technical Memorandum NMFS-F/SPO-69, Washington, D.C.

Blann, K. L., J. L. Anderson, G. R. Sands, and B. Vondracek. 2009. Effects of agricultural drainage on aquatic ecosystems: a review. *Critical Reviews in Environmental Science and Technology* 39:909–1001.

Boehm, H. I. A., J. C. Gostiaux, G. J. A. Hansen, J. M. Hennessy, and D. A. Isermann. 2020. Indexing age-0 walleye abundance in northern Wisconsin lakes before fall. *North American Journal of Fisheries Management* 40:910–921.

Bogue, M. B. 2000. *Fishing the Great Lakes: an environmental history, 1783–1933.* University of Wisconsin Press, Madison.

Bootsma, M. L., L. Miller, G. G. Sass, P. T. Euclide, and W. A. Larson. 2021. The ghosts of propagation past: haplotype information clarifies the relative influence of stocking history and phylogeographic processes on contemporary population structure of walleye (*Sander vitreus*). *Evolutionary Applications* 14:1124–1144.

Bowles, E., K. Marin, S. Mogensen, P. MacLeod, and D. J. Fraser. 2019. Size reductions and genomic changes within two generation in wild walleye population: associated with harvest? *Evolutionary Applications* 13:1128–1144.

Bozek, M. A., D. A. Baccante, and N. P. Lester. 2011a. Walleye and sauger life history. Pages 233–301 *in* B. A. Barton, editor. *Biology, management, and culture of walleye and sauger.* American Fisheries Society, Bethesda, Maryland.

Bozek, M. A., T. J. Haxton, and J. K Raabe. 2011b. Walleye and sauger habitat. Pages 133–197 *in* B. A. Barton, editor. *Biology, management, and culture of walleye and sauger.* American Fisheries Society, Bethesda, Maryland.

Braekevelt, C. R., D. B. McIntyre, and F. J. Ward. 1989. Development of the retinal tapetum lucidum of the walleye (*Stizostedion vitreum vitreum*). *Histology and Histopathology* 4:63–70.

Brahney, J., M. Hallerud, E. Heim, M. Hahnenberger, and S. Sukumaran. 2020. Plastic rain in protected areas of the United States. *Science* 368:1257–1260.

Brand, S. 1999. *The clock of the long now.* Basic Books, New York.

Brandt, E. J., Z. S. Feiner, A. W. Latzke, and D. A. Isermann. 2022. Similar environmental conditions are associated with walleye and yellow perch recruitment success in Wisconsin lakes. North American Journal of Fisheries Management. In press.

Bruch, R. M. 2008. Lake sturgeon use of the Eureka dam fishway, upper Fox River, Wisconsin, USA. Pages 88–94 *in* H. Rosenthal, P. Bronzi, M. Spezia, and C. Poggioli, editors. *Passages for fish: overcoming barriers for large migratory species.* World Sturgeon Conversation Society, Special Publication Number 2.

Bruner, J. C. 2021. *Stizostedion* Rafinesque, 1820 (Percidae) is the valid generic name for walleye, sauger, and Eurasian pikeperch. *Fisheries* 46:298–302.

Bulkowski, L., and J. W. Meade. 1983. Change in phototaxis during early development of walleye. *Transactions of the American Fisheries Society* 112:445–447.

Bunnell, D. B., S. A. Ludsin, R. L. Knight, L. G. Rudstam, C. E. Williamson, T. O. Höök, P. C. Collingsworth, B. M. Lesht, R. P. Barbiero, A. E. Scofield, E. S. Rutherford, L. Gaynor, H. A. Vanderploeg, and M. A. Koops. 2021. Consequences of changing water clarity on the fish and fisheries of the Laurentian Great Lakes. *Canadian Journal of Fisheries and Aquatic Sciences* 78:1524–1542.

Cahill, C. L., S. C. Anderson, A. J. Paul, L. MacPherson, M. G. Sullivan, B. van Poorten, C. J. Walters, and J. R. Post. 2020. A spatial-temporal approach to modeling somatic growth across inland recreational fisheries landscapes. *Canadian Journal of Fisheries and Aquatic Sciences* 77:1822–1835.

Cahill, C. L., C. J. Walters, A. J. Paul, M. G. Sullivan, and J. R. Post. 2022. Unveiling the recovery dynamics of walleye after the invisible collapse. *Canadian Journal of Fisheries and Aquatic Sciences*. In press.

Callicott, J. B., and E. T. Freyfogle, editors. 1999. *Aldo Leopold: for the health of the land. Previously unpublished essays and other writings.* Island Press/ Shearwater Books, Washington, D.C.

Callicott, J. B., L. B. Crowder, and K. Mumford. 1999. Current normative concepts in conservation. *Conservation Biology* 13:22–35.

Campbell, E. A. 1998. Predation by small walleyes on yellow perch: effects of prey size distribution. *Transactions of the American Fisheries Society* 127:588–597.

Carlin, C., S. A. Schroeder, and D. C. Fulton. 2012. Site choice among Minnesota walleye anglers: the influence of resource conditions, regulations and catch orientation on lake preference. *North American Journal of Fisheries Management* 32:299–312.

Carlson, A. K., P. E. Bailey, M. J. Fincel, and B. D. S. Graeb. 2016. Otoliths as elemental tracers of walleye environmental history: insights for interjurisdictional fisheries management. *Lake and Reservoir Management* 32:329–340.

Carpenter, S. R. 2008. Phosphorus control is critical to mitigating eutrophication. *Proceedings of the National Academy of Science of the United States of America* 105:11039–11040.

Carpenter, S. R., and J. F. Kitchell. 1993. *The trophic cascade in lakes.* Cambridge University Press, New York.

Carpenter, S. R., N. F. Caraco, D. L. Correll, R. W. Howarth, A. N. Sharpley, and V. H. Smith. 1998. Nonpoint pollution of surface waters with phosphorus and nitrogen. *Ecological Applications* 8:559–568.

Carpenter, S. R., E. H. Stanley, and M. J. Vander Zanden. 2011. State of the world's freshwater ecosystems: physical, chemical, and biological changes. *Annual Review of Environment and Resources* 36:75–99.

Carpenter, S. R., W. A. Brock, G. J. A. Hansen, J. F. Hansen, J. M. Hennessy, D. A. Isermann, E. J. Pedersen, K. M. Perales, A. L. Rypel, G. G. Sass, T. D. Tunney, and M. J. Vander Zanden. 2017. Defining a safe operating space for inland recreational fisheries. *Fish and Fisheries* 18:1150–1160.

Casselman, S. J., A. I. Schulte-Hostedde, and R. Montgomerie. 2006. Sperm quality influences male fertilization success in walleye *(Sander vitreus)*. *Canadian Journal of Fisheries and Aquatic Sciences* 63:2119–2125.

Castañeda, R. A., C. M. M. Burliuk, J. M. Casselman, S. J. Cooke, K. M. Dunmall, L. S. Forbes, C. T. Hasler, K. L. Howland, J. A. Hutchings, G. M Klein, V. M Nguyen, M. H. H. Price, A. J. Reid, J. D. Reist, J. D. Reynolds, A. Van Nynatten, and N. E. Mandrak. 2020. A brief history of fisheries in Canada. *Fisheries* 45:303–318.

Chen, K.-Y., S. A. Ludsin, B. J. Marcek, J. W. Olesik, and E. A. Marschall. 2020. Otolith microchemistry shows natal philopatry of walleye in western Lake Erie. *Journal of Great Lakes Research* 46:1349–1357.

Chevalier, J. R. 1973. Cannibalism as a factor in first year survival of walleye in Oneida Lake, 1973. *Transactions of the American Fisheries Society* 102:739–744.

Chevalier, J. R. 1977. Changes in walleye *(Stizostedion vitreum vitreum)* population in Rainy Lake and factors in abundance. *Journal of the Fisheries Research Board of Canada* 34:1696–1702.

Christie, G. C., and H. A. Regier. 1988. Measures of optimal thermal habitat and their relationship to yields for four commercial fish species. *Canadian Journal of Fisheries and Aquatic Sciences* 45:301–314.

Chu, C., C. K. Minns, J. E. Moore, and E. S. Millard. 2004. Impact of oligotrophication, temperature, and water levels on walleye habitat in the Bay of Quinte, Lake Ontario. *Transactions of the American Fisheries Society* 133:868–879.

Chu, C., L. Ellis, and D.T. de Kerckhove. 2018. Effectiveness of terrestrial protected areas for lake fish community conservation. *Conservation Biology* 32:607–618.

Cialdini, R. B. 2006. *Influence: the psychology of persuasion*, revised edition. HarperCollins, New York.

Cichosz, T. A. 2021. Wisconsin Department of Natural Resources 2019–2020 Ceded Territory fishery assessment report. Wisconsin Department of Natural Resources, Bureau of Fisheries Management, Administrative Report 95, Madison.

Clair, T. A., I. F. Dennis, and R. Vet. 2011. Water chemistry and dissolved organic carbon trends in lakes from Canada's Atlantic Provinces: no recovery from acidification measured after 25 years of lake monitoring. *Canadian Journal of Fisheries and Aquatic Sciences* 68:663–674.

Cobb, E. W. 1923. Pike-perch propagation in northern Minnesota. *Transactions of the American Fisheries Society* 53:95–105.

Cohen, Y., and P. Radomski. 1993. Water level regulations and fisheries in Rainy Lake and the Namakan Reservoir. *Canadian Journal of Fisheries and Aquatic Sciences* 50:1934–1945.

Colby, P. J., R. E. McNicol, and R. A. Ryder. 1979. Synopsis of biological data on the walleye *Stizostedion v. virtreum* (Mitchill 1918). Food and Agriculture Organization of the United Nations, Fisheries Synopsis 119, FAO, Rome.

Colby, P. J., P. A. Ryan, D. H. Schupp, and S. L. Serns. 1987. Interaction in north-temperate lake fish communities. *Canadian Journal of Fisheries and Aquatic Sciences* 44:104–128.

Cook, M. F., T. J. Goeman, P. J. Radomski, J. A. Younk, and P. C. Jacobson. 2001. Creel limits in Minnesota: a proposal for change. *Fisheries* 26(5):19–26.

Cooke, S. J., and H. L. Schramm. 2007. Catch-and-release science and its application to conservation and management of recreational fisheries. *Fisheries Management and Ecology* 14:73–79.

Cooke, S. J., S. Hinch, M. C. Lucas, and M. Lutcavage. 2012. Passive capture techniques. Pages 819–881 *in* A. V. Zale, D. L. Parrish, and T. M. Sutton, editors. *Fisheries techniques*, 3rd edition. American Fisheries Society, Bethesda, Maryland.

Cooke, S. J., V. M. Nguyen, J. M. Dettmers, R. Arlinghaus, M. C. Quist, D. Tweddle, O. L. F. Weyl, R. Raghavan, M. Portocarreo-Aya, E. Agudelo Cordoba, and I. G. Cowx. 2016. Sustainable inland fisheries—perspectives from the recreational, commercial and subsistence sectors from around the globe. Pages 467-505 *in* G. P. Closs, M. Krkosek, and J. D. Olden, editors. *Conservation of Freshwater Fishes.* Cambridge University Press, Cambridge, UK.

Corbett, B. W., and P. M. Powles. 1986. Spawning and larval drift of sympatric walleyes and white suckers in an Ontario stream. *Transactions of the American Fisheries Society* 115:41–46.

Cox, S., T. D. Beard Jr., and C. Walters. 2002. Harvest control in open-access sport fisheries: hot rod or asleep at the reel? *Bulletin of Marine Science* 70:749–761.

Currie, L. K., and D. C. Fulton. 2001. Managing Minnesota's fisheries resources: a review of angler and resort owner attitudes towards bag limits. Minnesota Cooperative Fish and Wildlife Research Unit. Report submitted to Minnesota Department of Natural Resources, St. Paul.

Czajkowski, S. P. 1993. Distribution, movement, and population statistics of walleyes *Stizostedion vitreum* in the Lake Winnebago System, Wisconsin. Master's thesis, University of Wisconsin–Stevens Point.

Daily, J. B. 1996. Pond culture of fingerlings in undrainable ponds. Pages 147–150 *in* R. C. Summerfelt, editor. *Walleye culture manual.* NCRAC Culture Series 1010, North Central Regional Aquaculture Center Publications Office, Iowa State University, Ames.

Darwin, C. 1859. *On the origin of species by means of natural selection, or the preservation of favoured races in the struggle for life.* John Murray, London, UK.

Davis, M. A., M. K. Chew, R. J. Hobbs, A. E. Lugo, J. J. Ewel, G. J. Vermeij, J. H. Brown, M. L. Rosenzweig, M. R. Gardener, S. P. Carroll, K. Thompson, S. T. A. Pickett, J. C. Stromberg, P. Del Tredici, K. N. Suding, J. G. Ehrenfeld, J. P. Grime, J. Mascaro, and J. C. Briggs. 2011. Don't judge species on their origins. *Nature* 474(7350):153–154.

Dembkowski, D. J., D. A. Isermann, and R. P. Koenigs. 2017. Walleye age estimation using otoliths and dorsal spines: preparation techniques and sampling guidelines based on sex and total length. *Journal of Fish and Wildlife Management* 8:474–486.

Dembkowski, D. J., D. A. Isermann, S. R. Hogler, W. A. Larson, and K. N. Turnquist. 2018. Stock structure, dynamics, demographics, and movements of walleyes spawning in four tributaries to Green Bay. *Journal of Great Lakes Research* 44:970–978.

Dengle, E. L. 2017. Minnesota at a glance: Quaternary glacial geology. University of Minnesota, Minnesota Geological Survey, St. Paul.

Deroba, J. J., M. J. Hansen, N. A. Nate, and J. M. Hennessy. 2007. Temporal profiles of walleye angling effort, harvest rate, and harvest in northern Wisconsin lakes. *North American Journal of Fisheries Management* 27:717–727.

Diamond, J. 1999. *Guns, germs and steel: fates of human societies.* W. W. Norton, New York.

Diamond, J. 2005. *Collapse: how societies choose to fail or succeed.* Viking, New York.

Di Giulio, R. T., and D. E. Hinton, editors. 2008. *The toxicology of fishes.* CRC Press, Boca Raton, Florida.

Dippold, D. A., N. R. Aloysius, S. C. Keitzer, H. Yen, J. G. Arnold, P. Daggupati, M. E. Fraker, J. F. Martin, D. M. Robertson, S. P. Sowa, M-V. V. Johnson, M. J. White, and S. A. Ludsin. 2020. Forecasting the combined effects of anticipated climate change and agricultural conservation practices on fish recruitment dynamics in Lake Erie. *Freshwater Biology* 65:1487–1508.

Divay, J. D., and A. M. Murray. 2013. A mid-Miocene ichthyofauna from the Wood Mountain Formation, Saskatchewan, Canada. *Journal of Vertebrate Paleontology* 33:1269–1291.

Dobie, J. 1956. Walleye pond management in Minnesota. *Progressive Fish-Culturist* 18:51–57.

Downing, J. A., S. Polasky, S. M. Olmstead, and S. C. Newbold. 2021. Protecting local water quality has global benefits. *Nature Communications* 12:2709.

Dugan, H. A., S. L. Bartlett, S. M. Burke, J. P. Doubek, F. E. Krivak-Tetley, N. K. Skaff, J. C. Summers, K. J. Farrell, I. M. McCullough, A. M. Morales-Williams, D. C. Roberts, Z. Ouyang, F. Scordo, P. C. Hanson, and K. C. Weathers. 2017. Salting our freshwater lakes. *Proceedings of the National Academy of Science of the United States of America* 114:4453–4458.

Eddy, S., and J. C. Underhill. 1974. *Northern fishes*. University of Minnesota Press, Minneapolis.

Elliott, C. W., M. S. Ridgway, E. Brown, and B. L. Tufts. 2022. Spatial ecology of Bay of Quinte walleye (*Sander vitreus*): annual timing, extent, and patterns of migration in eastern Lake Ontario. *Journal of Great Lakes Research* 48:159–170.

Elliott, S. M., M. E. Brigham, K. E. Lee, J. A. Banda, S. J. Choy, D. J. Gefell, T. A. Minarik, J. N. Moore, and Z. G. Jorgenson. 2017. Contaminants of emerging concern in tributaries to the Laurentian Great Lakes: I. Patterns of occurrence. *PLOS ONE* 12(9):e0182868.

Ellis, D. V., and M. A. Giles. 1965. The spawning behavior of walleye, *Stizostedion vitreum. Transactions of the American Fisheries Society* 94:358–362.

Embke, H. S., A. L. Rypel, S. R. Carpenter, G. G. Sass, D. Ogle, T. Cichosz, J. Hennessy, T. E. Essington, and M. J. Vander Zanden. 2019. Production dynamics reveal hidden overharvest of inland recreational fisheries. *Proceedings of the National Academy of Science of the United States of America* 116:24676–24681.

Embke, H. S., T. D. Beard Jr., A. J. Lynch, and M. J. Vander Zanden. 2020. Fishing for food: quantifying recreational fish harvest in Wisconsin lakes. *Fisheries* 45:647–655.

Engel, S., M. H. Hoff, and S. P. Newman. 2000. Walleye fry hatching, diet, growth, and abundance in Escanaba Lake, Wisconsin. Wisconsin Department of Natural Resources, Research Report 184, Madison.

Enger, P. S., H. E. Karlsen, F. R. Knudsen, and O. Sand. 1993. Detection and reaction of fish to infrasound. *ICES Marine Science Symposia* 196:108–112.

Fang, X., P. C. Jacobson, H. G. Stefan, S. R. Alam, and D. L. Pereira. 2012. Identifying cisco refuge lakes in Minnesota under future climate scenarios. *Transactions of the American Fisheries Society* 141:1608–1621.

Fayram, A. H., and P. J. Schmalz. 2006. Evaluation of a modified bag limit for walleyes in Wisconsin: effects of decreased angler effort and lake selection. *North American Journal of Fisheries Management* 26:606–611.

Fayram, A. H., M. J. Hansen, and T. J. Ehlinger. 2005. Interactions between walleyes and four fish species with implications for walleye stocking. *North American Journal of Fisheries Management* 25:1321–1330.

Feiner, Z. S., S. L. Shaw, and G. G. Sass. 2018. Influences of female body condition on recruitment success in Wisconsin lakes. *Canadian Journal of Fisheries and Aquatic Sciences* 76:2131–2144.

Fellegy, J. 1973. *Walleyes and walleye fishing*. Dillon Press, Minneapolis.

Fenton, R., J. A. Mathias, and G. E. E. Moodie. 1996. Recent and future demand for walleye in North America. *Fisheries* 21(1):6–12.

Ficke, A. D., C. A. Myrick, and L. J. Hansen. 2007. Potential impacts of global climate change on freshwater fisheries. *Reviews in Fisheries Biology and Fisheries* 17:581–613.

Fielder, D. G., J. S. Schaeffer, and M. Thomas. 2007. Environmental and ecological conditions surrounding the production of large year classes of walleye (*Sander vitreus*) in Saginaw Bay, Lake Huron. *Journal of Great Lakes Research* 33:118–132.

Filazzola, A., K. Blagrave, M. A. Imrit, and S. Sharma. 2020. Climate change drives increases in extreme events for lake ice in the Northern Hemisphere. *Geophysical Research Letters* 47:e2020GL089608.

Fisheries and Oceans Canada. 2019. Survey of recreational fishing in Canada, 2015. Fisheries and Oceans Canada, Catalogue No. Fs42–1/2015E-PDF, Ottawa, Ontario.

Foley, J. A., N. Ramankutty, K. A. Brauman, E. S. Cassidy, J. S. Berber, M. Johnston, N. D. Mueller, C. O'Connell, D. K. Ray, P. C. West, C. Balzer, E. M. Bennett, S. R. Carpenter, J. Hill, C. Monfreda, S. Polasky, J. Rockström, J. Sheehan, S. Siebert, D. Tilman, and D. P. M. Zaks. 2011. Solutions for a cultivated planet. *Nature* 478:337–342.

Foley, M. M., J. R. Bellmore, J. E. O'Connor, J. J. Duda, A. E. East, G. E. Grant, C. W. Anderson, J. A. Bountry, M. J. Collins, P. J. Connolly, L. S. Craig, J. E. Evans, S. L. Greene, F. J. Magilligan, C. S. Magirl, J. J. Major, G. R. Pess, T. J. Randle, P. B. Shafroth, C. E. Torgersen, D. Tullos, and A. C. Wilcox. 2017a. Dam removal: listening in. *Water Resources Research* 53:5229–5246.

Foley, M. M., F. J. Magilligan, G. E. Torgersen, J. J. Major, C. W. Anderson, P. J. Connolly, D. Wieferich, P. B. Shafroth, J. E. Evans, D. Infante, and L. S. Craig. 2017b. Landscape contact and the biophysical response of rivers to dam removal in the United States. *PLOS ONE* 12(7):e0180107.

Forney, J. L. 1974. Interactions between yellow perch abundance, walleye predation, and survival of alternate prey in Oneida Lake, New York. *Transactions of the American Fisheries Society* 103:15–24

Forney, J. L. 1976. Year-class formation in the walleye population of Oneida Lake, New York, 1966–73. *Journal of the Fisheries Research Board of Canada* 33:783–792.

Forney, J. L. 1977. Evidence of inter- and intraspecific competition as factors regulating walleye *(Stizostedion vitreum vitreum)* biomass in Oneida Lake, New York. *Journal of the Fisheries Research Board of Canada* 34:1812–1820.

Forney, J. L. 1980. Evolution of a management strategy for the walleye in Oneida Lake, New York. *New York Fish and Game Journal* 27:105–141.

Frelich, L. E., and P. B. Reich. 2010. Will environmental changes reinforce the impact of global warming on the prairie-forest border of central North America? *Frontiers in Ecology and the Environment* 8:371–378.

Gaeta, J. W., B. Bearmore, A. W. Latzka, B. Provencher, and S. R. Carpenter. 2013. Catch-and-release rates of sport fishes in northern Wisconsin from an angler diary survey. *North American Journal of Fisheries Management* 33:606–614.

Gaeta, J. W., T. D. Ahrenstorff, J. S. Diana, W. W. Fetzer, T. S. Jones, Z. J. Lawson, M. C. McInerny, V. J. Santucci, Jr, and M. J. Vander Zanden. 2018. Go big or . . . don't? A field-based diet evaluation of freshwater piscivore and prey fish size relationships. *PLoS ONE* 13(3):e0194092.

Galarowicz, T. L., J. A. Adams, and D. H. Wahl. 2006. The influence of prey availability on ontogenetic diet shifts of a juvenile piscivore. *Canadian Journal of Fisheries and Aquatic Sciences* 63:1722–1733.

Gatch, A. J., S. T. Koenigbauer, E. F. Roseman, and T. O. Höök. 2020. The effect of sediment cover and female characteristics on hatching success of walleye. *North American Journal of Fisheries Management* 40:293–302.

Gíslason, D., R. B. McLaughlin, and B. W. Robinson. 2021. Synchronous changes in length of maturity across four species of Lake Erie fish with different harvest histories. *Canadian Journal of Fisheries and Aquatic Sciences* 78:721–737.

Gleick, J. 1987. *Chaos: making a new science.* Viking, New York.

GLFC. 2007. A joint strategic plan for management of Great Lakes fisheries (adopted in 1997 and supersedes 1981 original). Great Lakes Fisheries Commission. Miscellaneous Publication 2007-01, Ann Arbor, Michigan.

GLIFWC. 2007. *A guide to understanding Ojibwe treaty rights.* Great Lakes Indian Fish and Wildlife Commission, Odanah, Wisconsin.

Gorman, A. M., R. T. Kraus, L. F. G. Gutowsky, C. S. Vandergoot, Y. Zhao, C. T. Knight, M. D. Faust, T. A. Hayden, and C. C. Krueger. 2019. Vertical habitat use by adult walleye conflicts with expectations from fishery-independent surveys. *Transactions of the American Fisheries Society* 148:592–604.

Gostiaux, J. C., H. I. A. Boehm, N. J. Jaksha, D. J. Dembkowski, J. M. Hennessy, and D. A. Isermann. 2022. Recruitment bottlenecks for age-0 walleye in northern Wisconsin lakes. *North American Journal of Fisheries Management.* In press.

Grade, T., P. Campbell, T. Cooley, M. Kneeland, E. Leslie, B. MacDonald, J. Melotti, J. Okoniewski, E. J. Permley, C. Perry, H. Vogel, and M. Pokras. 2019. Lead poisoning from ingestion of fishing gear: a review. *Ambio* 48:1023–1038.

Graham, D., and W. G. Sprules. 1992. Size and species selection of zooplankton by larval and juvenile walleye (*Stizostedion vitreum vitreum*) in Oneida Lake, New York. *Canadian Journal of Zoology* 70:2059–2067.

Grant, G. C., P. Radomski, and C. S. Anderson. 2004a. Using underwater video to directly estimate gear selectivity: the retention probability for walleye (*Sander vitreus*) in gill nets. *Canadian Journal of Fisheries and Aquatic Sciences* 61:168–174.

Grant, G. C., Y. Schwartz, S. Weisberg, and D. H. Schupp. 2004b. Trends in abundance and mean size of fish captured in gill nets from Minnesota lakes, 1983–1997. *North American Journal of Fisheries Management* 24:417–428.

Grausgruber, E. E., and M. J. Weber. 2020. Is bigger better? Evaluation of size-selective predation on age-0 walleye. *North American Journal of Fisheries Management* 40:726–732.

Green, D. J., and A. J. Derksen. 1984. The past, present and projected demands on Manitoba's freshwater fish resources. MS Report #84–4. Fisheries Branch, Manitoba Department of Natural Resources, Winnipeg, Canada.

Gutowsky, L. F. G., H. C. Giacomini, D. T de Kerckhove, R. Mackereth, D. McCormick, and C. Chu. 2019. Quantifying multiple pressure interactions affection populations of a recreationally and commercially important freshwater fish. *Global Change Biology* 25:1049–1062.

Haberl, H., K.-H. Erb, F. Krausmann, V. Gaube, A. Bondeau, C. Plutzar, S. Gingrich, W. Lucht, and M. Fisher-Kowalski. 2007. Quantifying and mapping the human appropriation of net primary production in earth's terrestrial ecosystems. *Proceedings of the National Academy of Sciences of the United States of America* 104:12942–12947.

Haberl, H., K.-H. Erb, F. Krausmann, and M. McGinley. 2012. Global human appropriation of net primary production (HANPP). *In* C. J. Cleveland, editor. *Encyclopedia of Earth.* Environmental Information Coalition, National Council for Science and the Environment, Washington, D.C.

Hacker, V. 1982. *A fine kettle of fish: rough fish, crayfish and turtles; how to catch and prepare them—and why.* Wisconsin Department of Natural Resources, Wisconsin Natural Resources Magazine, Madison.

Haglund, J. M., D. A. Isermann, and G. G. Sass. 2016. Walleye population and fishery responses after elimination of legal harvest on Escanaba Lake,

Wisconsin. *North American Journal of Fisheries Management* 36:1315–1324.

Hale, C. M., L. E. French, P. B. Reich, and J. Pastor. 2005. Effects of European earthworm invasion on soil characteristics in northern hardwood forests of Minnesota, USA. *Ecosystems* 8:911–927.

Halverson, M. A. 2008. Stocking trends: a quantitative review of governmental fish stocking in the United States, 1931–2004. *Fisheries* 33(2):69–75.

Hansen, G. J. A., S. R. Carpenter, J. W. Gaeta, J. M. Hennessy, M. J. Vander Zanden, and K. Tierney. 2015a. Predicting walleye recruitment as a tool for prioritizing management actions. *Canadian Journal of Fisheries and Aquatic Sciences* 72:661–672.

Hansen, G. J. A., J. W. Gaeta, J. F. Hansen, and S. R. Carpenter. 2015b. Learning to manage and managing to learn: sustaining freshwater recreational fisheries in a changing environment. *Fisheries* 40(2):56–64.

Hansen, G. J. A., J. M. Hennessy, T. A. Cichosz, and S. W. Hewett. 2015c. Improved models for predicting walleye abundance and setting safe harvest quotas in northern Wisconsin lakes. *North American Journal of Fisheries Management* 35:1263–1277.

Hansen, G. J. A., S. R. Midway, and T. Wagner. 2017a. Walleye recruitment success is less resilient to warming water temperatures in lakes with abundant largemouth bass populations. *Canadian Journal of Fisheries and Aquatic Sciences* 75:106–115.

Hansen, G. J. A., J. S. Read, J. F. Hansen, and L. A. Winslow. 2017b. Projected shifts in fish species dominance in Wisconsin lakes under climate change. *Global Change Biology* 23:1463–1476.

Hansen, G. J. A., L. A. Winslow, J. S. Read, M. Treml, P. J. Schmalz, and S. R. Carpenter. 2019. Water clarity and temperature effects on walleye safe harvest: an empirical test of the soft operating space concept. *Ecoshpere* 10(5):e02737.

Hansen, G. J. A., T. D. Ahrenstorff, B. J. Bethke, J. D. Dumke, J. Hirsch, K. E. Lovalenko, J. F. LeDuc, R. P. Maki, H. M. Rantala, and T. Wagner. 2020. Walleye growth declines following zebra mussel and *Bythotrephes* invasion. *Biological Invasions* 22:1481–1495.

Hansen, G. J. A., J. Ruzich, C. A. Krabbenhoft, H. Kundel, S. Mahlum, C. I. Rounds, A. O. Van Pelt, L. D. Slinger, D. E. Logsdon, and D. A. Isermann. 2022. It's complicated and it depends: a review of the effects of ecosystem changes on walleye and yellow perch populations in North America. *North American Journal of Fisheries Management.* In press.

Hansen, J. F., A. H. Fayram, and J. M. Hennessy. 2012. The relationship between age-0 walleye density and adult year-class strength across northern Wisconsin. *North American Journal of Fisheries Management* 32:663–670, errata 38:971–994.

Hansen, M. J. 1989. A walleye population model for setting harvest quotas. Wisconsin Department of Natural Resources, Fish Management Report 143, Madison.

Hansen, M. J., M. D. Staggs, and M. H. Hoff. 1991. Derivation of safety factors for setting harvest quotas on adult walleyes from past estimates of abundance. *Transactions of the American Fisheries Society* 120:620–628.

Hansen, M. J., M. A. Bozek, J. R. Newby, S. P. Newman, and M. D. Staggs. 1998. Factors affecting recruitment of walleyes in Escanaba Lake, Wisconsin, 1958–1995. *North American Journal of Fisheries Management* 18:764–774.

Hansen, M. J., T. D. Beard Jr., and S. W. Hewett. 2000. Catch rates and catchability of walleyes in angling and spearing fisheries in northern Wisconsin lakes. *North American Journal of Fisheries Management* 25:1011–1015.

Hansen, M. J., A. H. Fayram, and S. P. Newman. 2011. Natural mortality in relation to age and fishing mortality on walleyes in Escanaba Lake, Wisconsin, during 1956–2009. *North American Journal of Fisheries Management* 31:506–514.

Hanson, Z. J., J. A. Zwart, S. E. Jones, A. F. Hamlet, and D. Bolster. 2021. Projected changes of regional lake hydrologic characteristics in response to 21st century climate change. *Inland Waters* 11:335–350.

Haponski, A. E., and C. A. Stepien. 2013. Phylogenetic and biogeographical relationships of the Sander pikeperches (Percidae: Perciformes): patterns across North America and Eurasia. *Biological Journal of the Linnean Society* 10:156–179.

Haponski, A. E., and C. A. Stepien. 2014. A population genetic window in the past and future of the walleye *Sander vitreus:* relation to historic walleye and the extinct "blue pike" *S. v. "glaucus." BMC Evolutionary Biology* 14:133.

Harari, Y. N. 2015. *Sapiens: a brief history of humankind.* HarperCollins, New York.

Harari, Y. N. 2017. *Homo deus: a brief history of tomorrow.* HarperCollins, New York.

Hasnain, S. S., C. K. Minns, and B. J. Shuter. 2010. Key ecological temperature metrics for Canadian freshwater fishes. Ontario Ministry of Natural Resources, Applied Research and Development Branch, Climate Change Research Report CCCRR-17, Peterborough.

Hayden, T. A., T. R. Binder, C. M. Holbrook, C. S. Vandergoot, D. G. Fielder, S. J. Cooke, J. M. Dettmers, and C. C. Krueger. 2018. Spawning site fidelity and apparent annual survival of walleye *(Sander vitreus)* differ between a Lake Huron and Lake Erie tributary. *Ecology of Freshwater Fish* 27:339–349.

Henderson, B. A., N. Collins, G. E. Morgan, and A. Vaillancourt. 2003. Sexual size dimorphism of walleye *(Stizostedion vitreum vitreum). Canadian Journal of Fisheries and Aquatic Sciences* 60:1345–1352.

Henderson, B. A., G. E. Morgan, and A. Vaillancourt. 2004. Growth, ingestion rates and metabolic activity of walleye in lakes with and without lake herring. *Journal of Fish Biology* 64:1270–1282.

Henny, C. J., and K. P. Burnham. 1976. A reward band study of mallards to estimate reporting rates. *Journal of Wildlife Management* 40:1–14.

Herbst, S. J., B. S. Stevens, and D. B. Hayes. 2017. Influence of movement dynamics on walleye harvest management in intermixed fisheries in a chain of lakes. *North American Journal of Fisheries Management* 37:467–479.

Herwig, B. R., K. D. Zimmer, and D. F. Staples. 2022. Using stable isotope data to quantify niche overlap and diets of muskellunge, northern pike and walleye in a deep Minnesota lake. *Ecology of Freshwater Fish* 31:60–71.

Higgins, S. N., and M. J. Vander Zanden. 2010. What a difference a species makes: a meta-analysis of dreissenid mussel impacts on freshwater ecosystems. *Ecological Monographs* 80:179–196.

Hilborn, R. 2011. Future directions in ecosystem based fisheries management: a personal perspective. *Fisheries Research* 108:235–239.

Hilborn, R., and E. Litzinger. 2009. Causes of decline and potential recovery of Atlantic cod populations. *Open Fish Science Journal* 2:32–38.

Hilborn, R., and C. J. Walters. 1992. *Quantitative fisheries stock assessment: choice, dynamics, and uncertainty.* Kluwer Academic Publishers, Norwell, Massachusetts.

Hilborn, R., and C. J. Walters. 2021. Steep recruitment relationships result from modest changes in egg to recruit mortality rates. *Fisheries Research* 237:105872.

Hmielewski, K. 2019. Open water spearing in 1837 and 1842 ceded territories in Wisconsin by Ojibwe Indians during 2018. Administrative Report 19–04. Great Lakes Indian Fish and Wildlife Commission, Odanah, Wisconsin.

Hoffman, M. J., and E. Hittinger. 2017. Inventory and transport of plastic debris in the Laurentian Great Lakes. *Marine Pollution Bulletin* 115:273–281.

Holbrook, B. V., B. J. Bethke, M. D. Bacigalupi, and D. F. Staples. 2022. Assessing Minnesota's changing yellow perch populations using length-based metrics. *North American Journal of Fisheries Management.* In press.

Holling, C. S. 1973. Resilience and stability of ecological systems. *Annual Review of Ecology and Systematics* 4:1–23.

Honsey, A. E., Z. S. Feiner, and G. J. A. Hansen. 2020. Drivers of walleye recruitment in Minnesota's large lakes. *Canadian Journal of Fisheries and Aquatic Sciences* 77:1921–1933.

Hoxmeier, R. J. H., D. H. Wahl, R. C. Brooks, and R. C. Heidinger. 2006. Growth and survival of age-0 walleye (*Sander vitrus*): interactions among walleye size, prey availability, predation, and abiotic factors. *Canadian Journal of Fisheries and Aquatic Sciences* 63:2173–2182.

Hubert, W. A., K. L. Pope, and J. M. Dettmers. 2012. Passive capture techniques. Pages 223–265 *in* A. V. Zale, D. L. Parrish, and T. M. Sutton, editors. *Fisheries techniques*, 3rd edition. American Fisheries Society, Bethesda, Maryland.

Hudson, P. L., and L. T. Lesko. 2003. Free-living and parasitic copepods of the Laurentian Great Lakes: keys and details on individual species. U.S.G.S. Great Lakes Science Center, Ann Arbor, Michigan.

Hug, L. A., B. J. Baker, K. Anantharaman, C. T. Brown, A. J. Probst, C. J. Castelle, C. N. Butterfield, A. W. Hernsdorf, Y. Amano, K. Ise, Y. Suzuki, N. Dudek, D. A. Relman, K. M. Finstad, R. Amundson, B. C. Thomas, and J. F. Banfield. 2016. A new view of the tree of life. *Nature Microbiology* 1(5):16048.

Hunt, R. L. 1966. Production and angler harvest of wild brook trout in Lawrence Creek, Wisconsin. Wisconsin Department of Natural Resources, Technical Bulletin 35, Madison.

Inskip, P. D., and J. J. Magnuson. 1983. Changes in fish populations over an 80-year period: Big Pine Lake, Wisconsin. *Transactions of the American Fisheries Society* 112:378–389.

International Rainy and Namakan Lakes Rule Curves Study Board. 2017. Managing water levels and flows in the Rainy River Basin: a report to the International Joint Commission. Washington, D.C., and Ottawa.

Isermann, D. A. 2007. Evaluating walleye length limits in the face of population variability: case histories from western Minnesota. *North American Journal of Fisheries Management* 27:551–568.

Isermann, D. A., J. R. Meerbeek, G. D. Scholten, and D. W. Willis. 2003. Evaluation of three different structures used for walleye age estimation with emphasis on removal and processing times. *North American Journal of Fisheries Management* 23:625–631.

Jackson, J. R., J. C. Boxrucker, and D. W. Willis. 2004. Trends in agency use of propagated fish as a management tool in inland fisheries. Pages 121–138 *in* M. J. Nickum, editor. *Propagated fish in resource management.* American Fisheries Society, Symposium 44, Bethesda, Maryland.

Jacobson, P. C. 2004. Contribution of stocked walleyes *(Sander vitreus)* to the statewide harvest in Minnesota. Pages 113–114 *in* T. P. Barry and J. A. Malison, editors. *Proceedings of PERCIS III: the third international percid fish symposium.* University of Wisconsin, Sea Grant Institute, Madison.

Jacobson, P. C. 2014. Evolution of a fisheries scientist: from population dynamics to ecosystem integration. Pages 279–283 *in* W. W. Taylor, A. J. Lynch, and N. J. Léonard, editors. *Future of fisheries: perspectives for emerging professionals.* American Fisheries Society, Bethesda, Maryland.

Jacobson, P. C., and C. S. Anderson. 2007. Optimal stocking densities of walleye fingerlings in Minnesota lakes. *North American Journal of Fisheries Management* 27:650–658.

Jacobson, P. C., H. G. Stefan, and D. L. Pereira. 2010. Coldwater fish oxythermal habitat in Minnesota lakes: influence of total phosphorus, July air temperature, and relative depth. *Canadian Journal of Fisheries and Aquatic Sciences* 67:2002–2013.

Jacobson, P. C., T. K. Cross, J. Zandlo, B. N. Carlson, and D. L. Pereira. 2012. The effects of climate change and eutrophication on cisco *Coregonus artedi* abundance in Minnesota lakes. *Advances in Limnology* 63:417–427.

Jacobson, P. C., T. K. Cross, D. L. Dustin, and M. Duval. 2016. A fish habitat conservation framework for Minnesota lakes. *Fisheries* 41:302–317.

Jacobson, P. C., G. J. A. Hansen, B. J. Bethke, and T. K. Cross. 2017. Disentangling the effects of a century of eutrophication and climate warming on freshwater lake fish assemblages. *PLOS ONE* 12(8):e0182667.

Jacobson, P. C., K. D. Zimmer, R. Grow, and R. L. Eshenroder. 2020. Morphological variation of cisco across gradients of lake productivity. *Transactions of the American Fisheries Society* 149:462–473.

Jane, S. F., G. J. A. Hansen, B. M. Kraemer, P. R. Leavitt, J. L. Mincer, R. L. North, R. M. Pilla, J. T. Stetler, C. E. Williamson, R. L. Woolway, L. Arvola, S. Chandra, C. L. DeGasperi, L. Diemer, J. Dunalska, O. Erina, G. Flaim, H.-P. Grossart, K. Da. Hambright, C. Heln, J. Hehzlar, L. L. Janus, J.-P. Jenny, J. R. Jones, L. B. Knoll, B. Leoni, E. Mackay, S.-I. S. Matsuzaki, C. McBride, D. C. Müller-Navarra, A. M. Paterson, D. Pierson, M. Rogora, J. A. Rusak, S. Sadro, E. Saulnier-Talbot, M. Schmid, R. Sommaruga, W Thiery, P. Verburg, K. C. Weathers, G. A. Weyhenmeyer, K. Yokota, and K. C. Rose. 2021. Widespread deoxygenation of temperate lakes. *Nature* 594:66–70.

Jarvis, L. A., B. C. McMeans, H. C. Giacomini, and C. Chu. 2020. Species-specific preferences drive the differential effects of lake factors in fish production. *Canadian Journal of Fisheries and Aquatic Sciences* 77:1625–1637.

Jennings, M. J., J. E. Claussen, and D. P. Philipp. 1996. Evidence for heritable preferences for spawning habitat between two walleye populations. *Transactions of the American Fisheries Society* 125:978–982.

Jenny, J.-P., O. Anneville, F. Arnaud, Y. Baulaz, D. Bouffard, I. Domaizon, S. A. Bocaniov, N. Chèvre, M. Dittrich, J.-M. Dorioz, E. S. Dunlop, G. Dur, J. Guillard, T. Guinaldo, S. Jacquet, A. Jamoneau, Z. Jawed, E. Jeppesen, G. Krantzberg, J. Lenters, B. Leoni, M. Meybeck, V. Nava, T. Nõges, P. Nõges, M. Patelli, V. Pebbles, M.-E. Perga, S. Rasconi, C. R. Ruetz III, L. Rudstam, N. Salmaso, S. Sapna, D. Straile, O. Tammeorg, M. R. Twiss, D. G. Uzarski, A.-M. Ventelä, W. F. Vincent, S. W. Wilhelm, S.-Å. Wängberg, and G. A. Weyhenmeyer. 2020. Scientists' warning to humanity: rapid degradation of the world's large lakes. *Journal of Great Lakes Research* 46:686–702.

Jiang, L., X. Fang, H. G. Stefan, P. C. Jacobson, and D. L. Pereira. 2012. Oxy-thermal habitat parameters and identifying cisco refuge lakes in Minnesota under future climate scenarios using variable benchmark periods. *Ecological Modelling* 232:14–27.

Jimenez Cisneros, B. E., T. Oki, N. W. Arnell, G. Benito, J. G. Conley, P. Döll, T. Jiang, and S. S. Mwakalila. 2014. Freshwater resources. Pages 229–269 *in* C. B. Field, V. R. Barros, D. J. Dokken, K. J. Mach, M. D. Mastrandrea, T. E. Bilir, M. Chatterjee, K. L. Ebi, Y. O. Estrada, R. C. Genova, B. Girma, E. S. Kissel, A. N. Levy, S. MacCracken, P. R. Mastrandrea, and L. L. White, editors. *Climate change 2014: impacts, adaptation and vulnerability. Contribution of Working Group II to the Fifth Assessment Report of the Intergovernmental Panel on Climate Change.* Cambridge University Press, New York.

Johnson, F. H. 1961. Walleye egg survival during incubation on several types of bottoms in Lake Winnibigoshish, Minnesota, and connecting waters. *Transactions of the American Fisheries Society* 90:312–322.

Johnson, F. H., and J. G. Hale. 1977. Interrelations between walleye (*Stizostedion vitreum vitreum*) and smallmouth bass (*Micropterus dolomieui*) in four northeastern Minnesota lakes, 1948–69. *Journal of the Fisheries Research Board of Canada* 34:1626–1632.

Johnson, M. G., J. H. Leach, C. K. Minns, and C. H. Olver. 1977. Limnological characteristics of Ontario Lakes in relation to associations of walleye (*Stizostedion vitreum vitreum*), northern pike (*Esox lucius*), lake trout (*Salvelinus namaycush*), and smallmouth bass (*Micropterus dolomieui*). *Journal of the Fisheries Research Board of Canada* 34:1592–1601.

Johnston, T. A. 1997. Within-population variability in egg characteristics of walleye (*Stizostedion vitreum*) and white sucker (*Catostomus commersoni*). *Canadian Journal of Fisheries and Aquatic Sciences* 54:1006–1014.

Johnston, T. A., and W. C. Leggett. 2002. Maternal and environmental gradients in the egg size of an iteroparous fish. *Ecology* 83:1777–1791.

Johnston, T. A., and J. A. Mathias. 1994. Feeding ecology of walleye, *Stizostedion vitreum,* larvae: effects of body size, zooplankton abundance, and zooplankton composition. *Canadian Journal of Fisheries and Aquatic Sciences* 51:2077–2089.

Johnston, T. A., M. N. Gaboury, R. A. Janusz, and L. R. Janusz. 1995. Larval fish drift in the Valley River, Manitoba: influence of abiotic and biotic factors, and relationships with future year-class strengths. *Canadian Journal of Fisheries and Aquatic Sciences* 52:2423–2431.

Johnston, T. A., M. D. Wiegand, W. C. Leggett, R. J. Pronyk, S. D. Dyal, K. E. Watchorn, S. Kollar, and J. M. Casselman. 2007. Hatching success of walleye embryos in relation to maternal and ova characteristics. *Ecology of Freshwater Fish* 16:295–306.

Johnston, T. A., A. J. Harry, R. D. Montgomerie, M. D. Wiegand, G. A. Spiers, J. M. Casselman, and W. C. Leggett. 2021. Maternal effects on embryonic development and survival of walleye of Lake Nipissing, Ontario. *Transactions of the American Fisheries Society* 150:777–791.

Jones, L. P., S. T. Turvey, D. Massimino, and S. K. Papworth. 2020. Investigating the implications of shifting baseline syndrome on conservation. *People and Nature* 2:1131–1144.

Jones, T. S., and G. R. Montz. 2020. Population increase and associated effects of zebra mussels *Dreissena polymorpha* in Lake Mille Lacs, Minnesota, U.S.A.. *BioInvasions Records* 9:772–792.

Joseph, L. N., R. F. Maloney, and H. P. Possingham. 2009. Optimal allocation of resources among threatened species: a project prioritization protocol. *Conservation Biology* 23:328–338.

Kahneman, D. 2011. *Thinking fast and slow*. Farrar, Straus, and Giroux, New York.

Kamaszewski M., and T. Ostaszewska. 2015. Development of the sense organs in Percid fishes. Pages 227–237 *in* P. Kestemont, K. Dabrowski, and R. Summerfelt, editors. *Biology and culture of Percid fishes*. Springer, Dordrecht.

Kampa, J. M., and G. R. Hatzenbeler. 2009. Survival and growth of walleye fingerlings stocked at two sizes in 24 Wisconsin lakes. *North American Journal of Fisheries Management* 29:996–1000.

Kaufman, S. D., J. M. Gunn, and G. E. Morgan. 2009. The role of ciscoes as prey in the trophy growth potential of walleyes. *North American Journal of Fisheries Management* 29:468–477.

Kayle, K., J. Francis, C. Murray, and J. Markham. 2015. Lake Erie walleye management plan (2015–2019). Great Lakes Fishery Commission, Ann Arbor, Michigan.

Kerr, S. J. 2001. Stocking and marking: lessons learned over the past century. Pages 423–449 *in* B. A. Barton, editor. *Biology, management, and culture of walleye and sauger*. American Fisheries Society, Bethesda, Maryland.

Kerr, S. J. 2008. A survey of walleye stocking activities in North America. Ontario Ministry of Natural Resources, Fish and Wildlife Branch, Peterborough.

Keyler, T. D. 2018. Visual sensitivity, behavior, and habitat of select North American fishes. Doctoral dissertation, University of Minnesota, Duluth.

Kitchell, J. F., M. G. Johnson, K. Minns, K. H. Loftus, L. Grieg, and C. H. Olver. 1977a. Percid habitat: the river analogy. *Journal of the Fisheries Research Board of Canada* 34:1936–1940.

Kitchell, J. F., D. J. Stewart, and D. Weininger. 1977b. Applications of a bioenergetics model to yellow perch (*Perca flavescens*) and walleye (*Stizostedion vitreum vitreum*). *Journal of the Fisheries Research Board of Canada* 34:1922–1935.

Klein, N. 2014. *This changes everything: capitalism vs. the climate.* Simon and Schuster, New York.

Kline, K. S., R. M. Bruch, F. P. Binkowski, and B. Rashid. 2009. *People of the sturgeon: Wisconsin's love affair with an ancient fish.* Wisconsin Historical Society Press, Madison.

Kling, G. W., K. Hayhoe, L. B. Johnson, J. J. Magnuson, S. Polasky, S. K. Robinson, B. J. Shuter, M. M. Wander, D. J. Wuebbles, D. R. Zak, R. L. Lindroth, S. C. Moser, and M. L. Wilson. 2003. Confronting climate change in the Great Lakes Region: impacts on our communities and ecosystems. Union of Concerned Scientists, Cambridge, Massachusetts, and Ecological Society of America, Washington, D.C.

Knapp, A. K., and C. D'Avanzo. 2010. Teaching with principles: toward more effective pedagogy in ecology. *Ecosphere* 1(6):1–10.

Knight, R. L., F. J. Margraf, and R. F. Carline. 1984. Piscivory by walleyes and yellow perch in western Lake Erie. *Transaction of the American Fisheries Society* 113:677–693.

Koenigs, R. P., R. M. Bruch, and K. K. Kamke. 2013. Impacts of anchor tag loss on walleye management in the Winnebago system. *North American Journal of Fisheries Management* 33:909–916.

Koenigs, R. P., D. J. Dembkowski, C. D. Lovell, D. A. Isermann, and A. D. Nickel. 2021. Diets of double-crested cormorants in the Lake Winnebago System, Wisconsin. *Fish Management and Ecology* 28:183–193.

Koenst, W. M., and L. L. Smith Jr. 1976. Thermal requirements of the early life history stages of walleye, *Stizostedion vitreum vitreum,* and sauger, *Stizostedion canadense. Journal of the Fisheries Research Board of Canada* 33:1130–1138.

Kumar, R., D. Varkey, and T. Pitcher. 2016. Simulation of zebra mussels (*Dreissena polymorpha*) invasion and evaluation of impacts on Mille Lacs Lake, Minnesota: an ecosystem model. *Ecological Modeling* 331:68–76.

Kumar, R., T. J. Pitcher, and D. A. Varkey. 2017. Ecosystem approach to fisheries: exploring environmental and trophic effects on Maximum Sustainable Yield (MSY) reference point estimates. *PLOS ONE* 12(9):e0185575.

Kurlansky, M. 1997. *Cod: a biography of the fish that changed the world.* Walker Publishing, New York.

Laarman, P. W. 1978. Case histories of stocking walleye in inland lakes, impoundments, and the Great Lakes—100 years with walleyes. Pages 254–260 *in* R. L. Kendall, editor. *Selected coolwater fishes of North America.* American Fisheries Society, Special Publication 11, Bethesda, Maryland.

Lackey, R. 1998. Seven pillars of ecosystem management. *Landscape and Urban Planning* 40:21–30.

Lake Erie Walleye Task Group. 2021. Report of the Lake Erie walleye task group to the standing technical committee. Lake Erie Committee of the Great Lakes Fishery Commission.

Lamothe, K. A., K. M. Alofs, and C. Chu. 2019. Evaluating functional diversity conservation for freshwater fishes resulting from terrestrial protected areas. *Freshwater Biology* 64:2057–2070.

Lantry, B. F., L. G. Rudstam, J. L. Forney, A. J. Vandevalk, E. L. Mills, D. J. Stewart, and J. V. Adams. 2008. Comparisons between consumption estimates from bioenergetics simulations and field measurements for walleyes from Oneida Lake, New York. *Transactions of the American Fisheries Society* 137:1406–1421.

Latif, M. A., R. A. Bodaly, T. A. Johnston, and R. J. P. Fudge. 1999. Critical stage in developing walleye eggs. *North American Journal of Aquaculture* 61:34–37.

Lawson, Z. J., A. W. Latzka, and L. Eslinger. 2022. Stocking practices and lake characteristics influence probability of stocked walleye survival in Wisconsin's Ceded Territory lakes. *North American Journal of Fisheries Management.* In press.

Lemm, L. P. 2002. Characterization of the Canadian commercial walleye fishery. Master's thesis, North Dakota State University, Fargo.

Leopold, A. 1949. *A Sand County almanac and sketches here and there.* Oxford University Press, New York. Reissued in an enlarged edition in 1966, *A Sand County almanac with essays on conservation from Round River* by Oxford University Press. Enlarged edition issued in paperback by Ballentine Books, New York.

Lester, N. P., A. J. Dextrase, R. S. Kushneriuk, M. R. Rawson, and P. A. Ryan. 2004. Light and temperature. key factors affecting walleye abundance and production. *Transactions of the American Fisheries Society* 133:588–605.

Lester, N. P., B. J. Shuter, P. Venturelli, and D. Nadeau. 2014. Life-history plasticity and sustainable exploitation: a theory of growth compensation applied to walleye management. *Ecological Applications* 24:38–54.

Li, J., Y. Cohen, D. H. Schupp, and I. R. Adelman. 1996a. Effects of walleye stocking on population abundance and fish size. *North American Journal of Fisheries Management* 16:830–839.

Li, J., Y. Cohen, D. H. Schupp, and I. R. Adelman. 1996b. Effects of walleye stocking on year-class strength. *North American Journal of Fisheries Management* 16:840–850.

Lilienthal, J. D. 1996. Distribution of walleye fry and fingerlings. Pages 85–87 *in* R. C. Summerfelt, editor. *Walleye culture manual.* NCRAC Culture Series 1010, North Central Regional Aquaculture Center Publications Office, Iowa State University, Ames.

Loew, P. 2014. *Seventh generation earth ethics: native voices of Wisconsin.* Wisconsin Historical Society Press, Madison.

Logsdon, D., and D. Schultz. 2017. A report from the Walleye Technical Committee on the status of fingerling stocking and associated fish populations in lakes with stocking increased in response to recommendations under the Accelerated Walleye Program or Walleye Stocking Operational Plan 2010–2015. Minnesota Department of Natural Resources, St. Paul.

Logsdon, D. E., B. J. Pittman, and G. C. Barnard. 2004. Oxytetracycline marking of newly hatched walleye fry. *North American Journal of Fisheries Management* 22:985–994.

Logsdon, D., C. S. Anderson, and L. M. Miller. 2016. Contribution and performance of stocked walleye in the recovery of the Red Lakes, Minnesota, fishery. *North American Journal of Fisheries Management* 36:828–843.

Lopez, L. S., B. A. Hewitt, and S. Sharma. 2019. Reaching a breaking point: how is climate change influencing the timing of ice breakup in lakes across the northern hemisphere? *Limnology and Oceanography* 64:2621–2631.

Lynch, A. J., S. J. Cooke, A. M. Deines, S. D. Bower, D. B. Bunnell, I. G. Cowx, V. M. Nguyen, J. Nohner, K. Phouthavong, B. Riley, and M. W. Rogers. 2016a. The social, economic, and environmental importance of inland fish and fisheries. *Environmental Reviews* 24:115–121.

Lynch, A. J., B. J. Myers, C. Chu, L. A. Eby, J. A. Falke, R. P. Kovach, T. J. Krabbenhoft, T. J. Kwak, J. Lyons, C. P. Paukert, and J. Whitney. 2016b. Climate change effects on North American inland fish populations, assemblages, and aquatic communities. *Fisheries* 41:346–361.

Lyons, J. 1987. Distribution, abundance, and mortality of small littoral-zone fishes in Sparkling Lake, Wisconsin. *Environmental Biology of Fishes* 8:93–107.

Lyons, J., T. P. Parks, K. L. Minahan, and A. S. Ruesch. 2018. Evaluation of oxythermal metrics and benchmarks for the protection of cisco (*Coregonus artedi*) habitat quality and quantity in Wisconsin lakes. *Canadian Journal of Fisheries and Aquatic Sciences* 75:600–608.

Maclean, Norman. *A River Runs Through It and other stories.* Chicago: University of Chicago Press, 1976.

Madenjian, C. P., and S. R. Carpenter. 1991. Individual-based model for growth of young-of-the-year walleye: a piece of the recruitment puzzle. *Ecological Applications* 1:268–279.

Madenjian, C. P., J. T. Tyson, R. L. Knight, M. W. Kershner, and M. J. Hansen. 1996. First-year growth, recruitment, and maturity of walleyes in western Lake Erie. *Transactions of the American Fisheries Society* 125:821–830.

Madenjian, C. P., C. Wang, T. P. O'Brien, M. J. Holuszko, L. M. Ogilvie, and R. G. Stickel. 2010. Laboratory evaluation of a walleye (*Sander vitreus*) bioenergetics model. *Fish Physiology and Biochemistry* 36:45–53.

Magnuson, J. J. 2002. Signals from ice cover trends and variability. Pages 3–14 *in* N. A. McGinn, editor. *Fisheries in a changing climate*. American Fisheries Society, Symposium 32, Bethesda, Maryland.

Magnuson, J. J., D. M. Robertson, B. J. Benson, R. H. Wynne, D. M. Livingstone, T. Arai, R. Assel, R. G. Barry, V. Card, E. Kuusisto, N. G. Granin, T. D. Prowse, K. M. Stewart, and V. S. Vuglinski. 2000. Historical trends in lake and river ice cover in the northern hemisphere. *Science* 289:1743–1746.

Mahdiyan, O., A. Filazzola, L. A. Molot, D. Gray, and S. Sharma. 2021. Drivers of water quality changes within the Laurentian Great Lakes region over the past 40 years. *Limnology and Oceanography* 66:237–254.

Malison, J. A., L. S. Procarione, T. P. Barry, A. R. Kapuscinski, and T. B. Kayes. 1994. Endocrine and gonadal changes during the annual reproductive cycle of the freshwater teleost, *Stizostedion vitreum*. *Fish Physiology and Biochemistry* 13:473–484.

Maloney, J. E., and F. H. Johnson. 1957. Life histories and interrelationships of walleye and yellow perch, especially during their first summer, in two Minnesota lakes. *Transactions of the American Fisheries Society* 85:191–202.

Margenau, T. L., S. T. Schram, and W. H. Blust. 1988. Lymphocystis in a walleye population. *Transactions of the American Fisheries Society* 117:308–310.

Marshall, C. T., C. L. Needle, A. Thorsen, O. S. Kjesbu, and N. A. Yaragina. 2006. Systematic bias in estimates of reproductive potential of an Atlantic cod (*Gadus morhua*) stock: implications for stock–recruit theory and management. *Canadian Journal of Fisheries and Aquatic Sciences* 63:980–994.

Marshall, T. R., and P. A. Ryan. 1987. Abundance patterns and community attributes of fishes relative to environmental gradients. *Canadian Journal of Fisheries and Aquatic Sciences* 44(Supplement 2):198–215.

Martell, S. J. D., and C. J. Walters. 2002. Implementing harvest rate objective by directly monitoring exploitation rates and estimating changes in catchability. *Bulletin of Marine Science* 70:695–713.

Massie, D. L., G. J. A. Hansen, Y. Li, G. G. Sass, and T. Wagner. 2021. Do lake-specific characteristics mediate the temporal relationship between walleye growth and warming water temperatures? *Canadian Journal of Fisheries and Aquatic Sciences* 78:913–923.

Masson-Delmotte, V., P. Zhai, A. Pirani, S. L. Connors, C. Péan, S. Berger, N. Caud, Y. Chen, L. Goldfarb, M. I. Gomis, M. Huang, K. Leitzell, E. Lonnoy, J. B. R. Matthews, T. K. Maycock, T. Waterfield, O. Yelekçi, R. Yu, and B. Zhou, editors. 2021. *Climate change 2021: the physical science basis. Contribution of Working Group I to the Sixth Assessment Report of the Intergovernmental Panel on Climate Change*. Cambridge University Press, New York.

Mathias, J. A., and S. Li. 1982. Feeding habits of walleye larvae and juveniles: comparative laboratory and field studies. *Transactions of the American Fisheries Society* 111:722–735.

Matley, J. K, M. D. Faust, G. D, Raby, Y. Zhao, J. Robinson, T. MacDougall, T. A. Hayden, A. T. Fisk, C. S. Vandergoot, and C. C. Krueger. 2020. Seasonal habitat use difference among Lake Erie's walleye stocks. *Journal of Great Lakes Research* 46:609–621.

May, C. J., S. A. Ludsin, D. C. Glover, and E. A. Marschall. 2020. The influence of larval growth rate on juvenile recruitment in Lake Erie walleye *(Sander vitreus)*. *Canadian Journal of Fisheries and Aquatic Sciences* 77:548–555.

McHarg, I. 1969. *Design with nature.* Natural History Press, Garden City. Reissued in 1995 by Wiley, Hoboken, New Jersey.

McMahon, T. E., and D. H. Bennett. 1996. Walleye and northern pike: boost or bane to northwest fisheries? *Fisheries* 21(8):6–13.

MDNR. 1995a. Elements in a management procedure for Mille Lacs Lake. Minnesota Department of Natural Resources, St. Paul.

MDNR. 1995b. Methods for estimating yield and assessment of the Mille Lacs Lake fishery. Minnesota Department of Natural Resources, St. Paul.

MDNR. 1996. Walleye stocking guidelines for Minnesota fisheries managers. Minnesota Department of Natural Resources, Fisheries Special Publication 150, St. Paul.

MDNR. 2016. Walley stocking operation plan 2016-2020. Minnesota Department of Natural Resources, St. Paul.

MDNR. 2017. Manual for instructions for lake survey. Minnesota Department of Natural Resources, Fisheries Special Publication 180, St. Paul.

MDNR. 2020. Walleye stocking operation plan 2021–2025. Minnesota Department of Natural Resources, St. Paul.

MDNR and Ontario Ministry of Natural Resources. 1992. Minnesota-Ontario boundary waters fisheries atlas for Lake of the Woods, Rainy River, Rainy Lake, and Namakan Lake. Minnesota Department of Natural Resources, St. Paul.

Meadows, D. H. 2007. *Leverage points: places to intervene in a system.* The Sustainability Institute, Hartland, Vermont.

Meadows, D. H. 2008. *Thinking in systems: a primer.* Chelsea Green Publishing, White River Junction, Vermont.

Meine, C. 2019. The pragmatist's view: a conversation with Bryan Norton. *Minding Nature* 12(3):70–78.

Michaels, S. B. 2019. Open water spearing and netting in 1837 Minnesota ceded territory during the 2012–2013 quota year. Administrative Report 19–02. Great Lakes Indian Fish and Wildlife Commission, Odanah, Wisconsin.

Millennium Ecosystem Assessment. 2005. *Ecosystems and human well-being: synthesis.* Island Press, Washington, D.C.

Miranda, L. E., R. E. Brock, and B. S. Dorr. 2002. Uncertainty of exploitation estimates made from tag returns. *North American Journal of Fisheries Management* 22:1358–1363.

Monk, C. T., D. Bekkevold, T. Kelforth, T. Pagel, M. Palmer, and R. Arlinghaus. 2021. The battle between harvest and natural selection creates small and shy fish. *Proceedings of the National Academy of Sciences* 118:e2009451118.

Moodie, G. E. E., N. L. Loadman, M. D. Wiegand, and J. A. Mathias. 1989. Influence of eggs characteristics on survival, growth and feeding in larval walleye (*Stizostedion vitreum*). *Canadian Journal of Fisheries and Aquatic Sciences* 46:516–521.

Morgan, G. E., M. D. Malette, R. S. Kushneriuk, and S. E. Mann. 2003. Regional summaries of walleye life history characteristics based on Ontario's fall walleye index netting (FWIN) program, 1993 to 2001. Percid Community Synthesis, Diagnostics and Sampling Standards Working Group, Ontario Ministry of Natural Resources, Peterborough.

Moyle, J. B. 1957. A look at a barrel of rabbits. *Conservation Volunteer* 20:7–10.

Moyle, J. B., and C. R. Burrows. 1954. Manual instructions for lake survey. Minnesota Department of Natural Resources, Fisheries Special Publication 1, St. Paul. Revised in 1970 by W. J. Scidmore.

Mrnak, J. T., S. L. Shaw, L. D. Eslinger, T. A. Cichosz, and G. G. Sass. 2018. Characterizing the joint tribal spearing and angling walleye fisheries in the Ceded Territory of Wisconsin. *North American Journal of Fisheries Management* 38:1381–1393.

Muir, D. 2000. *Reflections in Bullough's Pond: economy and ecosystem in New England.* University Press of New England, Lebanon, New Hampshire.

Murry, A. M., and T. D. Divay. 2011. First evidence of percids (Teleostei: Perciformes) in the Miocene of North America. *Canadian Journal of Earth Sciences* 48:1419–1424.

Murry, A. M., S. L. Cumbaa, C. R. Harington, G. R. Smith, and N. Rybczynski. 2009. Early Pliocene fish remains from Arctic Canada support a pre-Pleistocene dispersal of percids (Teleostei: Perciformes). *Canadian Journal of Earth Sciences* 46:557–570.

Myers, R. A., M. W. Smith, J. M. Hoenig, N. Kmiecik, M. A. Luehring, M. T. Drake, P. J. Schmalz, and G. G. Sass. 2014. Size- and sex-specific capture and harvest selectivity of walleyes from tagging studies. *Transactions of the American Fisheries Society* 143:438–450.

Nash, C. H., J. S. Richardson, and S. G. Hinch. 1999. Spatial autocorrelation and fish production in freshwaters: a comment on Randall et al. (1995). *Canadian Journal of Fisheries and Aquatic Sciences* 56:1696–1699.

Nate N. A., M. A. Bozek, M. J. Hansen, and S. W. Hewett. 2000. Variation in walleye abundance with lake size and recruitment source. *North American Journal of Fisheries Management* 20:119–126.

Nate, N. A., M. A. Bozck, M. J. Hansen, and S. W. Hewett. 2001. Variation in adult walleye abundance in relation to recruitment and limnological variables in northern Wisconsin lakes. *North American Journal of Fisheries Management* 21:441–447.

Nate, N. A., M. A. Bozek, M. J. Hansen, C. W. Ramm, M. T. Bremigan, and S. W. Hewett. 2003. Predicting the occurrence and success of walleye populations from physical and biological features of northern Wisconsin lakes. *North American Journal of Fisheries Management* 23:1207–1214.

Nate, N. A., M. J. Hansen, L. G. Rudstam, R. L. Knight, and S. P. Newman. 2011. Population and community dynamics of walleye. Pages 321–374 *in* B. A. Barton, editor. *Biology, management, and culture of walleye and sauger.* American Fisheries Society, Bethesda, Maryland.

Nelson, J. S., T. C. Grande, and M. V. H. Wilson. 2016. *Fishes of the world*, 5th edition. John Wiley and Sons, Hoboken, New Jersey.

Nesper, L. 2002. *The walleye war: the struggle for Ojibwe spearfishing and treaty rights.* University of Nebraska Press, Lincoln.

Nevin, J. 1900. Hatching wall-eyed pike eggs. Pages 329–332 *in* F. Mather. *Modern fish culture in fresh and salt water.* Forest and Stream Publishing, New York.

Nickel, A. 2020. Lake Winnebago bottom trawling assessment report, 2020. Wisconsin Department of Natural Resources, Madison.

Nicollet. J. 1843. Hydrographical basin of the Mississippi River. Corps of Topographical Engineers, U.S. War Department, Washington, D.C.

Nieman, C. L., A. L. Oppliger, C. C. McElwain, and S. M. Gray. 2018. Visual detection thresholds in two trophically distinct fishes are compromised in algal compared to sedimentary turbidity. *Conservation Physiology* 6(1):coy044.

Nieman, C. L., and S. M. Gray. 2019. Visual performance impaired by elevated sedimentary and algal turbidity in walleye *Sander vitreus* and emerald shiner *Notropis atherinoides. Journal of Fish Biology* 95:186–199.

Nieman, C. L., J. T. Bruskotter, E. C. Braig IV, and S. M. Gray. 2020. You can't just use gold: elevated turbidity alters successful lure color for recreational walleye fishing. *Journal of Great Lakes Research* 46:589–596.

Nienhuis, S., T. J. Haxton, and T. C. Dunkley. 2014. An empirical analysis of the consequences of zebra mussel invasions on fisheries in inland, freshwater lakes in southern Ontario. *Management of Biological Invasions* 5:287–302.

Noble, R. L., and T. W. Jones. 1993. Managing fisheries with regulations. Pages 383–402 *in* C. C. Kohler and W. A. Hubert, editors. *Inland fisheries management in North America.* American Fisheries Society, Bethesda, Maryland.

Norton, B. G. 2003. *Searching for sustainability: interdisciplinary essays in the philosophy of conservation biology.* Cambridge University Press, Cambridge, UK.

Novotny, E. V., D. Murphy, and H. G. Stefan. 2008. Increase of urban lake salinity by road deicing salt. *Science of the Total Environment* 406:131–144.

NRC. 1998. *Improving fish stock assessments.* National Academy Press, Washington, D.C.

Oglesby, R. T., J. H. Leach, and J. Forney. 1987. Potential *Stizostedion* yield as a function of chlorophyll concentration with special reference to Lake Erie. *Canadian Journal of Fisheries and Aquatic Sciences* 44(Supplement 2):166–170.

Ollivier, F. J., D. A. Samuelson, D. E. Brooks, P. A. Lewis, M. E. Kallberg, and A. M. Komáromy. 2004. Comparative morphology of the tapetum lucidum (among selected species). *Veterinary Ophthalmology* 7(1):11–22.

Olson, D. E., and W. J. Scidmore. 1962. Homing behavior in spawning walleyes. *Transactions of the American Fisheries Society* 91:355–361.

Olson, D. E., D. H. Schupp, and V. Macins. 1978. An hypothesis of homing behavior of walleye as related to observed patterns of passive and active movements. Pages 52–57 *in* R. L. Kendall, editor. *Selected cool water fishes of North America.* American Fisheries Society, Special Publication 11, Bethesda, Maryland.

Oseid, D. M., and L. L. Smith Jr. 1971. Survival and hatching of walleye eggs at various dissolved oxygen levels. *Progressive Fish-Culturist* 33:81–85.

Ozersky, T., A. J. Bramburger, A. K. Elgin, H. A. Vanderploeg, J. Wang, J. A. Austin, H. J. Carrick, L. Chavarie, D. C. Depew, A, T, Fisk, S. F. Hampton, D. K. Hinchey, R. L. North, M. G. Wells, M. A. Xenopoulus, M. L. Coleman, B. B. Duhaime, A. Fujisaki-Manome, R. M. McKay, G. A. Meadows, M. D. Rowe, S. Sharma, M. R. Twiss, and A. Zastepa. 2021. The changing face of winter: lessons and questions from the Laurentian Great Lakes. *Journal of Geophysical Research: Biogeosciences* 126:e2021JG006247.

Page, K. S., and P. Radomski. 2006. Compliance with sport fishery regulations in Minnesota as related to regulation awareness. *Fisheries* 31(4):166–178.

Page, K. S., G. C. Grant, P. Radomski, T. S. Jones, and R. E. Bruesewitz. 2004. Fish total length measurement error from recreational anglers: causes and consequences for the Mille Lacs walleye fishery. *North American Journal of Fisheries Management* 24:939–951.

Page, K. S., R. D. Zweifel, G. Carter, N. Radabaugh, M. Wilkerson, M. Wolfe, M. Greenlee, and K. Brown. 2012. Do anglers know what they catch? Identification accuracy and its effect on angler survey-derived catch estimates. *North American Journal of Fisheries Management* 32:1080–1089.

Palmer, G. C., B. R. Murphy, and E. M. Hallerman. 2005. Movements of walleyes in Claytor Lake and the Upper New River, Virginia, indicate distinct lake and river populations. *North American Journal of Fisheries Management* 25:1448–1455.

Palmer, M. E., N. D. Yan, A. M. Paterson, and R. E. Girard. 2011. Water quality changes in south-central Ontario lakes and the role of local factors in regulating lake response to regional stressors. *Canadian Journal of Fisheries and Aquatic Sciences* 68:1038–1050.

Pannell, D. J. 2015. Ranking environmental projects. University of Western Australia School of Agricultural and Resource Economics Working Paper 1506, Crawely.

Parker, T. S., and C. H. Nilon. 2008. Gray squirrel density, habitat suitability, and behavior in urban parks. *Urban Ecosystems* 11:243–255.

Parsons, B. G., and D. L. Pereira. 1997. Dispersal of walleye fingerlings after stocking. *North American Journal of Fisheries Management* 21:801–808.

Paukert, C., J. D. Olden, D. D. Breshears, R. C. Chambers, C. Chu, M. Daley, K. L. Dibble, J. Falke, D. Issak, P. Jacobson, and O. P. Jensen. 2021. Climate change effects on North American fish and fisheries to inform adaptation strategies. *Fisheries* 46:449–464.

Paul, A. J., C. L. Cahill, L. MacPherson, M. G. Sullivan, and M. R. Brown. 2021. Are Alberta's northern pike populations at risk from walleye recovery? *North American Journal of Fisheries Management* 41:399–409.

Pauly, D. 1980. On the interrelationships between natural mortality, growth parameters, and mean environmental temperature in 175 fish stocks. *Journal du Conseil international pour l'Exploration de la Mer* 39:175–192.

Pauly, D. 1995. Anecdotes and the shifting baseline syndrome of fisheries. *Trends in Ecology and Evolution* 10:430.

Pauly, D., V. Christensen, S. Guénette, T. J. Pitcher, U. Rashid Sumulla, C. J. Walters, R. Watson, and D. Zeller. 2002. Towards sustainability in world fisheries. *Nature* 418:689–695.

Peake, S., R. S. McKinely, and D. A. Scruton. 2000. Swimming performance of walleye (*Stizostedion vitreum*). *Canadian Journal of Zoology* 78:1686–1690.

Pedersen, E. J., D. Goto, J. W. Gaeta, G. J. A. Hansen, G. G. Sass, M. J. Vander Zanden, T. A. Cichosz, and A. L. Rypel. 2018. Long-term growth trends in northern Wisconsin walleye populations under changing biotic and abiotic conditions. *Canadian Journal of Fisheries and Aquatic Sciences* 75:733–745.

Pereira, D. L., and M. J. Hansen. 2003. A perspective on challenges to recreational fisheries management: summary of the symposium on active management of recreational fisheries. *North American Journal of Fisheries Management* 23:1276–1282.

Pierce, R. B. 2012. *Northern pike: ecology, conservation, and management history.* University of Minnesota Press, Minneapolis.

Pister, E. P. 1987. A pilgrim's progress from group A to group B. Pages 221–232 *in* J. Baird Callicott, editor. *Companion to a Sand County almanac.* University of Wisconsin Press, Madison.

Pister, E. P. 2001. Wilderness fish stocking: history and perspective. *Ecosystems* 4:279–286.

Pitcher, T. J. 2001. Fisheries managed to rebuild ecosystems? Reconstructing the past to salvage the future. *Ecological Applications* 11:601–617.

Polasky, S., A.-S. Crépin, R. Biggs, S. R. Carpenter, C. Folke, G. Peterson, M. Scheffer, S. Barrett, G. Daily, P. Ehrlich, R. B. Howarth, T. Hughes, S. A. Levin, J. F. Shogren, M. Troell, B. Walker, A. Xepapadeas. 2020. Corridors of clarity: four principles to overcome uncertainty paralysis in the Anthropocene. *BioScience* 70:1139–1144.

Pollock, K. H., J. M. Hoenig, W. S. Hearn, and B. Calingaert. 2001. Tag reporting rate estimation I: an evaluation of the high-reward tagging method. *North American Journal of Fisheries Management* 21:521–532.

Post, J. R., M. Sullivan, S. Cox, N. P. Lester, C. J. Walters, E. A. Parkinson, A. J. Paul, L. Jackson, and B. J. Shuter. 2002. Canada's recreational fisheries: the invisible collapse? *Fisheries* 27(1):6–17.

Prentice, J. A., and R. D. Clark Jr. 1978. Walleye fishery management program in Texas—a system approach. Pages 408–416 *in* R. L. Kendall, editor. *Selected cool water fishes of North America.* American Fisheries Society, Special Publication 11, Bethesda, Maryland.

Priegel, G. R. 1963. Food of walleye and sauger in Lake Winnebago, Wisconsin. *Transactions of the American Fisheries Society* 92:312–313.

Priegel, G. R. 1966. *Lake Puckaway walleye.* Wisconsin Department of Natural Resources, Research Report 19, Madison.

Priegel, G. R. 1968. The movement, rate of exploitation and homing behavior of walleyes in Lake Winnebago and connecting waters, Wisconsin, as determined by tagging. *Transactions of the Wisconsin Academy of Sciences, Arts, and Letters* 56:207–233.

Priegel, G. R. 1969a. Age and growth of the walleye in Lake Winnebago. *Transactions of the Wisconsin Academy of Sciences, Arts, and Letters* 57:121–133.

Priegel, G. R. 1969b. Food and growth of young walleyes in Lake Winnebago, Wisconsin. *Transactions of the American Fisheries Society* 98:121–124.

Priegel, G. R. 1970. *Reproduction and early life history of the walleye in the Lake Winnebago region.* Wisconsin Department of Natural Resources, Technical Bulletin 45, Madison.

Pryor, S. C., D. Scavia, C. Downer, M. Gaden, L. Iverson, R. Nordstrom, J. Patz, and G. P. Robertson. 2014. Midwest. Pages 418–440 *in* J. M. Melillo, T. C. Richmond, and G. W. Yohe, editors. *Climate change impacts in the United States: The third national climate assessment.* U.S. Global Change Research Program, Washington, D.C.

Pulliam, H. R., and N. M. Haddad. 1994. Human population growth and the carrying capacity concept. *Bulletin of the Ecological Society of America* 75(3):141–157.

Quinn, T. J., II, and R. B. Deriso. 1999. *Quantitative fish dynamics.* Oxford University Press, New York.

Quist, M. C., C. S. Guy, R. J. Bernot, and J. L. Stephen. 2002. Seasonal variation in condition, growth and food habits of walleye in a Great Plains reservoir and simulated effects of an altered thermal regime. *Journal of Fish Biology* 61:1329–1344.

Quist, M. C., C. S. Guy, R. D. Schultz, and J. L. Stephen. 2003. Recruitment dynamics of walleyes *(Stizostedion vitreum)* in Kansas reservoirs: generalities with natural systems and effects of a centrarchid predator. *Canadian Journal of Fisheries and Aquatic Sciences* 60:830–839.

Quist, M. C., C. S. Guy, R. J. Bernot, and J. L. Stephen. 2004. Factors related to growth and survival of larval walleyes: implications for recruitment in a southern Great Plains reservoir. *Fisheries Research* 67:215–225.

Raabe, J. K., and M. A. Bozek. 2012. Quantity, structure and habitat selection of natural spawning reefs by walleyes in a north temperate lake: a multiscale analysis. *Transactions of the American Fisheries Society* 141:1097–1108.

Raabe, J. K., and M. A. Bozek. 2015. Influence of wind, wave, and water level dynamics on walleye eggs in a north temperate lake. *Canadian Journal of Fisheries and Aquatic Resources* 72:570–581.

Raabe, J. K., J. A. VanDeHey, D. L. Zentner, T. K. Cross, and G. G. Sass. 2020. Walleye inland lake habitat: considerations for successful natural recruitment and stocking in North Central North America. *Lake and Reservoir Management* 36:335–359.

Radomski, P. J. 1999. Commercial fishing and property rights. *Fisheries* 24(6):22–29.

Radomski, P. 2003. Initial attempts to actively manage recreational fishery harvest in Minnesota. *North American Journal of Fisheries Management* 23:1329–1342.

Radomski, P. 2017. Personal observation on the management of the Mille Lacs walleye fishery. Minnesota Department of Natural Resources, St. Paul.

Radomski, P., and K. Carlson. 2018. Prioritizing lakes for conservation in lake-rich areas. *Lake and Reservoir Management* 34:401–416.

Radomski, P. J., and T. J. Goeman. 1995. The homogenizing of Minnesota lake fish assemblages. *Fisheries* 20(7):20–23.

Radomski, P., and D. Perleberg. 2019. Avoiding the invasive trap: policies for aquatic non-indigenous plant management. *Environmental Values* 28(2):211–232.

Radomski, P. J., and K. Van Assche. 2014. *Lakeshore living: designing lake places and communities in the footprints of environmental writers.* Michigan State University Press, East Lansing, Michigan.

Radomski, P. J., G. C. Grant, P. C. Jacobson, and M. F. Cook. 2001. Visions for recreational fishing regulations. *Fisheries* 26(5):7–18.

Radomski, P., J. R. Bence, and T. J. Quinn II. 2005. Comparison of a virtual population analysis and a statistical kill-at-age analysis for a recreational kill-dominated fishery. *Canadian Journal of Fisheries and Aquatic Sciences* 62:436–452.

Radomski, P., T. Heinrich, T. Jones, P. Rivers, and P. Talmage. 2006. Estimates of tackle loss for five Minnesota walleye fisheries. *North American Journal of Fisheries Management* 26:206–212.

Radomski, P., C. S. Anderson, R. E. Bruesewitz, A. J. Carlson, and B. D. Borkholder. 2020. An assessment model for a standard gill net incorporating direct and indirect selectivity applied to walleye. *North American Journal of Fisheries Management* 40:105–124.

Rainy Lake and Namakan Reservoir Water Level International Steering Committee. 1993. Final report and recommendations (Volume 1 and 2). Fort Frances, Ontario, and International Falls, Minnesota.

Ramsey F. P. 1928. A mathematical theory of saving. *Economic Journal* 38:543–559.

Ramstack, J. M., S. C. Fritz, and D. R. Engstrom. 2004. Twentieth century water quality trends in Minnesota lakes compared with presettlement variability. *Canadian Journal of Fisheries and Aquatic Sciences* 61:561–576

Randall, R. G., J. R. M. Kelso, and C. K. Minns. 1995. Fish production in freshwaters: are rivers more productive than lakes? *Canadian Journal of Fisheries and Aquatic Sciences* 52:631–643.

Reeves, K. A., and R. E. Bruesewitz. 2007. Factors influencing the hooking mortality of walleye caught by recreational anglers on Mille Lacs, Minnesota. *North American Journal of Fisheries Management* 27:443–452.

Reid, A. J., L. E. Eckert, J-F. Lane, N. Young, S. G. Hinch, C. T. Darimont, S. J. Cooke, N. C. Ban, and A. Albert. 2020. "Two-Eyed Seeing": an indigenous framework to transform fisheries research and management. *Fish and Fisheries* 21:1–19.

Reinl, K. L., J. D. Brookes, C. C. Carey, T. D. Harris, B. W. Ibelings, A. M. Morales-Williams, L. D. De Senerpont Domis, K. S. Atkins, P. D. F. Isles, J. P. Mesman, R. L. North, L. G. Rudstam, J. A. A. Stelzer, J. J. Venkiteswaran, K. Yokota, and Q. Zhan. 2021. Cyanobacterial blooms in oligotrophic lakes: shifting the high-nutrient paradigm. *Freshwater Biology* 66:1846–1859.

Renik, K. M., M. J. Jennings, J. M. Kampa, J. Lyons, T. P. Parks, and G. G. Sass. 2020. Status and distribution of cisco (*Coregonus artedi*) and lake whitefish

(*Coregonus clupeaformis*) in inland lakes of Wisconsin. *Northeastern Naturalist* 27:469–484.

Reverter, M., N. Tapissier-Bontemps, D. Lecchini, B. Banaigs, and P. Sasal. 2018. Biological and ecological roles of external fish mucus: a review. *Fishes* 3(4):41.

Reynolds, J. B., and J. C. Dean. 2020. Development of electrofishing for fisheries management. *Fisheries* 45:229–237.

Reynolds, J. B., and A. L. Kolz. 2012. Electrofishing. Pages 305–361 *in* A. V. Zale, D. L. Parrish, and T. M. Sutton, editors. *Fisheries techniques*, third edition. American Fisheries Society, Bethesda.

Ricker, W. E. 1946. Production and utilization of fish populations. *Ecological Monographs* 16:373–391.

Ricker, W. E. 1975. *Computation and interpretation of biological statistics of fish populations.* Fisheries Research Board of Canada, Bulletin 191, Ottawa, Ontario. Reissued in 2010 by Blackburn Press, Caldwell, New Jersey.

Rieger, P. W., and R. C. Summerfelt. 1998. Microvideography of gas bladder inflation in larval walleye. *Journal of Fish Biology* 53(1):93–99.

Rigler, F. H., and J. A. Downing. 1984. The calculation of secondary production. Pages 19–58 in J. A. Downing and F. H. Rigler, editors. *A manual on the methods for the assessment of secondary production in fresh waters.* Blackwell, Boston.

Robertson, D. M., and M. W. Diebel. 2020. Importance of accurately quantifying internal loading in developing phosphorus reduction strategies for a chain of shallow lakes. *Lake and Reservoir Management* 36:391–411.

Robertson, D. M., B. J. Siebers, M. W. Diebel, and A. J. Somor. 2018. Water-quality response to changes in phosphorus loading of the Winnebago Pool Lakes, Wisconsin, with special emphasis on the effects of internal loading in a chain of shallow lakes. U.S. Geological Survey Scientific Investigations Report 2018–5099, Washington, D.C.

Rose, K. C., L. A. Winslow, J. S Read, and G. J. A. Hansen. 2016. Climate-induced warming of lakes can be either amplified or suppressed by trends in water clarity. *Limnology and Oceanography Letters* 1:44–53.

Roseman, E. F., R. Drouin, M. Gaden, R. Knight, J. Tyson, and Y. Zhao. 2012. Managing inherent complexity for sustainable walleye in Lake Erie. Pages 475–494 *in* W. W. Taylor, A. J. Lynch, and N. J. Léonard, editors. *Great Lakes fisheries policy and management: a binational perspective.* Michigan State University Press, East Lansing, Michigan.

Rottiers, D. V., and C. A. Lemm. 1985. Movement of underyearling walleyes in response to odor and visual cues. *Progressive Fish-Culturist* 47:34–41.

Rudstam, L. G., A. J. VanDeValk, C. M. Adams, J. T. H. Coleman, J. L. Forney, and M. E. Richmond. 2004. Cormorant predation and the population dynamics of walleye and yellow perch in Oneida Lake. *Ecological Applications* 14:149–163.

Ryan, S. F., J. M. Deines, J. Mark Scriber, M. E. Pfrender, S. E. Jones, A. J. Emrich, and J. J. Hellmann. 2018. Climate-mediated hybrid zone movement revealed with genomics, museum collection, and simulation modeling. *Proceedings of the National Academy of Sciences* 115: E2284–E2291.

Ryder, R. A. 1961. Lymphocystis as a mortality factor in a walleye population. *Progressive Fish-Culturist* 23:183–186.

Ryder, R. A. 1977. Effects of ambient light variations on behavior of yearling, subadult, and adult walleyes (*Stizostedion vitreum vitreum*). *Journal of the Fisheries Research Board of Canada* 34:1481–1491.

Ryder, R. A., and S. R. Kerr. 1978. The adult walleye in the percid community—a niche definition based on feeding behavior and food specificity. Pages 39–51 *in* R. L. Kendall, editor. *Selected coolwater fishes of North America.* American Fisheries Society, Special Publication 11, Bethesda, Maryland.

Ryder, R. A., S. R. Kerr, K. H. Loftus, and H. A. Regier. 1974. The morphoedaphic index, a fish yield estimator—review and evaluation. *Journal of the Fisheries Research Board of Canada* 31:663–688.

Rypel, A. 2021. Spatial versus temporal heterogeneity in abundance of fishes in north-temperate lakes. *Fundamental and Applied Limnology* 195:173–185.

Rypel, A. L., and S. R. David. 2017. Pattern and scale in latitude-production relationships for freshwater fishes. *Ecosphere* 8(1):e01660.

Rypel, A. L., D. Goto, G. G. Sass, and M. J. Vander Zanden. 2015. Production rates of walleye and their relationship to exploitation in Escanaba Lake, Wisconsin, 1965–2009. *Canadian Journal of Fisheries and Aquatic Sciences* 72:834–844.

Rypel, A. L., J. Lyons, J. D. T. Griffin, and T. D. Simonson. 2016. Seventy-year retrospective on size-structure changes in the recreational fisheries of Wisconsin. *Fisheries* 41:230–243.

Rypel, A. L., D. Goto, G. G. Sass, and M. J. Vander Zanden. 2018. Eroding productivity of walleye populations in northern Wisconsin lakes. *Canadian Journal of Fisheries and Aquatic Sciences* 75:2291–2301.

Sackett, D. K., and M. Catalano. 2017. Spatial heterogeneity, variable rewards, tag loss, and tagging mortality affect the performance of mark-recapture designs to estimate exploitation: an example using red snapper in the northern Gulf of Mexico. *North American Journal of Fisheries Management* 37:558–573.

Sackett, D. K., M. Catalano, M. Drymon, S. Powers, and M. A. Albins. 2018. Estimating exploitation rates in the Alabama red snapper fishery using a high-reward tag-recapture approach. *Marine and Coastal Fisheries: Dynamics, Management, and Ecosystem Science* 10:536–549.

Sagoff, M. 2019. Fact and value in invasion biology. *Conservation Biology* 34:581–588.

Sanzo, D., and S. J. Hecnar. 2006. Effects of road de-icing salt (NaCl) on larval wood frogs (*Rana sylvatica*). *Environmental Pollution* 140:247–256.

Sass, G. G., and M. S. Allen, editors. 2014. *Foundations of fisheries science.* American Fisheries Society, Bethesda, Maryland.

Sass, G. G., and S. L. Shaw. 2018. Walleye population responses to experimental exploitation in a northern Wisconsin lake. *Transactions of the American Fisheries Society* 147:869–878.

Sass, G. G., and S. L. Shaw. 2019. Catch-and-release influences on inland recreational fisheries. *Reviews in Fisheries and Aquaculture* 28:211–227.

Sass, G. G., A. L. Rypel, and J. D. Stafford. 2017. Inland fisheries habitat management: lessons learned from wildlife ecology and a proposal for change. *Fisheries* 42:197–209.

Sass, G. G., Z. S. Feiner, and S. L. Shaw. 2021. Empirical evidence for depensation in freshwater fisheries. *Fisheries* 46:266–276.

Sass, G. G., S. L. Shaw, and K. M. Renik. 2022a. Celebrating 75 years of Wisconsin's Northern Highland Fishery Research Area: the past, present, and future. *Fisheries.* In press.

Sass, G. G., S. L. Shaw, L. W. Sikora, M. Lorenzoni, and M. Luehring. 2022b. Plasticity in abundance and demographic responses of walleye to elevated exploitation in a north-temperate lake. *North American Journal of Fisheries Management.* In press.

Scalet, C. G., L. D. Flake, and D. W. Willis. 1996. *Introduction to wildlife and fisheries: an integrated approach.* W. H. Freeman, New York.

Schindler, D. W. 2001. The cumulative effects of climate warming and other human stresses on Canadian freshwaters in the new millennium. *Canadian Journal of Fisheries and Aquatic Sciences* 58:18–29.

Schindler, D. W., R. E. Hecky, D. L. Findlay, M. P. Stainton, B. R. Parker, M. J. Paterson, K. G. Beaty, M. Lyng, and S. E. M. Kasian. 2008. Eutrophication of lakes cannot be controlled by reducing nitrogen input: results of a 37-year whole-ecosytem experiment. *Proceedings of the National Academy of Science of the United States of America* 105:11254–11258.

Schmalz, P. J., A. H. Fayram, D. A. Isermann, S. P. Newman, and C. J. Edwards. 2011. Harvest and exploitation. Pages 375–401 *in* B. A. Barton, editor. *Biology, management, and culture of walleye and sauger.* American Fisheries Society, Bethesda, Maryland.

Schneider, J. C., T. J. Lychwick, E. J. Trimberger, J. H. Peterson, R. O'Neal, and P. J. Schneeberger. 1991. Walleye rehabilitation in Lake Michigan, 1969–1989. Pages 23–61 *in* P. J. Colby, C. A. Lewis, and R. L. Eshenroder, editors, *Status of walleye in the Great Lakes: case studies prepared for the*

1989 workshop. Great Lakes Fisheries Commission, Special Publication 91–1, Ann Arbor, Michigan.

Schneider, K. N., R. M. Newman, V. Card, S. Weisberg, and D. L. Pereira. 2010. Timing of walleye spawning as an indicator of climate change. *Transactions of the American Fisheries Society* 139:1198–1210.

Schultz, D. W., A. J. Carlson, S. Mortensen, and D. L. Pereira. 2013. Modeling population dynamics and fish consumption of a managed double-crested cormorant colony in Minnesota. *North American Journal of Fisheries Management* 33:1283–1300.

Schupp, D. H. 1992. An ecological classification of Minnesota lakes with associated fish communities. Minnesota Department of Natural Resources Investigational Report 417, St. Paul.

Schupp, D. H. 2002. What does Mt. Pinatubo have to do with walleyes? *North American Journal of Fisheries Management* 22:1014–1020.

Schupp, D. H., and V. Macins. 1977. Trends in percid yields from Lake of the Woods, 1888–1973. *Journal of the Fisheries Research Board of Canada* 34:1784–1791.

Scott, W. B., and E. J. Crossman. 1973. *Freshwater fishes of Canada*. Fisheries Research Board of Canada, Bulletin 184, Ottawa.

Seibert, M. K., and W. E. Rees. 2021. Through the eye of a needle: an eco-heterodox perspective on the renewable energy transition. *Energies* 14:4508.

Serns, S. L. 1982. Influence of various factors on density and growth of age-0 walleyes in Escanaba Lake, Wisconsin, 1958–1980. *Transactions of the American Fisheries Society* 111:299–306.

Sharma, S., K. Blagrave, J. J. Magnuson, C. M. O'Reilly, S. Oliver, R. D. Batt, M. R. Magee, D. Straile, G. A. Weyhenmeyer, L. Winslow, and R. L. Woolway. 2019. Widespread loss of lake ice around the northern hemisphere in a warming world. *Nature Climate Change* 9:227–231.

Sharma, S., K. Blagrave, A. Filazzola, M. A. Imrit, and H.-J. Hendricks Franssen. 2021a. Forecasting the permanent loss of lake ice in the Northern Hemisphere within the 21st century. *Geophysical Research Letters* 48:e2020GL091108.

Sharma, S., D. C. Richardson, R. I. Woolway, M. A. Imrit, D. Bouffard, K. Blagrave, J. Daly, A. Filazzola, N. Granin, and J. Johanna. 2021b. Loss of ice cover, shifting phenology, and more extreme events in Northern Hemisphere lakes. *Journal of Geophysical Research: Biogeosciences* 126:e2021JG006348.

Shaw, S. L., G. G. Sass, and J. A. VanDeHey. 2018. Maternal effects better predict walleye recruitment in Escanaba Lake, Wisconsin, 1957–2015: implications for regulations. *Canadian Journal of Fisheries and Aquatic Sciences* 75:2320–2331.

Shaw, S. L., K. M. Renik, and G. G. Sass. 2021. Angler and environmental influences on walleye *Sander vitreus* and muskellunge *Esox masquinongy* angler catch in Escanaba Lake, Wisconsin 2003-2015. *PLoS One* 16(9):e0257882.

Shelton, A. O., S. B. Munch, D. Keith, and M. Mangel. 2012. Maternal age, fecundity, egg quality, and recruitment: linking stock structure to recruitment using an age-structured Ricker model. *Canadian Journal of Fisheries and Aquatic Sciences* 69:1631–1641.

Shepard, P. 1998. *Nature and madness.* University of Georgia Press, Athens, Georgia.

Shmueli, G. 2010. To explain or to predict? *Statistical Science* 25:289–310.

Smith, C. L. 1990. Resource scarcity and inequality in the distribution of catch. *North American Journal of Fisheries Management* 10:269–278.

Smith, L. L., and J. B. Moyle. 1945. Factors influencing production of yellow pike-perch, *Stizostedion vitreum vitreum,* in Minnesota rearing ponds. *Transactions of the American Fisheries Society* 73(1943):243–261.

Staggs, M. D. 1989. *Walleye angling in the ceded territory, Wisconsin, 1980-1987.* Wisconsin Department of Natural Resources, Fisheries Management Report 144, Madison.

Staudinger, M. D., A. J. Lynch, S. K. Gaichas, M. G. Fox, D. Gibson-Reinemer, J. A. Langan, A. K. Teffer, S. J. Thackeray, and I. J. Windfield. 2021. How does climate change affect emergent properties of aquatic systems. *Fisheries* 46:423–441.

Stefan, H. G., M. Hondzo, X. Fang, J. G. Eaton, and J. H. McCormick. 1996. Simulated long-term temperature and dissolved oxygen characteristics of lakes in the north-central United States and associated fish habitat limits. *Limnology and Oceanography* 41:1124–1135.

Stepien, C. A., O. J. Sepulveda-Villet, and A. E. Haponski. 2015. Comparative genetic diversity, population structure, and adaptations of walleye and yellow perch across North America. Pages 643–689 *in* P. Kestemont, K. Dabrowski, and R. C. Summerfelt, editors. *Biology and Culture of Percid Fishes.* Springer, Dordrecht.

Stern, N. H., S. Peters, V. Bakhshi, A. Bowen, C. Cameron, S. Catovsky, D. Crane, S. Cruickshank, S. Dietz, N. Edmonson, S.-L. Garbett, L. Hamid, G. Hoffman, D. Ingram, B. Jones, N. Patmore, H. Radcliffe, R. Sathiyarajah, M. Stock, C. Taylor, T. Vernon, H. Wanjie, and D. Zenghelis. 2006. *Stern Review: the economics of climate change.* Cambridge University Press, Cambridge, UK.

Sternberg, T. 2015. Water mega-projects in deserts and drylands. *International Journal of Water Resources Development* 32(2):301–320.

Sternberg, T. 2017. Water towers: security risks in a changing climate. Pages 20–27 *in* C.E. Werrell and F. Femia, editors. *Epicenters of climate and security: the new geostrategic landscape of the anthropocene.* Center for Climate and Security, Washington, D.C.

Stone, C. D. 1972. Should trees have standing? Toward legal rights for natural objects. *Southern California Law Review* 45:450–501.

Stone, J. P., K. L. Pangle, S. A. Pothoven, H. A. Vanderploeg, S. B. Brandt, T. O. Höök, T. H. Johengen, and S. A. Ludsin. 2020. Hypoxia's impact on pelagic fish populations in Lake Erie: a tale of two planktivores. *Canadian Journal of Fisheries and Aquatic Sciences* 77:1131–1148.

Su, Z., and J. X. He. 2013. Analysis of Lake Huron recreation fisheries data using models dealing with excessive zeros. *Fisheries Research* 148:81–89.

Sullivan, M. G. 2003a. Active management of walleye fisheries in Alberta: dilemmas of managing recovering fisheries. *North American Journal of Fisheries Management* 23:1343–1358.

Sullivan, M. G. 2003b. Exaggeration of walleye catches by Alberta anglers. *North American Journal of Fisheries Management* 23:573–580.

Summerfelt, R. C., J. A. Johnson, and C. P. Clouse. 2011. Culture of walleye, sauger, and hybrid walleye. Pages 451–570 *in* B. A. Barton, editor. *Biology, management, and culture of walleye and sauger.* American Fisheries Society, Bethesda, Maryland.

Sunstein, C. R., and R. Hastie. 2015. *Wiser: getting beyond groupthink to make groups smarter.* Harvard Business Review Press, Boston.

Swenson, W. A., and L. L. Smith Jr. 1976. Influence of food competition, predation, and cannibalism on walleye *(Stizostedion vitreum vitreum)* and sauger *(S. canadense)* populations in Lake of the Woods, Minnesota. *Journal of the Fisheries Research Board of Canada* 33:1946–1954.

Taleb, N. N. 2007. *The black swan.* Random House, New York.

Taleb, N. N. 2010. *The bed of Procrustes: philosophical and practical aphorisms.* Random House, New York.

Taleb, N. N. 2012. *Antifragile.* Random House, New York.

Taleb, N. N. 2018. *Skin in the game.* Random House, New York.

Talmage, P. J., and D. F. Staples. 2011. Mortality of walleyes angled from the deep water of Rainy Lake, Minnesota. *North American Journal of Fisheries Management* 31:826–831.

Thomas, L. M., Z. G. Jorgenson, M. E. Brigham, S. J. Choy, J. N. Moore, J. A. Banda, D. J. Gefell, T. A. Minarik, and H. L. Schoenfuss. 2017. Contaminants of emerging concern in tributaries to the Laurentian Great Lakes: II. Biological consequences of exposure. *PLoS ONE* 12(9):e0184725.

Thompson, D. 1996. Stripping, fertilizing, and incubating walleye eggs at a Minnesota hatchery. Pages 41–44 *in* R. C. Summerfelt, editor. *Walleye culture manual.* NCRAC Culture Series 1010, North Central Regional Aquaculture Center Publications Office, Iowa State University, Ames.

Thorson, J. T., S. B. Munch, J. M. Cope, and J. Gao. 2017. Predicting life history parameters for all fishes worldwide. *Ecological Applications* 27:2262–2276.

Tingley, R. W., J. F. Hansen, D. A. Isermann, D. C. Fulton, A. Musch, and C. P. Paukert. 2019. Characterizing angling preferences for largemouth bass, bluegill, and walleye fisheries in Wisconsin. *North American Journal of Fisheries Management* 39:676–692.

Treuer, A. 2010. *Ojibwe in Minnesota*. Minnesota Historical Society Press, St. Paul.

Treuer, A. 2015. *Warrior nation: a history of the Red Lake Ojibwe*. Minnesota Historical Society Press, St. Paul.

Trochta, J. T., M. Pons, M. B. Rudd, M. Krigbaum, A. Tanz, and R. Hilborn. 2018. Ecosystem-based fisheries management: perception on definitions, implementations, and aspirations. *PLOS ONE* 13(1):e0190467.

Tsehaye, I., B. M. Roth, and G. G. Sass. 2016. Exploring optimal walleye exploitation rates for northern Wisconsin Ceded Territory lakes using a hierarchical Bayesian age-structured model. *Canadian Journal of Fisheries and Aquatic Sciences* 73:1413–1433.

Turchin, P. 2001. Does population ecology have general laws? *Oikos* 94:17–26.

Twardek, W. M., R. J. Lennox, M. J. Lawrence, J. M. Logan, P. Szekeres, and S. J. Cooke. 2018. The postrelease survival of walleye following ice-angling on Lake Nipissing, Ontario. *North American Journal of Fisheries Management* 38:159–169.

U.S. Army Corps of Engineers. 2010. *Lake Winnebago: Fox-Wolf River basin*. USACE, Detroit.

USDOI (U.S. Department of the Interior), U.S. Fish and Wildlife Service, and U.S. Department of Commerce, U.S. Census Bureau. 2011. 2011 national survey of fishing, hunting, and wildlife-associated recreation. Washington, D.C.

USDOI (U.S. Department of the Interior), U.S. Fish and Wildlife Service, and U.S. Department of Commerce, U.S. Census Bureau. 2016. 2016 national survey of fishing, hunting, and wildlife-associated recreation. Washington, D.C.

Valentinčič, T. 2004. Taste and olfactory stimuli and behavior in fishes. Pages 90–108 *in* G. von der Emde, J. Mogdans, and B. G. Kapoor, editors. *The senses of fish*. Springer, Dordrecht.

Van Assche, K., J. Van Biesebroeck, and J. Holm. 2014. Governing the ice: ice fishing villages on Lake Mille Lacs and the creation of environmental governance institutions. *Journal of Environmental Planning and Management* 57:1122–1144.

Vandenbyllaardt, L., F. J. Ward, C. R. Braekevelt, and D. B. McIntyre. 1991.

Relationships between turbidity, piscivory, and development of the retina in juvenile walleyes. *Transactions of the American Fisheries Society* 120:382–390.

VanOosten, J., and H. J. Deason. 1957. History of Red Lakes fishery, 1917–1938, with observations on population status. United States Bureau of Fisheries, Special Scientific Report 229.

van Poorten, B. T., and C. J. MacKenzie. 2020. Using decision analysis to balance angler utility and conservation in a recreational fishery. *North American Journal of Fisheries Management* 40:29–47.

Van Zuiden, T. M., and S. Sharma. 2016. Examining the effects of climate change and species invasions on Ontario walleye populations: can walleye beat the heat? *Diversity and Distributions* 22:1069–1079.

Van Zuiden, T. M., M. M. Chen, S. Stefanoff, L. Lopez, and S. Sharma. 2016. Projected impacts of climate change on three freshwater fishes and potential novel competitive interactions. *Diversity and Distributions* 22:603–614.

Vaugeois, M., P. A. Venturelli, S. L. Hummel, and V. E. Forbes. 2021. A simulation-based evaluation of management actions to reduce the risk of contaminants of emerging concern (CECs) to walleye in the Great Lakes Basin. *Science of the Total Environment* 768:144326.

Venturelli, P. A., N. P. Lester, T. R. Marshall, and B. J. Shuter. 2010a. Consistent patterns of maturity and density-dependent growth among populations of walleye *(Sander vitreus)*: application of the growing degree-day metric. *Canadian Journal of Fisheries and Aquatic Sciences* 67:1057–1067.

Venturelli, P. A., C. A. Murphy, B. J. Shuter, T. A. Johnston, P. J. van Coeverden de Groot, P. T. Boag, J. M. Casselman, R. Montegomerie, M. D. Wiegand, and W. C. Leggett. 2010b. Maternal influences on population dynamics: evidence from an exploited freshwater fish. *Ecology* 91:2003–2012.

Venturelli, P., J. R. Bence, T. O. Brenden, N. P. Lester, and L. G. Rudstam. 2014. Mille Lacs walleye blue ribbon panel data review and recommendations for future data collection and management. Report submitted to the Minnesota Department of Natural Resources, St. Paul.

Vincent, E. R. 1987. Effects of stocking catchable-size hatchery rainbow trout on two wild trout species in the Madison River and O'Dell Creek, Montana. *North American Journal of Fisheries Management* 7:91–105.

Vitousek, P. M., P. R. Ehrlich, A. H. Ehrlich, and P. A. Matson. 1986. Human appropriation of the products of photosynthesis. *Bioscience* 36:368–373.

Vitousek, P. M., H. A. Mooney, J. Lubchenco, and J. M. Melillo. 1997. Human domination of Earth's ecosystems. *Science* 227:494–499.

Walters, C. J., and S. J. D. Martell. 2004. *Fisheries ecology and management.* Princeton University Press, Princeton, New Jersey.

Walters, C. J., R. Hilborn, and V. Christensen. 2008. Surplus production dynamics in declining and recovering fish populations. *Canadian Journal of Fisheries and Aquatic Sciences* 65:2536–2551.

WDNR. 1997. A chronology of the Chippewa treaty rights issue. Wisconsin Department of Natural Resources, Publication PUB-FH-825, Madison.

WDNR. 2004. Water quality in the Lake Winnebago Pool. Wisconsin Department of Natural Resources, Publication FH-229–04, Madison.

WDNR. 2018. Winnebago walleye management plan. Wisconsin Department of Natural Resources, Madison.

Weber, M. J., R. E. Weber, E. E. Ball, and J. R. Meerbeek. 2020. Using radio-telemetry to evaluate poststocking survival and behavior of large fingerling walleye in three Iowa, USA, lakes. *North American Journal of Fisheries Management* 40:48–60.

Weitzman, M. L. 1998. Why the far-distant future should be discounted at its lowest possible rate. *Journal of Environmental Economics and Management* 36:201–208.

Weitzman, M. L. 2007. A review of the Stern Review on the economics of climate change. *Journal of Economic Literature* 45:703–724.

Wetzel, R. G. 2001. *Limnology: lake and river ecosystems*, 3rd edition. Academic Press, San Diego.

Whitinger, J. A., T. G. Zorn, and B. S. Gerig. 2022. Stable isotope signatures and displacement patterns of walleye change following establishment of dreissenid mussels in a Lake Michigan embayment. *North American Journal of Fisheries Management*. In press.

Whyte, K. P. 2015. How similar are indigenous North American and Leopoldian environmental ethics? SSRN Paper 2022038.

Whyte, W. H. 1988. *City: rediscovering the center*. Doubleday, New York. Republished in 2002 by the University of Pennsylvania Press, Philadelphia.

Wiegand, M. D., T. A. Johnston, W. C. Leggett, K. E. Watchorn, A. J. Ballevona, L. R. Porteous, and J. M. Casselman. 2007. Contrasting strategies of ova lipid provisioning in relation to maternal characteristics in three walleye (*Sander vitreus*) populations. *Canadian Journal of Fisheries and Aquatic Sciences* 64:700–712.

Williams, T. A., C. J. Cox, P. G. Foster, G. J. Szöllősi, and T. M. Embley. 2020. Phylogenomics provides robust support for a two-domains tree of life. *Nature Ecology and Evolution* 4:138–147.

Williamson, C. E., E. P. Overholt, J. A. Brentrup, R. M. Pilla, T. H. Leach, S. G. Schladow, J. D. Warren, S. S. Urmy, S. Sadro, S. Chandra, and P. J. Neale. 2016. Sentinel responses to droughts, wildfires, and floods: effects of UV radiation on lakes and their ecosystem services. *Frontiers in Ecology and the Environment* 14:102–109.

Winslow, L. A., J. S. Read, G. J. A. Hansen, and P. C. Hanson. 2015. Small lakes show muted climate change signal in deepwater temperatures. *Geophysical Research Letters* 42:355–361.

WMO. 2019. Statement on the state of the global climate in 2019. World Meteorological Organization, WMO-No. 1248, Geneva, Switzerland.

Woolway, R. I., and C. J. Merchant. 2019. Worldwide alteration of lake mixing regimes in response to climate change. *Nature Geoscience* 12:271–276.

Woolway, R. I., B. M. Kraemer, J. D. Lenters, C. J. Merchant, C. M. O'Reilly, and S. Sharma. 2020. Global lake responses to climate change. *Nature Reviews Earth and Environment* 1:388–403.

Woolway, R. I., E. J. Anderson, and C. Albergel. 2021a. Rapidly expanding lake heatwaves under climate change. *Environmental Research Letters* 16:094013.

Woolway, R. I., S. Sharma, G. A. Weyhenmeyer, A. Debolskiy, M. Golub, D. Mercado-Bettín, M. Perroud, V. Stepanenko, Z. Tan, L. Grant, R. Ladwig, J. Mesman, T. N. Moore, T. Shatwell, I. Vanderkelen, J. A. Austin, C. L. DeGasperi, M. Dokulil, S. La Fuente, E. B. Mackay, S. G. Schladow, S. Watnaabe, R. Marcé, D. C. Pierson, W. Thiery, and E. Jennings. 2021b. Phenological shifts in lake stratification under climate change. *Nature Communications* 12:2318.

Writer, J. H., L. B. Barber, G. K. Brown, H. E. Taylor, R. L. Kiesling, M. L. Ferrey, N. D. Jahns, S. E. Bartell, and H. L. Schoenfuss. 2010. Anthropogenic tracers, endocrine disrupting chemicals, and endocrine disruption in Minnesota lakes. *Science of the Total Environment* 409:100–111.

Xu, C., T. A. Kohler, T. M. Lenton, J.-C. Svenning, and M. Scheffer. 2020. Future of the human climate niche. *Proceedings of the National Academy of Sciences* 117:11350–11355.

Zar, J. H. 1999. *Biostatistical analysis*. Prentice-Hall, Englewood Cliffs, New Jersey.

Zentner, D. L., J. K. Raabe, T. K. Cross, and P. C. Jacobson. 2022. Machine learning applied to lentil habitat use by spawning walleye demonstrates the benefits of considering multiple spatial scales in aquatic research. *Canadian Journal of Fisheries and Aquatic Sciences*. In press.

Zhang, F., K. B. Reid, and T. D. Nudds. 2018. Effects of walleye predation on variation in the stock-recruitment relationship of Lake Erie yellow perch. *Journal of Great Lakes Research* 44:805–812.

Zhao, Y., D. W. Einhouse, and T. M. MacDougall. 2011. Resolving some of the complexity of a mixed-origin walleye population in the east basin of Lake Erie using a mark-recapture study. *North American Journal of Fisheries Management* 31:379–389.

Zhao, H., K. Silliman, M. Lewis, S. Johnson, G. Kratina, S. J. Rider, C. A. Stepien,

E. M. Hallerman, B. Beck, A. Fuller, and E. Peatman. 2020. SNP analyses highlight a unique, imperiled southern walleye *(Sander vitreus)* in the Mobile River Basin. *Canadian Journal of Fisheries and Aquatic Sciences* 77:1366–1378.

Zuur, A. F., E. N. Ieno, N. J. Walker, A. A. Saveliev, and G. M. Smith. 2009. *Mixed effects models and extensions in ecology with R.* Springer, New York.

INDEX

abundance, 12, 42, 45–46, 133, 140–41, 158–59, 163, 271n1; habitat relationship, 50–51; recruitment effects, 37, 154–56, 161–65, 257n74, 270n54, 277n17

acid rain, 122

age, 38–39, 157–58

age-0 fish, 34–38; habitat, 34

age at maturity, 38–39, 45, 158, 256n43; sex differences, 39, 256n46

age class, 245

aging, 5, 221, 251n12

agriculture, 43, 122–25, 266n36

Alberta, 23, 257n73, 269n27; exploitation management, 145–46, 270n39

algae, 50, 52, 121, 123, 128, 153, 201, 251n7, 258n2, 260n37, 278n39

angling, vii, ix, 3, 9, 12, 17, 23–26, 49–60, 70–80, 82–83, 146, 172, 188, 192–96

angling regulations, 90, 131–46, 173, 180–82, 217–18, 226, 230–31, 235, 268n11, 269n23

aquatic plants, 38, 50, 52, 71, 125, 201, 264n46

area closure, 145, 182, 245

Arrowood, Mike, 176–81

bacteria diseases, 42–43

bait, 73, 75, 77–80

bait shop, 57

Barnard, Gary, 206, 214–17, 221–22, 224, 228, 230–33

bass, 12, 23, 26, 50, 52, 62, 70, 105, 111–12, 128–29, 152, 188, 212, 267n48, 268n57, 278n38;

interactions with walleye, 36, 42, 133, 201, 270n54

bioenergetics models, 40–41

biomass, 50, 131, 158, 159, 161–65, 199–208, 224–30, 235, 245, 249, 271n8, 280n19

bird predation, 42, 257n62

bluegill, 12, 30, 128, 212

blue walleye, 20, 253n35

bluntnose minnow, 37, 80, 188, 261n44

bobber fishing, 75–76

body condition, 37, 202, 204–5, 277n17

bow and arrow fishing, 60–61

brook trout, 3, 78, 160, 272n41

Brown, Pat, 214–22, 224, 226, 228–32, 235–36

bullheads, 37, 71, 102, 128, 212

burbot, 26, 76, 188, 212, 252n13, 267n48

by-catch, 62, 67, 102

camera trap, 80–81

Canada, ix, 12, 14–15, 22, 53, 149, 239; commercial fisheries, 20, 23, 143; recreational fisheries, 22, 24, 132

cannibalism, 35, 37–38, 40, 162, 202, 204, 229

carrying capacity, 33, 45, 115, 161, 163, 199–206, 245, 263n39, 264n6, 245

Carson, Rachel, 241–42

catch, 3, 13, 21–23, 25, 49–50, 57, 60, 62, 63–65, 70–74, 78, 81–83, 111–12, 136, 139, 152, 181, 207, 209

catchability, 51, 196, 245, 273n43

catch-and-release, 17, 26, 104–5, 146, 206, 253n49; fishery, 205, 207,

stock-recruitment, 154–56; relationships, 155, 231, 249, 271n8. *See also*
recruitment curves
subsistence fisheries, 15, 17, 143, 146,
218, 226
summerkill, 123
surplus production, 87, 132, 160, 231,
234–35, 249, 273n42, 273n43,
274n50. *See also* sustainable harvest
surveys, 18, 59, 69, 140–42, 163, 172,
189–90, 226. *See also* creel surveys
survival: adult, 146, 155–57, 209; egg,
30–33, 171 255n18; fingerling, 37,
101–2, 201, 204, 255n25; fry, 171;
juvenile, 154–55, 158, 165, 188, 202,
204, 206–7, 272n11
sustainability, 250
sustainable harvest, 160–64
swimming speed, 41

tackle, 55, 57, 71, 192, 195, 253n47,
260n37; non-toxic, 72, 260n36
tags, 4, 60, 69, 143–44, 172–73, 175,
180–82, 247, 275n12
Taleb, Nassim Nicholas, 139, 208
Tamarac River, Minnesota, 216
tapetum lucidum, 251n9
teeth, 6–7, 10, 66
thermal preferences, 46, 58, 163,
255n18, 256n42, 274n47, 274n49
thermal stratification, 52, 58, 128,
274n47
Thunberg, Greta, 130
total length, 6, 158, 250
total mortality rate, 245, 250, 258n84,
272n23, 273n26
trap net, 13, 61–63, 65, 93, 95, 102, 212
treaties, 15, 146, 186, 211, 252n26
treaty rights: for hunting, fishing, and
gathering, 15, 16, 17–18, 146, 186–87,
276n12, 276n12

tribal fisheries, 13–20, 143, 146,
186–87, 189, 210–15, 226–27, 230,
236, 259n17
trolling, 57, 73–74, 193, 195–96
trophic level, 153, 250
trout, 3, 9, 26, 30, 70, 78, 253n49,
261n1, 262n4
trout-perch, 171, 188, 212
turbid water, 10, 38, 59, 78, 251n7,
260n37

Vermont, vii, 260n36
vision, 6–8, 77, 251n7, 255n27,
260n38
von Bertalanffy growth equation,
158
vulnerability, 38, 136, 196, 250. *See
also* catchability

walleye chop, 72. *See also* waves;
wind effects: on fishing
walleye fry. *See* fry
Walters, Carl J., 149
water chemistry, 58, 255n18, 258n2,
266n31
water clarity, 128, 159, 169, 187–88,
202, 212, 274n47, 276n5
water depth, 7, 52, 57–59, 82, 128,
251n7, 254n51, 274n47
water pollution, viii, 11, 43, 53, 82–83,
115, 117, 122–25, 127–29, 242,
260n36, 266n25, 281n9, 281n15
water quality, 122–26
watershed, 117, 122, 125, 169, 184, 250,
264n10
water temperature, 52; climate
change impacts, 128, 133; egg development, 31–32, 107, 255n18;
growth effects, 39, 41, 157, 256n42;
hooking mortality effects, 82,
254n51; productivity effects, 163;

Paul J. Radomski is a fisheries biologist and lake ecology scientist with the Minnesota Department of Natural Resources. He has worked for more than thirty-five years on fisheries and lake management issues and is Minnesota's lead scientific expert on lakeshore habitat management. He writes scientific articles on walleye population dynamics, fisheries management, lakeshore habitat, and conservation, and he is coauthor of *Lakeshore Living*.

He loves to fish and enjoys trips to Rainy Lake, Namakan Lake, and the headwaters of Itasca State Park. He lives on an eighty-acre old farm site in the Brainerd lakes area, and the forestation of this retired farmland is his current obsession.